WATSUJI ON NATURE

Northwestern University
Studies in Phenomenology
and
Existential Philosophy

General Editor Anthony J. Steinbock

WATSUJI
ON NATURE

Japanese Philosophy
in the Wake of Heidegger

David W. Johnson

Northwestern University Press
Evanston, Illinois

Northwestern University Press
www.nupress.northwestern.edu

Printed in the United States of America

10 9 8 7 6 5 4 3 2 1

Library of Congress Cataloging-in-Publication Data

Title: Watsuji on nature : Japanese philosophy in the wake of Heidegger /
David W. Johnson.
Other titles: Northwestern University studies in phenomenology & existential
philosophy.
Description: Evanston, Illinois : Northwestern University Press, 2019. | Series:
Northwestern University studies in phenomenology and existential philosophy
Identifiers: LCCN 2019007708| ISBN 9780810140462 (paper text : alk. paper) |
ISBN 9780810140479 (cloth text : alk. paper) | ISBN 9780810140486 (e-book)
Subjects: LCSH: Watsuji, Tetsurō, 1889–1960. | Heidegger, Martin, 1889–1976—
Influence. | Philosophy of nature.
Classification: LCC B5244.W354 J64 2019 | DDC 181.12—dc23
LC record available at https://lccn.loc.gov/2019007708

Contents

Acknowledgments

A number of individuals and institutions have provided me with the kind of support necessary to see a project like this through, and I wish to thank them here. I want first to express my gratitude to the Philosophy Department and to the dean of the College of Arts and Sciences at Boston College for arranging the extended periods of research leave that allowed me to complete this book. Jim Heisig of the Nanzan Institute for Religion and Culture in Nagoya, Japan, generously furnished me with difficult to obtain Japanese texts and provided feedback on my work, reference letters that made possible extended research stays at other institutions, and multiple opportunities to present my ideas to other visitors to Nanzan. Among the latter, I want to thank Tom Kasulis for encouraging me to write this book when it was still in embryonic form; Peter Liederbach for the informative questions, comments, and conversations on the topic of Watsuji's philosophy; and the indefatigable Takeshi Morisato for organizing the workshop on Watsuji held at Nanzan in 2016.

During the 2015–2016 academic year I was a visiting researcher at the International Research Center for Japanese Studies (Nichibunken) in Kyoto. I want to express my gratitude to Inaga Shigemi for sponsoring my visit and to Nichibunken for the use of their library, which enabled me to access important Japanese-language material. Patricia Fister of Nichibunken also deserves my thanks for organizing an evening seminar around my work on Watsuji. In the spring of 2018 I had the opportunity to finish the manuscript of this book as a Haas Fellow at the Bibliotheca Mystica et Philosophica Alois M. Haas in Barcelona, thanks to a grant awarded by the Haas Association. I owe a special debt of gratitude to Raquel Bouso of Pompeu Fabra University for organizing my stay there under the auspices of her international research project in Japanese philosophy, and for her invitations to present my arguments and ideas to a wide-ranging audience. Invitations to present my research also came from Philip Ivanhoe (then at the Center for East Asian and Comparative Philosophy at the City University of Hong Kong) and Choong-Su Han (then at the Institute of Philosophical Research at Seoul National University). I thank them and those who attended my talks for the useful and lively discussions of my work.

The lengthy process of writing this book also brought me into contact and association with an array of helpful individuals outside of these particular institutional contexts. While it is not possible to acknowledge everyone here, there are several people that I would like to single out for thanks: Dennis Schmidt, for his assistance, counsel, and advocacy over the years; John Maraldo, for his early and supportive interest in my work; Augustin Berque, for offering illuminating comments on a foundational essay that anticipates some of the main themes of this book; William Britt and Magnus Ferguson, for committing to the laborious task of both commenting on and proofreading the manuscript; the two anonymous readers for Northwestern University Press, for the time and attention they gave to reading this text and for their uplifting affirmation of it; and Trevor Perri, who has been so prompt, effective, and helpful in his capacity as my editor at Northwestern. I thank my students, both undergraduate and graduate, for being such good interlocutors and for being—in their own fashion—such good teachers.

Portions of this manuscript were published as "Self in Nature, Nature in the Lifeworld: A Reinterpretation of Watsuji's Concept of *Fūdo,*" *Philosophy East and West* 68, no. 4 (2018); "Watsuji's Topology of the Self," *Asian Philosophy* 26, no. 3 (2016); and "*Fūdo* as the Disclosure of Nature: Re-Reading Watsuji with Heidegger," in *Critical Perspectives on Japanese Philosophy,* edited by Takeshi Morisato (Nagoya: Nanzan Institute Press, 2016). I thank each of these venues for permission to republish material here.

This book is dedicated to my wife, Akiko, for being the sheltering world that has made all of this possible.

WATSUJI ON NATURE

Introduction

The Japanese philosopher Watsuji Tetsurō (1889–1960) was a thinker whose work extended across a remarkable range of topics in cultural theory, intellectual history, religion, the arts, and, above all, philosophy. Watsuji's overall philosophical project can be understood as an attempt to reconceive the relations between selfhood, ethical life, and the natural world by reinterpreting and interweaving philosophical concepts found in Confucianism and Buddhism with ideas drawn from Western philosophy, especially hermeneutics, phenomenology, and the philosophy of Hegel. This is a way of approaching the human and natural worlds that opens genuinely original themes and questions, while also offering a creative array of responses to these issues.

This study focuses on Watsuji's philosophy of nature. At the heart of his thinking about nature is the novel and radical claim that nature as it is experienced and lived through is part of the very structure of human existence, such that the self is immersed in, and continuous with, this dimension of nature. This means that the human being can be what it is only through its living in, incorporating, and giving cultural expression to a region of nature, and, furthermore, that a particular region of nature can fully be what *it* is only through its being part of and disclosed through the world of human culture. Watsuji calls this geocultural environment, which we both open up and belong to, a *fūdo* 風土.

This concept is built upon an ordinary Japanese word whose usage and history is connected to texts, practices, and ways of thinking that link self with place, and nature with culture, and whose constituent sinographs extend the semantic range and depth of these associations. Watsuji draws on this background and these connotations to express the way nature and subjectivity are ontologically interwoven with rather than exterior to one another. While he sets out this philosophical interpretation of *fūdo* primarily in response to related problems and themes he encounters in the work of Herder and, above all, Heidegger, the importance of this idea for philosophical inquiry extends well beyond these concerns.

The Relational Self

The central claim of this study is that the concept of *fūdo* has significant implications for two important issues in contemporary philosophy. The first question concerns how we understand the self; the second, how we understand our experience of nature. In the former case, the claim that the lived experience of nature is part of the very structure of subjectivity challenges the problematic modern understanding of the self as a self-contained, individuated center, completely encased in a biological profile that fully divides it from the world. Instead the notion of *fūdo* enables us to uncover the way in which the self, in, for instance, its sensibility, preferences, imagination, has its being in the places and spaces of the natural world. This mode of being also makes possible an essential form of self-understanding, one that varies across regions of nature.

Thus rather than an individual subject decoupled and sealed off from that which surrounds it, such that it remains the same in all places and in any set of circumstances, we find that the self is continuous with its environment in and through a space that is constitutive of its being rather than external to it. Because this relational space is also an intersubjective one, we discover that we have our being in others, too. The self is present to, overlaps with, extends into, and is continuous with others who help to compose it. In uncovering this dimension of the basic space and place in and through which the self is able to be continuous with the human and natural worlds, Watsuji advances a new conception of the self as a relational structure open to that which is constitutive for it. This understanding of the self allows us to circumvent central aspects of ontological dualism and, by doing so, to dispense with some of the philosophical difficulties and problems that this dichotomy entails.

Fūdo and the Reenchantment of Nature

The concept of *fūdo* also has significant consequences for the pressing question of the appropriate relation between what has been called the "manifest" image of nature, or nature as it appears to us, with its characteristic qualities, meanings, and values, and the scientific image of nature, or the qualitatively bald and value-free world of nature as described by science. When these images collide, the dominant approach to resolving this conflict has been to fold the manifest image into the scientific one. The consequences of this move are immense and manifold; numbered among them is the abolition of a large expanse of the world of meaningful human experience. Yet this approach has also become entangled in serious philosophical difficulties, such as in the various problems posed by the attempt to account for mental states from the external or third-person standpoint of physicalism, or in the controversies generated by naturalistically reductive accounts of ethical and aesthetic experience. As many have argued, the attempt to reduce lived experience to purely objective elements has led to incoherence, to the loss of insight, and even to the loss of the phenomenon that was to be explained.

I argue that Watsuji's work contains an account of the appearances of nature that avoids these difficulties by showing that the essential reality of nature in this dimension is neither merely phenomenal and subjective, nor is it "really" an objective domain of bare entities, independent, self-contained, and complete in themselves. Rather nature as it appears in the lifeworld possesses a nascent intelligibility that is completed only in the experience of those who encounter and perceive it. This experience is not, however, an encounter with a "pristine" nature standing outside of all mediation. Watsuji's work can be situated within a hermeneutical tradition that includes Herder, Humboldt, Heidegger, and Gadamer, one that, as John Maraldo has observed, has now become international. For Watsuji and other thinkers in this tradition, the intelligibility of nature, like the whole content of human experience, is disclosed and so mediated through our language, practices, and culture, and brought in this way to a kind of expressive articulation. And because the intelligibility of nature is completed in culture, it can be said that nature has a history—as many histories as there are cultures.

So disclosure as expressive articulation is not simply the articulation of something already known and fully formed; in this process there is a complex interaction of making and showing, discovery and creation. Yet insofar as the disclosive activity of the self and the being of nature unfold together in *fūdo*, nature as it appears in the lifeworld is not an "objective" entity onto which we project "subjective" meanings; rather it is an always already meaningful setting in which subjective and objective elements form a unity.

In this regard, the concept of *fūdo* returns us to a richer, premodern conception of experience, one that, by restoring the "weight" of the things, holds out the promise of a partial reenchantment of nature. Although the philosophical implications of the concept of *fūdo* are novel, wide-ranging, and dramatic, the idea that the appearances of nature are "saved" in the event of disclosure is only incipient but never fully realized in Watsuji's thought. This study shows that this aspect of Watsuji's philosophy of nature can be more fully developed through a richer account of the disclosive capacity of actions, practices, language, and emotions.

Watsuji and Heidegger

The conversion of the ordinary Japanese term *fūdo* into a philosophical concept that alters our understanding of self and nature in these ways is made possible by Watsuji's appropriation of Heidegger's early work—especially his concept of being-in-the-world. But this appropriation is also a transformation, since even as Watsuji draws on the notion of being-in-the-world, he revises and expands this structure at each of its poles. At the pole of Dasein, he proposes a more phenomenologically accurate conception of the self as constituted by its relations to others. The self that is so constituted is surprisingly strange: in certain modes of consciousness and interaction, it is able to overlap with, extend into, and be continuous with others who extend into and are continuous with it. At the other pole of this dyad, Watsuji incorporates nature as it is experienced and lived through, or *fūdosei*, into the ontological structure of the world. In this way, the continuity of the self with what surrounds it ultimately encompasses both nature *and* other selves. Watsuji thus approaches the relational space that constitutively links self and other, and both of these with nature, through the dyadic structure of Dasein and world laid down by Heidegger. But this is no mere borrowing: the way in which Watsuji builds on Heidegger results in something new; that is, it issues in what Gadamer calls a fusion of horizons.

This connection between Watsuji and Heidegger will come as no surprise to those familiar with the history of contact and mutual recognition between Heidegger and several of Nishida's students and associates in the first half of the twentieth century. Nishida's students Tanabe Hajime, Miki Kiyoshi, and Nishitani Keiji, and associates such as Kuki Shūzō, studied with Heidegger.[1] Tanabe appears to have been the first scholar in the world to write a commentary on Heidegger's thought, in 1924; Miki wrote essays on Heidegger in 1930 and 1933; Kuki published *Heidegger's Philosophy*, the first book-length study of Heidegger in any language, in 1933; Watsuji's *Climate and Culture*, which he began work on in 1928 and published in 1935, is explicitly both an appreciation and a critique of Heidegger's thought.[2] But the direction of interest and attention flowed both ways; Heidegger also showed a genuine interest in Japanese thought and culture. In his 1954 essay, "A Dialogue on Language between a Japanese and an Inquirer," he references Nishida and Kuki, and meditates on the Japanese words *iki* 粋 and *kotoba* 言葉. Reflecting on the prospects for cross-cultural dialogue, he observes that the concept of *das Nichts*, which appears in his essay "What Is Metaphysics?," was grasped immediately by Japanese thinkers because of the large presence in their own tradition of the Buddhist concept of emptiness.[3]

In his 1959 letter to the fifth East-West Philosophers' Conference at the University of Hawaii, Heidegger writes, "Again and again it has seemed urgent to me that a dialogue take place with the thinkers of what is to us the Eastern world."[4] And Gadamer, in private correspondence, has said that those who study Heidegger would do well to pursue comparisons of his work with Asian philosophies.[5] This mutual interest and admiration had its source in certain ideas that both sides recognized as shared philosophical ground. This is a very large subject, and one that it is not necessary for our purposes to enter fully into. Instead we will be concerned primarily with the way certain approaches and foundational concepts in Heidegger's philosophy form a bridge to Watsuji's work.

One of Heidegger's most valuable insights has been to see and show that a discrete approach to phenomena is a severely limited one, and so a way of doing philosophy that has led to any number of difficulties. To fully understand a phenomenon, it must be put in relation to the things that surround it, and these, in turn, must be situated in a larger contextual field. Jeff Malpas has called this dimension of Heidegger's approach a *topographic* mode of analysis, namely, one in which "the concepts at issue must be understood in terms of their interconnection rather than their reduction, through their interdependence rather than through their simplification."[6] These underlying interconnections, however, also make it difficult to "arrive at simple, univocal definitions. Significant terms will generally connect up with other terms in multiple ways and carry a range of connotations and meanings that cannot always be easily or precisely separated out."[7] Notwithstanding this, Malpas maintains that the desire for the univocity of meaning may well be a mistaken philosophical ideal in general. Moreover, one can argue that philosophical accounts that employ this kind of methodological holism are often more phenomenologically accurate in that they are better able to fully capture, and so do justice to, our experience.

This is surely one reason why Watsuji found himself attracted to Heidegger's thought; he too saw one of the central problems of philosophy as a problem of method; for him this difficulty appeared in the inability of thinkers—especially in the Western tradition—to see constitutive relationships. So while Watsuji's work, like almost all of the modern Japanese philosophy of the twentieth century, takes many of its concepts, themes, and approaches from Western models, it also stands in the conceptual space and implicit background of intelligibility which has its origins in Buddhism, Confucianism, and Shintoism, among other influences. Watsuji refashions and repurposes both the Confucian idea of the human being as existing at the intersection of a totality of inescapable relationships to specific others, and the Buddhist metaphysics of nondualism, to develop modes of constitutive relationality that bring together the self with others, and both of these with nature. Hence while he recognized the kind of philosophical breakthrough that Heidegger's notion of *In-der-Welt-sein* represented, Watsuji also saw that Heidegger's methodological holism did not go far enough, and that to really restore the fullness of both the self and the world, what was needed was a conception of Dasein as a being-in-relation-to-others (*aidagara* 間柄) and an understanding of world as grounded in the lived experience of nature (*fūdo*). While Heidegger himself will return in later works to rethink key elements of his early philosophy, Watsuji seems not to have given further consideration in print to the major developments in Heidegger's thought after *Being and Time*, turning his attention instead to studies in Buddhism, Confucianism, and ethical theory, as well as to issues and themes in Japanese political and intellectual history, and aesthetics. For this reason, our study will limit its commentary on Heidegger's philosophy to his prewar writings.

Watsuji in the West

Watsuji's philosophical work can hence be seen as focused primarily on establishing and developing two general claims. The first is that the self is constituted by its relational contact with others; the second is that the self is constituted by its relational contact with the wider geocultural environment. The two book-length treatments of Watsuji in English focus on the first claim, analyzing the link between forms of constitutive sociality and Watsuji's ethical theory. Erin McCarthy's *Ethics Embodied* compares the ethics of Watsuji and Luce Irigary, and Graham Mayeda's *Time, Space, and Ethics in the Philosophy of Watsuji Tetsurō, Kuki Shūzō, and Martin Heidegger* places the ethical thought of these three figures into dialogue. The studies in German and French tend to be more expansive in putting Watsuji to other uses. Hans Peter Liederbach's *Martin Heidegger im Denken Watsuji Tetsurōs* is both a work of intellectual history and an attempt to improve Watsuji's *Rinrigaku* in order to make its critique of Heidegger more effective. Bianca Boteva-Richter's *Der Methodentransfer nach Watsuji Tetsuro* draws on Watsuji's work to develop a dialectical method for doing comparative philosophy. Augustin Berque's *Écoumène: Introduction à l'étude des milieux humains* calls on Watsuji's concept of *fūdo* in developing an environmental ethics and a philosophical approach to the study of geography.

The approach in this work can be distinguished from these earlier efforts in several important ways. First, unlike the studies in English and

German, this study takes up the other great theme of Watsuji's work, namely, nature as a constituent element of selfhood. And although Watsuji's ethics is not the primary concern of this book, unlike the study in French I also attend to the claim at the ground of Watsuji's ethical theory that the self is constituted by its relational contact with others, and show how both the natural and social dimensions of this relationality work together to make the self what it is: the relational network of *aidagara* is always situated in a particular locale, and this means that *aidagara* is always positioned within and encompassed by a specific region of nature, or *fūdo*. The extensive attention we give to constitutive sociality will also allow us to relate Watsuji's philosophy of nature to the other major concepts in his philosophical work, bringing into view the frequently difficult to discern unity at the ground of Watsuji's thought.

Thinking with and after Watsuji

This book thus offers a critical interpretation of Watsuji's thought, but it does not aim to present an assessment of his oeuvre as a whole, or even to provide an interpretive reconstruction of the entirety of *Climate and Culture* (*Fūdo*), which is his main text on the theme of nature. To fully grasp Watsuji's theory of *fūdo*, *Climate and Culture* must be read together with the third volume of *Ethics* (*Rinrigaku* 倫理学). There Watsuji supplies many more of the ingredients needed to fill out the highly compressed philosophical insights that were presented in the preface, first chapter, and last chapter of *Climate and Culture*. Nevertheless my primary interest is less in the granular details of Watsuji's texts themselves than in what I see as fundamental and original philosophical insights that emerge from them concerning the relation between fact and value, the nature of the self, the structure and status of experience, and, at the end of this study, the implications of the concept of *fūdo* for problems in phenomenology, for questions in environmental ethics, and for the recent turn to place and space in contemporary philosophy. In this regard this book belongs among recent works that seek, as James Heisig observes, "to put the ideas of the Kyoto School to use in rephrasing a range of traditional philosophical questions. This, in turn, has led to a *creative rethinking of some of their core ideas* in order to accommodate them to new modes of thought and problems specific to our own times."[8]

This book is therefore not a scholarly synthesis of all of Watsuji's works, an attempt to work through a history of the development of his thought in order to arrive at a comprehensive presentation of his views.

The primary aim of this study is to make explicit what remains unthought in Watsuji's philosophy of nature. What remains unsaid, unarticulated, is the full philosophical significance of the concept of *fūdo*. The lived experience of *fūdo* is an event of disclosure, one that can be understood as overcoming a disenchanted nature. And while the concept of *fūdo* is the focal point of this work, it cannot be treated in isolation, because insofar as a *fūdo* is encountered and lived through, it is also a dimension of the self. Watsuji nevertheless had real difficulty in smoothly bringing together and integrating these themes into a coherent whole.[9] Megumi Sakabe observes that despite Watsuji's detailed and subtle investigation into the structure of the self as a relational field, the place of nature in this structure receives insufficient treatment. Moreover, Sakabe says, the tendency toward geographical determinism in Watsuji's thought may be viewed as a counterpart to the failure of his effort to establish the coherence of this relation. Sakabe's verdict, in sum, is that "in spite of his declared attempt to overcome modern European subjectivism or the dualism of subject and object, Watsuji was unable to free himself entirely from these tendencies. . . . Accordingly, if one is to refine and further develop the lines of thinking inaugurated by Watsuji, it will be absolutely necessary to undertake a fundamental reconsideration of the notions of subject (including intersubjective subject as 'between-ness' and so forth) and object (including nature) and finally the interrelationship between the two."[10] This, in fine, is what we set out to do through a sustained focus on the profound yet concrete and commonplace ways in which the self is continuous with the wider social and natural whole to which it is related. In moving through Watsuji's corpus, then, we will be primarily concerned with that part of his work that most directly addresses these questions rather than with reconstituting his thought in general.

Working through Watsuji's texts presents interpretive challenges that stem mostly from the fragmentary and scattered presentation of his arguments across multiple works and from the abbreviated quality of some of his most important philosophical claims. One often has to comb his texts and select concepts and passages that require fuller interpretation or clarifying explanations in order to build an adequate account of the relevant point. This is done not in order to produce a commentary on Watsuji's texts but to present a certain reading of Watsuji's philosophical project. This is a project faced with numerous problems—some of them of Watsuji's own making. Time and again, for instance, Watsuji opens a door to a room that he never fully enters, picking up an important interpretive thread only to let it go shortly afterward without, as is more often the case than one might wish, rigorous or sustained development. While this might be taken as a sign that his ideas are less than fully formed, and while it also means that his claims can be frustrating in their vagueness and lack of detail, some of the rooms he ushers us into amount to new precincts for philosophical investigation. When we turn on the light, we are greeted with insights that startle, flashes of vision in which we suddenly see what *fūdo* and *aidagara* come to: that we are in a place which is in us, that we are beings whose consciousness always already belongs together with others.

The critical and hermeneutic task will be to fill out and supplement these insights—in a spirit both generous and critical—with an account of what Watsuji said and was trying to say, what he failed to say, and what he could and should have said. In this process of speculative reconstruction, I use Watsuji's ideas as a platform to advance my own arguments and ideas about how to think about both our experience of others and our experience of nature. I carry this out along the lines laid down by Watsuji, but also in ways that go beyond what Watsuji actually said. This approach shows where Watsuji perhaps did not go himself, but where one could go with his thinking. It allows us—in the words that Merleau-Ponty used to speak so eloquently about another philosopher's shadow—to recommence his efforts "instead of simply repeating what he said. It allows us to resume, instead of his theses, the very movement of his thought."[11]

Chapter Overviews

The following summaries indicate the developmental arc of each chapter, as well as how this trajectory contributes to the book's overall narrative thread.

Chapter 1: *Fūdo*: History, Language, and Philosophy

The first chapter provides an explanatory overview of the concept of *fūdo*, beginning with a summary of its history and usage. Because the semantic and cultural density of the term poses serious obstacles to adequate translation, I elect to leave it untranslated. This decision is rooted in a hermeneutic conception of language and linguistic meaning found in Heidegger and Gadamer which is implicitly shared by Watsuji and which, as we will see at the end of this study, is decisive for a more fully realized conception of *fūdo* than Watsuji himself was able to achieve.

The reach and originality of Watsuji's rereading of *fūdo* also presents additional barriers to the full and faithful translation of this term. It accounts too for the difficulty Watsuji had in articulating this concept.

This has led to multiple and conflicting interpretations of the meaning of *fūdo*. The rest of the chapter adjudicates between these interpretations by addressing some of the most common misreadings and showing both how most fail to grasp the full range of what is covered in this notion and so miss what is really new in it. This requires us to explain how *fūdo* relates to and can be distinguished from the concept of nature and to address the charge that Watsuji uses the concept of *fūdo* to advance a nationalist "politics of nature." In the course of navigating these and other questions, we show the way Watsuji attempts to forge a new philosophical concept, one that brings together the semantic, cultural, and historical dimensions of *fūdo* and uncovers the manner in which self and nature belong together as aspects of a single, unitary phenomenon.

Chapter 2: The Scientific Image of Nature: Dualism and Disenchantment

This chapter begins with the sense in which the self belongs to a region of nature: it is immersed in and continuous with nature as it appears in the lifeworld—and so a nature replete with qualities and values. I demonstrate that insofar as contemporary philosophical prejudices presuppose a disenchanted conception of nature and a dualistic understanding of the self in relation to the natural world, they pose serious obstacles to bringing this understanding of *fūdo* fully into view.

Watsuji's criticisms of the forms of dualism and objectivism contained in these presuppositions culminate in a form of perspectivism in which what appears to a point of view is constitutively tied to this standpoint. The question of the status of our experience of nature will hence be inseparable from the overcoming of dualism achieved in this stance. The road back—or, rather, forward—to a reenchanted conception of nature must pass through an analysis of this reconfiguration of the relationship between subject and object, self and world.

Chapter 3: Beyond Objectivism: Watsuji's Path through Phenomenology

This chapter shows how the perspectivism with which chapter 2 closes is fully elaborated through the phenomenological thesis of intentionality, and later in the closely related concept of being-in-the-world. Watsuji finds the forms of continuity of the self with what surrounds it in both of these notions especially congenial. His reconstructive appropriation of Heidegger's concept of being-in-the-world in particular will ultimately enable us to account for the way self and nature form a relational whole, such that nature as it is experienced and lived through is part of the very structure of subjectivity.

This refashioning begins with his contention that the concept of Dasein is still too closely tied to an individuated conception of the self. Heidegger fails to see that the self not only opens on to and is continuous with a world, as Dasein is in being-in-the-world, but also that, in particular forms of consciousness and interaction, it opens at the same time on to and is continuous with other selves. This understanding of the self is so different, and so novel, that it requires a separate chapter to fully address.

Chapter 4: The Relational Self: A New Conception

Watsuji proposes what he takes to be a more phenomenologically accurate conception of the self as constituted by its relations to others and shows that essential modes of embodiment, consciousness, and identity necessarily require contact, association, and interaction with others. This constitutive sociality is a relational mode of being that Watsuji calls *aidagara* 間柄, or being-in-relation-to-others. *Aidagara* is the way in which I exist, and not an activity that I can choose or decline to undertake; I have to live this relatedness to others, which is ontologically constitutive of who and what I am.

The kind of self that is so constituted is far stranger and more radical than Dasein: in certain modes of consciousness and interaction we overlap with, extend into, and are continuous with others, who extend into and are continuous with us. Thus not only is the self social in that it depends upon others to be what it is; the self is also social in the sense that one self opens out onto another. While Watsuji offers a real critique of Heidegger here that will be welcomed by many, his notion of the self also coincides with Dasein in a crucial way: the self as *aidagara* also has an individual dimension. The self, then, is both individual and social. The next chapter, which charts the hybrid structure of the self, allows us to link this concept of the self with Watsuji's concept of a world as a social, historical, and natural structure.

Chapter 5: The Hybrid Self: Oscillation and Dialectic

Watsuji attempts to capture the hybrid nature of the self with his concept of the human being as *ningen sonzai* 人間存在. Human beings are hybrid beings in that they are individuated through an untranscendable and inescapable relation to specific others and to wider social structures. This relational mode of being allows me to be absorbed into a social whole, as well as to distinguish myself from it as an individual in a continually oscillating movement of interaction.

This alternating movement reveals that a form of existential spatiality belongs to the very structure of human existence and shows that the self is also linked to its surroundings insofar as this space is part of the relational structure of the self itself. This means that this existential space connects one self to another, and both of these to a world and to the lifeworldly dimension of nature that is disclosed through it. Since, as Heidegger had shown, self and world are inseparable, and, as Watsuji shows, one self exists in relational continuity with another, this space is an essential dimension of the connections between all of the entities in this configuration.

Chapter 6: The Space of the Self: Between Culture and Nature

The previous two chapters describe Watsuji's transformation of the pole of Dasein within the structure of being-in-the-world. This chapter examines the way he remakes the other pole in this structure by expanding the concept of world so that it encompasses the phenomenon of *fūdo*.

We begin where chapter 5 ended, showing that insofar as spatiality belongs to the structure of the self as *aidagara*, or being-in-relation-to-others, it must also belong to the world "in" which *aidagara* is. This space is opened up by what is expressed and understood between us in interaction. This shared understanding, as structured, retained, and expressed by the material infrastructure of a society, forms the basis for the common cultural space of a world. Hence space always already has a certain social and cultural character. Space also always already has a certain atmospheric character produced by light, temperature, humidity, and so forth, because this space is always located in and dependent on a place that precedes and outstrips it, namely, the place of nature. Space and place, then, belong partly to the self and partly to a world and to nature, neither purely subjective nor merely objective. Hence through the space and place of a world, the self as *aidagara* and a region of nature as *fūdo* are able to be continuous with and belong to one another.

Chapter 7: Self, World, and *Fūdo*: Continuity and Belonging

Because Watsuji expands the concept of world to include specific regions of nature in this way, there is also another important sense in which self and *fūdo* belong to and depend upon one another: in and through the phenomenon of world and the activities of self-understanding and disclosure that accompany it, each belongs to and depends upon the other to be what it is.

Thus, on the one hand, the essential roles, practices, and equipment we engage in and use to understand ourselves (e.g., coal mines, coal mining, and drilling equipment) as well as our tastes and preferences, our imagination and sensibility, are determined in large part by a natural region, so that *who* we are depends in essential ways upon *where* we are. On the other hand, *fūdosei*, or a *fūdo* as it is encountered in experience, as part of a world, is a particular region of nature as it is disclosed through the activities, practices, affective possibilities, and language that characterize a world. According to Watsuji, these forms of directedness originate in, and are most fully realized as, shared comportments, that is, comportments that make it possible for nature to show the same face to the I-as-we and we-as-I in a single, shared experience. Nature comes in this way to take on a certain appearance for those who belong to a shared culture. Self and *fūdo* thus depend on, and are continuous with, one another through these modes of self-interpretation and disclosure that belong to a cultural world.

Chapter 8: Self in Nature, Nature in the Lifeworld

Self and nature form a unitary whole in *fūdo*, but they are so closely identified with one another in self-understanding and disclosure that it is difficult to maintain them together in this unity without reducing one side to the other. The dependence of sensibility and self-understanding upon a *fūdo*, if too strongly construed, threatens to reduce the self to its natural setting; too forceful an emphasis on the way cultural modes of disclosure always mediate what appears as nature leads to the opposite kind of danger, namely, the reduction of our experience of nature to our cultural forms of making sense of and displaying it.

In the former case, the close identification of the self with a particular region of nature has prompted the criticism that Watsuji adheres to a form of determinism in which national characters are produced by particular geographical conditions; in response to this, I examine the human capacity to disclose nature in different ways over time and across cultures; I also detail an array of ways in which the individual self is capable of significantly transcending its *fūdo*.

In the latter case, the fact that it is *we* who disclose nature seems to entail a certain relativism and subjectivism about the content of this experience. I argue that these problems can be largely avoided by drawing on phenomenology, as well as on the Buddhist metaphysics of nondualism, to show the ways in which self and nature are ontologically continuous with and belong to one another. Here my subjectivity both "gives" me the natural world and is always already something given in and continuous with it. Because we are part of and belong to the very nature we encounter and disclose, experiencing self and experienced nature must be seen as two aspects of the same phenomenon. In this regard it becomes possible to understand our culturally mediated experience and expression of nature as the *self* disclosure of nature rather than as a process of subjective construal or projection. And because the appearances of nature as they show themselves to us through culture are replete with qualities and values, this radical, even uncanny conception of experience holds out the possibility of an at least partial reenchantment of nature, since it enables us to treat this qualitative fullness as belonging to nature itself. The concept of *fūdo*, then, overcomes the duality of nature and culture and returns us to a richer, premodern conception of experience.

Conclusion

The concluding remarks rehearse the contributions of this study to the problem of a disenchanted nature and to a new conception of the self. I also look to other lines of inquiry opened up by the concept of *fūdo*, including issues in phenomenology, environmental ethics, and the "spatial turn" in recent philosophy. Finally, I provide an overview of the conceptual links between Watsuji and other thinkers in the Kyoto School and delineate the ways in which *fūdo* provides a framework for what I call a *topology* of the self.

1

Fūdo: History, Language, and Philosophy

One of the most important and least well-understood notions in Watsuji Tetsurō's philosophical oeuvre is the concept of *fūdo* 風土. The aim of this chapter is to provide an explanatory overview of this concept. This task is made more difficult by the complexity, richness, and philosophical novelty of this notion, and by Watsuji's own piecemeal, inconsistent, and ambiguously formulated presentation of it. These factors have led to an array of conflicting interpretations concerning the scope and nature of this concept. These difficulties of understanding have been compounded by the widespread use of the word *climate* to translate *fūdo* into English, which is a misleading simplification that does not reflect the complex meaning that Watsuji attributed to this term. For this reason, as well as for reasons stemming from a specific conception of language and linguistic meaning, I have elected to leave *fūdo* untranslated throughout this study. While this approach allows us to avoid the distortion and loss of meaning that have plagued previous translations of *fūdo*, using a new and unfamiliar concept from a foreign language in a philosophical study also presents a different kind of challenge to the understanding.

In what follows, we will forge a path through the various difficulties of this terrain by showing how the semantic and philosophical dimensions of the term *fūdo*, as well as the cultural and historical background in which it is situated, come together for Watsuji in the coherent whole of a new philosophical concept.

I. *Fūdo*: History of a Concept

Fūdo is an ordinary Japanese word that indicates the natural environment peculiar to a given region—such as the fertility of its soil, its climate, and its topography—which adheres to and influences the life and culture of the people who live there. For most Japanese-language learners, this is a concept that opens a new window on the world, and so must be newly and somewhat laboriously acquired. There is no straightforward equivalent of this concept in English or, as far as I am aware, among the major Western languages. This is in part because *fūdo* does not merely designate a zone or region of nature *simpliciter*, as the English word *climate* does when speaking, for example, of the climate of the Arabian peninsula. *Fūdo* indicates an area of nature implicitly considered from a certain standpoint, namely, insofar as it shapes or determines a culture. The concept of *fūdo* hence represents one among many possible ways of looking at the natural world, just as a map does when it selects or highlights certain features of a terrain and omits others. Thus Antarctica, for instance, is characterized by a certain climate but not by a specific *fūdo*, since this is an expanse of the natural world without any connection to or influence on a particular human culture.

The association of the sinograph compound 風土 with human culture appears to be an ancient one in the East Asian cultural sphere. In Japan this term appears explicitly with these connotations in the early tenth century, when we find the first known reference to the *fudoki* 風土記, or the official eighth-century reports on the history, geography, and customs of the provinces. While the term *fudoki* itself derives from Chinese usage in the Later Han period and appears to have been associated with the title of a now-lost third-century work, the Japanese records likely took as their model official Sui and Tang dynasty compilations of maps and reports on local products and customs.[1] Translated literally, *fudoki* means "records of wind and land." But the character for wind (*fū* 風) in this term also stands metaphorically for "customs." Hence *fudoki* is more exactly rendered "records of lands and their customs." These records were compiled in compliance with an imperial edict issued in 713 by Empress Genmei. Of the several dozens of *fudoki* known to have been produced, only five have been preserved, while the rest (with the exception of fragments) have been lost. Thus what is known about these reports comes from these texts and fragments and from scattered quotes in poetic treatises and commentaries from the medieval era, such as the *Man'yōshū chūshaku* (*A Commentary on the Collection of Ten Thousand Leaves*) of 1269 and the *Shaku Nihongi* (*Annotated Edition of the Chronicles of Japan*) of the late thirteenth century. These sources show that the *fudoki* contained an array of information arranged according to region, including the origins of place-names, local products, and natural resources, geographical features such as the topography and productivity of the land in the area, scenic spots, regional customs and practices, religious edifices, and local folktales, legends, and myths.[2]

The *fudoki* thus initiated a long and venerable tradition of geographical writing in Japan. Some scholars have convincingly argued that the history of this literature can be usefully divided into two overlapping but still distinct genres.[3] The first is represented by the practice of belle-lettristic travel writing, which begins with the *Tosa Diary* (*Tosa nikki,* 935) and gains substantive shape and depth with Saigyō's travel poetry (1118–1190), and reaches its summit (though not its end) with Bashō's *Narrow Road to the Interior* (*Oku no hosomichi,* 1694). This tradition is characterized by an emotional, even sentimental approach, the obligatory mention of classical or famous place-names (*utamakura* and *meisho*), attempts to capture the mood, impressions, and atmosphere of an experience, and an effort to display a refined sense of taste. In contrast to the inward focus of these works, the texts belonging to the second genre of geographical writing direct their attention outward, toward the places and people of the world.[4] This tradition is intellectual and encyclopedic; it takes an interest in accumulating information about the various regions of Japan through, for example, geographical descriptions, accounts of the daily life of the local inhabitants, and reports of unknown and or unexplored regions. As successors to the *fudoki* in content and purpose, these works are more directly relevant to and central for the development of the concept of *fūdo.*

Like the *fudoki,* many of the works in this genre link particular kinds of products and customs—and even at times the character of the local inhabitants—to specific regions and their geographical features. Later the term *suido* 水土 (which contains the sinographs for *water* and *land*) came to be used for formal reports of this kind. Among the most important and well-known works of this type are topographical surveys such as the *Jinkokuki* (*Depictions of People and Customs according to Region,* circa sixteenth century), the *Shin jinkokuki* (*New Depictions of People and Customs according to Region,* 1700), and the *Nihon suidokō* (*Treatise on Japanese Geography,* 1720).[5] More personal and less formal forms of geographical writing, such as travelogues, also weave together the natural and the cultural, showing that this way of thinking about the relationship between human beings and nature was not confined to the topographical survey. In her commentary on Kaibara Ekiken's *Jinshin kikō* (*Account of Travels in the Year of Jinshin,* 1672) and Nagakubo Sekisui's *Nagasaki kōeki nikki* (*Diary of Official Travel to Nagasaki,* 1767), Marcia Yonemoto observes, for instance, that after describing the layout of the temple compound at Shoshazan (in present-day Himeji city), Kaibara "goes on to give a history and etymology of place-names in and around Shoshazan, recount the area's folklore, comment on the productivity of land and types of land ownership, and describes the local markets and products. He notes that in spite of the area's quiet setting the local people are industrious; they cultivate and market the bamboo that flourishes on the mountainside." Nagakubo, for his part, is attentive "to the details of material culture, making note of various local products and regional specialties or characteristics: a shrine in Izu is known for its calendars, the town of Kashiwahara for its fried eel, Imaizumi for its metal work, and Sakai for its palm trees."[6]

Although the term *fūdo* itself is not explicitly thematized in these texts, these works and others like them help to furnish a cultural background of associations and impressions that enrich and extend the semantic range of *fūdo*. This process continues into the modern period with the introduction in the eighteenth century of Western medical knowledge (including the science of hygiene) to Japan through the port of Nagasaki. By the late nineteenth century medical researchers—most prominent among them Mori Rintarō (Mori Ōgai)—began to include in their use of the term *fūdo* all aspects of the natural environment (including atmospheric conditions) that have an impact on the biological functioning of plants, animals, and human beings.[7]

The scope and suggestive power of the term *fūdo* is also amplified by the polysemy of the first sinograph in the compound 風土. When introducing the concept of *fūdo*, it is common for Western commentators to address the meaning of the individual sinographs by limiting themselves to the observation that *fūdo* 風土 is composed of the sinographs for wind, *kaze/fū* 風, and earth or land, *do* 土. But this description fails to address the semantic density that the character *kaze/fū* 風 imparts to 風土. Ikkai Tomoyoshi points out that *fū* 風 has an elusive and hence ambiguous and equivocal character or quality, associations it has long had. He notes, for instance, that in Buddhist cosmology, *kaze* 風, or wind, is one the four traditional elements that constitute the universe. Three of these—earth, water, and fire—are entities that are visible to the eye, whereas only the wind is not visible. He observes too that in the Japanese phrase *kachōfūgetsu* 花鳥風月, or "the beauties of nature," three of the beauties—flowers, birds, and the moon—all offer the viewer something that can be solidly and clearly apprehended; only the wind has this elusive, almost ungraspable quality.[8]

The idea that *fū* 風 tends to be used to describe or refer to phenomena that cannot be captured in a firm or concrete way seems also to be borne out by the other meanings this sinograph can possess. In addition to wind or breeze, *fū* 風 can also mean (1) appearance, air; (2) tendency; and (3) style, manner, way. While there are other sinographs that are close in meaning to (3) such as *shiki* 式 (style, form) and *ryū* 流 (way, style), *fū* 風 conveys a vaguer sense of the notions of style, manner, or way.[9] In short, the character *fū* 風 in the term *fūdo* 風土 also connotes the "sense" of a land or a region, that is, its appearance, atmosphere, and style—and even the "ways" of its inhabitants.

II. Translating *Fūdo*

The preceding account of the way the term *fūdo* has been carried into
the present by a long procession of historical and linguistic factors and
contexts exhibited the wide array of meanings that have sedimented into
this concept. Yet this semantic and cultural density also poses serious
obstacles to the adequate translation of this word. In my view, these barriers to full translation can be explained by a hermeneutic conception of
language and linguistic meaning that has deep intellectual and historical
affinities with Watsuji's own philosophical stance, namely, the holistic and
disclosive understanding of language and linguistic meaning found in
the hermeneutic phenomenology of Heidegger and Gadamer.

For a holistic conception of linguistic meaning, the full meaning of
the word *fūdo*—as we saw above—depends upon and emerges through
a wider background of etymological associations, forms of usage, and related terms, texts, and practices.[10] The claim that the meaning of a word
or sentence cannot be determined solely from the content it presents but
must rely on context, surrounding sentences, related words, and so on
is one with a long and complex genealogy. One thinks here of Saussure,
who makes the point that the value of a linguistic sign must "be assessed
against comparable values, by contrast with other words. The content of
a word is determined in the final analysis not by what it contains but by
what exists outside it";[11] of Frege, who claims that the meaning of words
must be accounted for in the context of the sentences in which they
occur; and of Wittgenstein, who observes, "It is only in language that
something is a proposition. To understand a proposition is to understand
a language."[12]

But the version of semantic holism that is closest and most relevant
to our concerns is to be found above all in the work of Gadamer and the
tradition from which he emerges, whose high-water marks are Herder,
Humboldt, and Heidegger. For these thinkers, even the most commonplace words rely on a (partly concealed) context in order to fully mean
what they do. Take, for instance, the word *book*. To identify or recognize something as a book I must already have in my lexicon neighboring
words that contrast with and situate this word. So, for example, I must
be able recognize other objects containing written material as nonbooks
and understand the words that identify its properties, such as paper and
binding; I must also be familiar with the language of the practices in
which books figure, such as the words associated with reading and writing. Moreover, there are still other, somewhat more distant words that
contribute significantly to the meaning of this word—in the case of the
word *book* these might be words from the practice of using libraries and

the world of publishing. This array of words, in turn, will depend in part for their meanings on yet another range of words, in an ever-widening circle of connections. In this regard, words depend for their meaning on an implicit background of associated words, objects, and practices that provide the broadest context for the words we speak and hear, read and write, giving them a particular direction and sense.

This kind of semantic holism accounts for the difficulty of fully and straightforwardly translating culturally specific terms such as *fūdo* into English, since whatever term is ultimately chosen to render *fūdo* will be encompassed by a very different kind of background whole from that of *fūdo*, one that extends from associated words to contexts of activity, all the way up to the very form of life in which all of these are embedded. Moreover the semantic holism I wish to argue for poses a further obstacle for the task of translation. I contend that the total horizon of meaning brought into play by words or expressions enables them to *disclose* the things of the world. Since different languages bring with them different such background wholes, one language can disclose something that cannot always be made manifest in another language.

This version of semantic holism, then, supports a conception of language as essentially disclosive rather than designative. According to this view, language primarily makes manifest or reveals the world rather than represents it. Although he does not set out his views in detail, Watsuji appears to share this conception of language, which originates with Herder and Humboldt and receives its fullest and most sophisticated statement in the work of Heidegger and Gadamer. The phenomenon of linguistic disclosure is a large topic that has significant consequences for Watsuji's thought, so this theme will be addressed in a separate chapter. Here I will give only a brief indication of what is involved in this conception of language in order to understand how it relates to the question of translation.

Language is disclosive insofar as it more fully articulates, increases, and completes the intelligibility of things so that they can make an appearance in our experience *as* what they are. This means that disclosure is an event that takes place at the point where separate domains of intelligibility intersect: the meanings that belong to things, on the one side, and those that belong to words, on the other. Although this understanding of language diverges in fundamental ways from the common and widespread view of language as a system of signs used to refer to and represent reality, it does not entail that language cannot (at times) refer to and represent things. The difference is that for this conception, language is not a tool that belongs to us, which we use to signify and represent the world; rather it is a disclosive medium to which *we* belong and in which we encounter the world. As such, language is a medium in which we live and through which things become manifest.[13] This means that, as Humboldt had already pointed out in the nineteenth century, language is a whole into which we are plunged and from which we cannot extract ourselves. As he puts it, "Every language draws about the people that possess it a circle whence it is possible to exit only by stepping over at once into the circle of another one."[14] Even if we leave our native language behind, we never leave language *as such* behind. We can never get outside of language and achieve the distance needed to objectify it, as in the conception of language as an instrument. Instead we must see that language is a holistic medium through which our whole experience of the world unfolds.

This capacity to unfold or disclose, moreover, is not a power that belongs to the individual word in isolation, or even to the whole sentence; my contention is that the capacity of words and sentences to reveal depends on the implicit and unexpressed whole that surrounds every word or expression. That is, the full meaning of the terms we use depends on a fusion of the expressed and the unexpressed; meaning cannot be wholly carried by and restricted to the explicit content of what is actually said or written. As we have seen, the meaning of words depends to some degree for their exact sense on a surrounding context of associated words, such as synonyms, antonyms, and other terms and expressions that situate and color these words in one respect or another—such as those connected to the related sentiments, ideas, and narratives of the great texts of the culture. The meaning of such words will depend, too, on their usage in proverbs, songs, and idioms and in the practices and institutions they help to constitute.

This coalescence of expressed and unexpressed meaning that belongs to the intelligibility of the word, then, gives the word a particular way of revealing the thing by constituting a specific standpoint from which the intelligibility of the thing is disclosed. The result is a partial and always incomplete articulation of the meanings of things rather than the full representation of a preexisting reality. I suggest we find here an explanation for why one language can fail to uncover in translation that which was disclosed in the original. Since different languages provide different contexts of associated words and practices for equivalent words and concepts, some languages are unable to furnish, through the equivalent term, the perspective on the thing that will reveal precisely the same meaning that is uncovered by the original language. Thus some of what gets lost in translation is what is *disclosed* by the original term or expression. This is especially true of translations involving the translation of concepts, values, and ideas specific to a culture and worldview.

All of this does not amount to the claim that rare or difficult terms such as *fūdo* are untranslatable; it only means that the complete meaning of this term cannot be fully grasped through whatever English words are used to translate it. This becomes apparent upon inspecting some earlier translations of this term. *Fūdo* has been variously translated into English as *climate and culture, climate,* and *milieu.* The problem with the term *climate* is that it does not register the connection to human life and culture that is intimated in the term *fūdo.* And while it focuses attention on the indispensable physical dimension of nature in *fūdo, climate* does not suggest much beyond the weather and other atmospheric and meteorological phenomena; other physical characteristics of *fūdo,* such as the soil type and the topographical features of the land, are not comprehended by this term. The phrase *climate and culture,* which was used to translate the title of Watsuji's book into English, has the virtue of indicating the way *fūdo* extends beyond the mere physicality of nature, but this pair is too cumbersome to use in translating every instance of the occurrence of the term *fūdo.* In addition, the use of a pair of terms to translate a single concept also gives the mistaken impression that *fūdo* consists of, or can be divided into, two distinct and separate entities. The geographer and theorist Augustin Berque—who is also the French translator of Watsuji's *Fūdo*—has made a case for translating *fūdo* as *milieu* in both French and English. This usage has certain advantages, especially in terms of moving the reader away from the idea of an objective "natural environment." On the other hand, in English *milieu* primarily connotes a social environment, and it does not really convey the vital and all-important sense of nature as the ground of *fūdo.*

These examples show that there is no exact equivalent of *fūdo* in English, no single word that is able to express what the Japanese term reveals. The unsatisfactory nature of these alternatives, and the difficulties involved in translating this concept, already give us good reasons to leave the term *fūdo* untranslated in this study. But another and even more important consideration in this regard is the philosophical significance of Watsuji's use of the term *fūdo.* Although he never really transforms *fūdo* into a full-fledged philosophical concept in the way that Heidegger, for instance, does with *Dasein,* Watsuji ultimately links *fūdo* to the being of the human being, so that this term functions in his work as an ontological concept. This use of the term is greatly facilitated by the way in which, in ordinary Japanese usage, *fūdo* conveys the sense of nature as implicated in the articulation of forms of human life and culture. Ordinary English words such as *climate, environment,* and *milieu,* on the other hand, are not quite able to capture this phenomenon. Moreover words such as *climate* and *environment* invite us to consider the spaces and sites of nature as objects or, when viewed in relation to human beings, as stages for or backdrops to human life and activity. This kind of dualism runs counter to the way in which the expression of human life and the activity of nature unfold together in *fūdo*. In this way, the translation of *fūdo* by one of these English words misses what is really new in this concept, just as would be the case, for example, if *Dasein* were translated by words such as *consciousness* or *subject*.

Watsuji was alert to the way this kind of loss in translation, as a loss of that which was disclosed in the original language, could have decisive philosophical consequences. He begins his major three-volume work in ethics, *Rinrigaku* 倫理学 (*Ethics*), for example, with the contention that words such as *anthropos, homo, man,* and *Mensch* cannot be used to express his conception of the human being, which he names with the Japanese word *ningen* 人間. These words always and only denote either the *individual* human being or human beings in general, whereas the etymology of *ningen* reveals that when appropriated as a concept for philosophical inquiry, it is able to express the hybrid character of human beings as simultaneously individual and social. We should point out here that even when we use the word *human being*, the rules of English usage require us to either signify the category that encompasses all human beings (e.g., the human being or human beings) or to pick out an individual (e.g., a human being) or a plurality of individuals (e.g., the human beings). In any case, we are not able to use this word to express exactly what the term *ningen* represents for Watsuji.

This sensitivity to the force and depth of certain words, to the importance of etymology, and to the difficulty of translation, both in this example as well as in other instances throughout his work, indicate the kind of hermeneutic considerations that are essential to Watsuji's philosophical method. As John Maraldo has shown, Watsuji's work can be situated within a hermeneutical tradition that has now become international.[15] Watsuji belongs in many respects to a lineage of thinkers that runs from Schleiermacher and Dilthey to Heidegger, Gadamer, and Ricoeur. His particular hermeneutic practice is oriented by the idea that the nature of things can be uncovered by the way we speak and have spoken about them. For this reason, some of his most important philosophical inquiries begin by excavating the range of historical meanings that have sedimented into the large concepts that structure the way we think about the world, such as *rinri* 倫理 (~ ethics), *ningen sonzai* 人間存在 (~ human existence), or *wakaru* 分かる (~ to understand).

This method of closely examining the root meanings of words that have been forgotten or covered over in order to recover their disclosive force has obvious parallels with, and is likely to have been influenced by, Heidegger's etymological method. The terms Watsuji appropriates in this way are, like Heidegger's own philosophical concepts, extremely difficult to translate fully. But this does not amount to the claim that the philosophical meaning of a concept like *fūdo* cannot be understood by someone who does not speak Japanese. This study is predicated on the notion that what is disclosed by *fūdo* as a philosophical concept can be made intelligible even—and perhaps especially—if this term is left untranslated. One does not need a translation of *Dasein* to see what this term makes manifest—one needs a translation of the philosophical account that accompanies and explains the use of this term. An English-language translation of the word *Dasein* is almost certain to cover over the phenomenon Heidegger wishes to set before us. Or, to take better known examples, the translation of *phronêsis* by *prudence*, and *arête* by *virtue* are just as likely to conceal as to convey what is contained in these concepts. In my view, we can come to a better and fuller understanding of both of these terms by leaving them untranslated, allowing their meanings to emerge through an explanatory account that links them to an array of related concepts that pertain to phenomena ranging from dispositions, emotions, and perception to habituation, judgment, and action. Likewise, rather than render *fūdo* into English, we will attempt, over the course of this study, to render what is made *manifest* by the use of this term.

III. The Emergence of *Fūdo* as a Philosophical Concept

In the preface to his 1935 book, *Fūdo: A Philosophical-Anthropological Study* (*Fūdo: Ningengakuteki kōsatsu* 風土−人間学的考察), Watsuji writes that he first came to reflect on the problem of *fūdosei* 風土, or the character and quality of *fūdo* as it is experienced and lived through, while reading Heidegger's *Sein und Zeit* in Berlin. He was especially intrigued by Heidegger's treatment of the structure of human existence in terms of temporality. He was struck at the same time by the way Heidegger seemed to overlook the spatial dimension of that structure. He noticed this, he surmises, because his mind was still filled with impressions from the various *fūdo* he encountered on a recently completed voyage by sea from Japan to Europe. This trip was sponsored by the Japanese Ministry of Education, as it was then required of imperial university associate professors to spend a period of time in Europe before their promotion to a full professorship. Thus in February 1927 Watsuji boarded a Japanese passenger liner which took him from Kobe to Marseille. Along the way his ship called at ports in Shanghai, Hong Kong, Penang, Singapore, Colombo, Aden, and the Suez

Canal. After arriving in Europe, Watsuji traveled extensively around Germany and Italy, but also spent time in France, Switzerland, and England.[16]

    The continuous shifts in locale during this trip seem to have foregrounded something for Watsuji that usually does not come to explicit notice, namely, the prodigious variety of natural spaces and places that compose the setting of the lifeworld. Moreover Watsuji was aided greatly by the fact that the Japanese language possesses a term that made it possible for him to pick out and name this phenomenon when he encountered it. Nevertheless, as he himself points out, his impressions of these locations would have remained exactly that, impressions, had he not read *Being and Time* shortly after his arrival in Europe.[17] Thanks to his reading of this text, his observations of these places, which he set down in notes as well as in letters home, would form the basis for his book-length philosophical study of *fūdo*.

    While *Fūdo* is explicitly both an appreciation and a critique of Heidegger's *Being and Time*, as a philosophical text it is also a response to a particular way of viewing culture and climate prevalent among the thinkers in the Western tradition whom Watsuji read while in Europe.[18] He observes that ancient Greek authors such as Hippocrates, Polybius, and Strabo, as well as later thinkers such as Bodin and Montesquieu, shared the view that environment and climate determine the characteristics and fate of different ethnic groups. He rejects this idea outright because it presupposes an understanding of *fūdo* as external to human beings. In his view, these thinkers fail to grasp the true nature (*honshitsu* 本質) of *fūdo*.[19] This point emerges most fully in his discussions of Montesquieu and Herder. He maintains that just as in the natural sciences, in Montesquieu's work nature and climate are treated as objects that impact human physiology rather than as what they properly are: part of the very structure of human existence.[20] As Christopher Goto-Jones explains with regard to this claim, because man does not and cannot exist cut off from or outside of space, "the environment is an integral part of his subjectivity."[21]

    Because Herder's concept of *Klima*, or climate, enables Watsuji to fill out this insight in greater detail, he turns in his account to a fuller consideration of Herder's work. For Watsuji, Herder is that singular and essential thinker in the history of Western philosophy who first sets forth the true character of the relation between human beings and the natural world. Despite the emergent scientific spirit of his age, Watsuji notes with approval, Herder does not treat *Klima* as an object of the natural sciences. This is in part because *Klima* cannot simply be identified with the meteorological phenomenon of climate, or even with the natural environment as a whole. Although *Klima* encompasses both of these, it also includes the humanly constructed environment, so that it amounts, in effect, to everything in the environment of a person that affects her existence. Herder gives as examples of the constituent elements of *Klima* not only the topography of the region one inhabits, the local products to be found there, and the food and drink one consumes, but also the type of work one engages in, the clothing one wears, the amusements one pursues, and the overall mode of life one adheres to.[22]

Watsuji views this concept of climate as something like an early, if imperfect, version of the concept of *fūdo*, and he uses the terms interchangeably in his analysis of Herder. This is somewhat puzzling, since *Klima* covers a far more expansive range of phenomena than *fūdo*. Nonetheless these concepts *do* overlap in essential ways. Both *Klima* and *fūdo* refer to an environment that functions as a nonobjectifiable medium in and through which we live and have our being. For Herder, as for Watsuji, this environment is plainly of a different order from the "natural environment" studied by geography. We arrive at the latter conception only by separating human beings and *fūdo*, as when we analyze the relation between the two in terms of mutual influences or causal connections. Watsuji contrasts these phenomena with one another in order to show that unlike the natural environment, which is external to human beings, the concept of *Klima* enables Herder to set *fūdo inside* of human existence. This will mean first, that the phenomenon of geographic climate, as an expression of human life, becomes an object of the understanding and not, as in conventional geography, an object of explanation. Second, as Herder shows in the course of setting out the principles of his philosophy of history, it means that our mentality and way of life themselves always already have a *fūdo*-like (*fūdoteki*) character or quality.[23]

Our mentality has the character and quality of a *fūdo* first, to the extent that our sensibility, our sense of and for things is climatic. Our palate, for instance, is closely linked to the water and temperatures of a place as well as to its flora and fauna. It develops as and is expressed in the cuisine specific to a region or land. Second, the power of the imagination is climatic. The concept of Santa Claus, Watsuji observes, was not invented in the tropics. Third, emotions and drives are climatic, so that, for example, there come to be a variety of ways in which human beings are brought together through bonds of affection.

Our form of life has the character and quality of a *fūdo* first, insofar as the practices we engage in vary with the *Klima* in which we live. The question of whether, for instance, the people who inhabit a place are nomadic or agricultural, or whether they engage primarily in fishing or in raising livestock, is a question settled by *Klima*. Second, the traditions, customs, and values that underpin our way of life are, in Herder's view, so intimately tied to *Klima* that he traces the differences between cultures in these areas to differing *Klimata*. Our idea of what constitutes happiness, for example, is to a large extent a function of climate. Hence modern Western (and, it must be said, modern Japanese) ideas about happiness are not appropriate criteria by which to assess ideas about human fulfillment that are found in very different climates. A person living in a modern nation is not necessarily happier in his pleasures, Watsuji points out, than someone in a less developed nation engaged in the quiet satisfactions of family life and a rustic existence.[24]

This descriptive and comparative analysis of the relation between *Klima*, mentality (*Geist des Klimas*), and *Lebensform* enables Herder to uncover the way in which divergent *Klimata* lead to significant differences in mentality and in forms of life, and hence to many of the important differences between the cultures and values of different peoples. Herder maintains that some of these values and cultures are incommensurable, and so cannot be compared with one another. In place of comparative judgments of superiority and inferiority in such cases, he expresses an appreciation for the specificity and singularity of mentalities, cultural values, and ways of life.

For most historians and philosophers, the value pluralism that emerges from Herder's philosophy of history is the most important aspect of his work on climate. For Watsuji, Herder's achievement does not end there. Through the concept of *Klima*, Herder shows that man is a climatic being: his sentiments, his labors and pleasures, his way of life, the very boundaries of his heart and mind—all of these are climatic, so that to take away his land is to take everything away from him.[25] This is an approach that moves beyond the dualism and objectification of standard geography to exhibit the way in which man and nature have their being in one another. Although Herder was not fully aware of it himself, Watsuji says, his work demonstrates the sense in which *fūdo* is a "moment" (*keiki* 契機) in the structure of human life (*ningen no sei no kōzō* 人間の生の構造).[26] Watsuji first employs this enigmatic expression in almost exactly the same form at the beginning of *Fūdo* to describe the principal theme of his book. The meaning of this complex and rather opaque formulation of the issue will gradually become clearer over the course of our own study. What is important to note here is the extent to which Watsuji saw his own project in Herder's earlier work on this topic. It is clear that he takes up much of what he found in Herder in the course of developing his own notion of *fūdo* as a distinct concept.

Watsuji's favorable, though qualified reception of Herder's ideas is rivaled only by a similar, though more extensive and complicated embrace of Heidegger's early thought—an event that will be one of the major concerns of this study. His appropriation of the work of both of these thinkers, together with the semantic depth and range of the term *fūdo*, are largely what make it possible for him to transform this ordinary word into a philosophical concept. So although Watsuji opens his study with an initial definition of *fūdo* as a term that designates the meteorological, geological, topographic, and scenic features of a given region of nature, he eventually expands upon this formulation in ways that show that *fūdo* goes far beyond this initial designation and amounts to one of the central philosophical concepts in his oeuvre.

Nevertheless Watsuji does not attempt to recover the meanings latent in this term in the same way, or to anywhere near the same extent, that he does for the various other concepts that feature so prominently in his thinking, such as *ningen* and *rinri*. This comes as something of a surprise, since he almost always uses this method to promote select terms from ordinary words to philosophical concepts, that is, concepts that bring to light new realities and give us novel ways of understanding the world. So while *fūdo* functions as a philosophical concept in this sense, Watsuji never sets out the precise meaning of this term in a thorough or systematic fashion. Instead an array of meanings emerges in piecemeal and at times cryptic fashion. Hans Peter Liederbach notes in this regard that although the text of *Fūdo* contains all of Watsuji's philosophical thinking *in nuce*, *fūdo* itself is an enigmatic phenomenon that always seems to escape conceptual clarification; its ontological status, he observes, is notoriously unclear.[27]

IV. The Conflict of Interpretations: Nature and Culture in *Fūdo*

The ambiguity and confusion surrounding this term has led to two very general kinds of misunderstandings on the part of Watsuji's interpreters. On the one side are those who inflate the significance of the cultural and subjective dimension of *fūdo* in their interpretations and either roundly criticize or are content to embrace what they view as Watsuji's subsumption of nature into culture. In moving through this group of interpreters, we begin with a brief overview of the primary complaints regarding Watsuji's extension of nature into culture before turning to the positive (though to varying degrees mistaken) assessments of this elision; proceeding in this manner will allow us to articulate the limits of a "cultural" reading of *fūdo* in a way that cuts across both kinds of misunderstandings.

It is not difficult to see where interpretations that overemphasize the subjective and cultural features of *fūdo* come from, since Watsuji is explicit in setting out *fūdo* as a category that blurs the usual boundaries between the natural and the cultural, the subjectivity of the human being and the objectivity of nature. This approach to the notion of *fūdo* has led some commentators to accuse Watsuji of suppressing the dimension of nature in *fūdo* in ways that distort and undermine the concept altogether. Takashima Zenya claims, for example, that the notion of *fūdo* lacks the concept of a true and living nature. Nature for Watsuji is nature for man, but not, as it should be, the nature of philosophical naturalism, which transcends man and takes a certain kind of priority.[28] Ikimatsu Keizō and Iizuka Kōji also maintain that Watsuji has overlooked the primacy of nature's materiality and transcendence. Ikimatsu contends that Watsuji denies to nature a priority that it should rightly have, and that he views the question of *fūdo* as merely a matter of human self-understanding. Iizuka maintains that even though it is "nature as such" that underlies *fūdo*, this dimension of nature remains hidden in Watsuji's account.[29]

Watsuji's own statements about the relation between culture and *fūdo* appear, at times, to substantiate such charges. He maintains, for instance, that "we can also find the phenomenon of *fūdo* [*fūdo no genshō* 風土の現象] in all of the expressions of human life, such as literature, art, religion, customs."[30] A certain way of reading this and similar assertions has led other commentators to conclude that *fūdo* extends beyond the natural environment to incorporate the cultural one, rather than that nature has somehow been concealed or overlooked in this concept. Robert Carter and Erin McCarthy are among those who share this view, maintaining that in addition to the natural environment of a locale, *fūdo* includes the social environment of the family, community, and wider culture.[31] Yoko Arisaka goes further than this and extends the notion of *fūdo* to cover more or less everything that environs and influences a person, including social and cultural phenomena such as family environment, class, and religion, so that *fūdo* comes to be equated with something like the totality of a milieu.[32] Pauline Couteau echoes this judgment, describing *fūdo* as, in sum, "the totality of what surrounds human beings living together in a given place."[33] Just as with the first group of commentators, such readings have a propensity to underscore the significance of the cultural and subjective dimensions of *fūdo*, although these interpretations are generally far more positive in their assessment of the way *fūdo* can be understood to encompass the human world.

While it is true that as a philosophical concept, *fūdo* transcends significant aspects of the duality between culture and nature, I want nevertheless to resist the equation of *fūdo* with *everything* that environs a human being. A full and rigorous accounting of the elements that would constitute a *fūdo* as the total human environment would require an inventory of literally everything we experience: weather, trees, plants, bodies of water, animals wild and domestic, topographic features of a terrain; but also practices, institutions, images, language, art, music, texts, architecture, communication and transportation networks, ceremonies, forms of entertainment, ideologies, religious creeds, political organizations, clothing styles, cuisines, scents, other people and their actions, gestures, moods, and habits, and so on almost ad infinitum. Since these things do not all have one and the same mode of being, the sense in which each of these entities "environs" us varies widely and includes visual, psychological, auditory, intellectual, gustatory, emotional, tactile, and olfactory forms of contact—all of which would also need to be analyzed and incorporated into this account. I maintain that to include everything that is part of the setting of our lives in the concept of *fūdo* is too broad an interpretation, one that would sharply reduce the explanatory power of *fūdo* and render this notion almost useless.

I suggest, instead, that we stay close to the basic meaning that Watsuji must surely have had in mind in choosing the word *fūdo*. The opening lines of his study give a fairly clear indication of his intentions in this regard: "What I am here calling *fūdo* is a general term which designates the climate, the weather conditions, the nature of the soil, and the geologic, topographic, and scenic [*keikan* 景観] features of a given land."[34] This characterization of *fūdo* does not differ on its face from the way this word is used in ordinary Japanese, namely, as referring primarily to a region of nature, albeit one that is woven into the fabric of human life. Watsuji underscores this sense of *fūdo* as having a material and physical ground in the next sentence, observing that the ancient Buddhist cosmological view of nature as constituted by the four elements of earth, water, fire, and wind lies behind the concept of *fūdo*. *Fūdo* at its core, then, for Watsuji, is that which environs us insofar as it belongs to or is part of a specific region of nature.

This definition of *fūdo* is further reinforced by the way much of the rest of this study is devoted to the descriptive explanation of three basic types of *fūdo*: monsoon, desert, and meadow. The monsoon *fūdo* (a fusion of heat and humidity, lush vegetation, violent storms and floods) comprises India (at that time including modern-day Pakistan, Bangladesh, and Myanmar) and the whole coastal belt of East Asia, including Japan and China. Arabia, northern Africa, and Mongolia belong to the desert *fūdo*, and the meadow *fūdo* (green pastureland and a synthesis of humidity and aridity) refers mainly to Europe. Watsuji posited these types on the basis of the impressions he received and observations he accumulated during his long journey to Europe and back. Later, in the second volume of *Ethics*, he adds the American (forests, prairies, powerful rainstorms, intense changes in temperature through the seasons) and the steppe (the endless and monotonous expanses of the Russian grasslands) as basic types of *fūdo*, while acknowledging that his work had also yet to treat the distinct climes of the African interior and the islands of the Pacific as other types of *fūdo*.[35]

While these points can serve to correct overly cultural and subjective construals of the notion of *fūdo*, they also introduce a set of difficulties and questions that must be resolved if this correction is to really succeed. There are, to begin with, two kinds of problems with Watsuji's system of classification—despite the general truths about the geographical and climatic patterns that characterize the world to be found in these descriptions. The first arises from Watsuji's overgeneralizations concerning the climate and flora of vast regions of the globe, which are considerably more diverse and complex in their physical geography than his account suggests. He seems to have left descriptive nuance aside in his haste to demonstrate a correspondence between these climatic regions and different ethnocultural personality types, such as the Indian, the Arab, the European, and so on. But he also draws a connection between *fūdo* and specific national characters, maintaining that certain allegedly Greek, American, Russian, Chinese, and, of course, Japanese national character traits naturally emerge from the region in which these peoples live. Claims of this sort have led to the charge of geographic determinism among commentators on Watsuji's work—a charge that we will shortly address.

Such assertions also raise questions about the range of peoples and places supposedly covered by these terms—for example, who counts as "Chinese" or "European"? Is it really possible to identify an ethnic personality type shared across all of the possible groups of people that might be placed into each of these categories? And how can the total geospheric environment of something like the entire Indian subcontinent, with its cold mountain and white salt deserts, with its mountain ranges and scrub forests, be summarily designated a monsoon clime? These and other doubts point toward the second problem, namely, that Watsuji has underdetermined the size and scope of a *fūdo*. Plainly, the mixing together here of continents and nations, of transcontinental populations and nationalities, shows that the concept of *fūdo* does not, to use Plato's metaphor, carve reality at its joints, so that it would be possible to see the convergence of nature and nation in each *fūdo*.

Watsuji may have wished to preserve a certain indeterminacy in the concept of *fūdo*, since this would have made it possible to capture a wider range of phenomena with this notion. Nevertheless criteria that can be used to specify the scale of a *fūdo* can be located in Watsuji's own descriptions of what is entailed by *fūdo* as a philosophical concept. I propose that we adhere to these criteria so as to avoid the kind of ambiguity that can undercut what was gained by initially deploying this concept in the first place. Although in later chapters we will fill in and further refine these criteria, an initial survey of such specifications will allow us to determine, if only in a general way, the scope and boundaries of a *fūdo*.

The primary criterion comes from nature itself, which is a kind of given that presents certain regions as articulated wholes around which boundaries can be drawn; this is what Watsuji attempts to express with his taxonomy of basic types of *fūdo*. But because *fūdo* is not a stand-alone concept, this classification needs to be more carefully carpentered. Watsuji's examination of the phenomenon of *fūdo* will reveal that the intelligibility of a region of nature is disclosed by the people who live there, even as the continuities of meaning that emerge from a *fūdo* shape their self-understanding. There is no clear or clean break in a *fūdo* between nature and culture; they are continuous with each other and are distinguished here only in order to identify a particular *fūdo*. At its ground, this is a place in nature distinct enough to engender correspondingly distinct, large-scale cultural forms, namely, structures that are relatively stable and self-sustaining over time.

A second criterion for what counts as a *fūdo* can thus be equated with this relational whole of disclosure, self-interpretation, and natural locale. While this eliminates small-scale locales such as the garden of a home or the fields around a farm as possible candidates for a *fūdo*, it leaves open the answer to what counts as an identifiably distinct, large-scale cultural form.[36] Watsuji's own descriptions and examples suggest that such forms could include local, regional, and national subcultures and cultures. And this, in turn, allows for a relatively wide range of sizes and scales of the regions of nature that might function as the ground of these cultural forms. Gary Snyder offers a close and informative explanation of why this kind of natural region necessarily varies in its scope:

> The total size of the region a group calls home depends on the land type. Every group is territorial, each moves within a given zone, even nomads stay within boundaries. A people living in a desert or grassland with great visible spaces that invite you to step forward and walk as far as you can see will range across tens of thousands of square miles. A deep old-growth forest may rarely be traveled at all. Foragers in gallery forests and grasslands will regularly move broadly, whereas people in a deep-soiled valley ideal for gardens might not go far beyond the top of the nearest ridge. The regional boundaries were roughly drawn by climate, which is what sets the plant-type zones—plus soil type and

landforms. Desert wastes, mountain ridges, or big rivers set a broad
edge to a region. We walk across or wade through the larger and
smaller boundaries. Like children first learning our homeland we can
stand at the edge of a big river, or on the crest of a major ridge, and
observe that the other side is a different soil, a change of plants and
animals, a new shape of barn roof, maybe less or more rain. The lines
between natural regions are never simple or clear, but vary according
to such criteria as biota, watersheds, landforms, elevation. . . . Still, we
all know—at some point—that we are no longer in the Midwest, say,
but in the West.[37]

Linking the notion of *fūdo* so closely to the materiality of nature
in these ways enables us to evade the criticisms as well as the difficulties
that originate with the different kinds of "cultural" misreadings of *fūdo*,
but this approach then raises the question of what we intend by the term
nature. To find our way safely through the maze of such a far-reaching
question, we can begin, as do many philosophers who think about the
topic of nature, with the classic distinction that Mill makes between two
basic senses of nature. The first is "the sum of all phenomena, together
with the causes which produce them; including not only all that happens,
but all that is capable of happening." The second is nature as opposed
to art, to artifact, and to what is artificial.[38] In referring to "nature," we
are not speaking about nature in the first, all-encompassing sense, since
this would return us to the kinds of difficulties that arise when *fūdo* is
equated with *everything* that environs a human being. Moreover such a
conception of nature would erase any meaningful distinction between
what is natural and what cultural or artificial, and so between something
like *nature* and *nonnature*. Hence this definition gives with one hand what
it takes away with the other, a comprehensive philosophical definition of
nature per se. Puzzles of this kind are quite representative of the seemingly endless and intractable difficulties of the terrain here. Fortunately
for us, securing a definitive concept of nature is not absolutely necessary before we can make meaningful use of this term. Instead our main
concern is to establish the inherent features, content, and scope of that
portion of nature that constitutes the basis of a *fūdo*, namely, nature as
place and space, and the processes that unfold in this domain. This much
narrower focus allows us to pass over the extensive debate concerning the
philosophical definition of nature and the perplexities and aporias that
ensue even in the byways of this discussion. References to "nature" in this
study are thus not to nature per se, but to those geographical expanses
of the natural places and spaces that can be encountered in perceptual
experience.

While this more narrowly circumscribed focus on the geospheric components of place and space appears to provide a straightforward way to demarcate nature from nonnature at a given location, this impression is quickly dispelled by the opacity and ambiguity that attends—even at this markedly reduced scale—every attempt to more fully specify what nature is, and so what is natural. We can see this when we try to describe the natural elements enumerated by Watsuji that make up a *fūdo*: weather, climate, and the pedospheric, topographic, geologic, and scenic characteristics of a given expanse of land. If a *fūdo* includes the scenic features of a land, it must comprise both bodies of water as well as vegetation. Bodies of water occur naturally but can also, of course, be artificially constructed in the form of reservoirs, canals, drainage ditches, decorative ponds, and so forth. And so much of the vegetation we encounter in a place has been replanted, reforested, replaced, cultivated, modified, domesticated (or otherwise altered, as in the case of GMOs) that the attempt to establish a coherent distinction between the natural and the nonnatural in this area is even more difficult than in the case of bodies of water.[39] The topography of many areas has also been reshaped by human hands, through slash-and-burn agriculture, mountaintop and pit mining, road and rail construction, the erection of levees, logging, and the soil erosion caused by the change of water flow over the land as a result of these activities. Even the atmosphere is not immune: the imprint of human activity is there in phenomena such as smog and man-made climate change.

In short, when we look upon nature, we are coming, increasingly, to see ourselves. If this is so, on what basis can one say, for example, that agricultural fields and canals belong to a *fūdo*, but the buildings and streets, bridges and dams in the same place do not? If *fūdo* excludes what Jacques Ellul calls "the technological milieu," we are faced with the question of how we are to distinguish between nature and artifice—which is the problem of how "nature" in Mill's second sense can be delineated.

The distinction between what belongs to nature and what to artifice in a given location, I suggest, can be made, first, on the basis of what is entailed in something like a place at all. We live in places and spaces—especially in the developed world—whose built environment seems all-embracing, from urban landscapes to the social, cultural, economic, and political spaces in which we act and move. Wesley Kort, whose argument I will be recapitulating (and who himself draws on Henri Lefebvre), shows that these humanly constructed and controlled places and spaces cannot be all-encompassing by their very nature, since they are structured according to particular human interests, goals, and values. What lies in the interstices and at the margins and limits of these configurations exposes what is always present but usually concealed: the kind of space and place that supports and provides a basis for humanly constructed places and spaces, one that antedates and reaches far beyond the borders of even the most extended places or massive social spaces. This space and place, as primary, fundamental, and encompassing, provides the most extensive context of human life; it is that which enables, supports, unifies, and endures. Here we encounter something not fully available to us, something that lies behind and ultimately beyond what we have laid down. Kort, citing Lefebvre, speaks about this kind of space and place as opening "out onto something more and directing attention to possible boundaries that are beyond depiction," and so something that "eludes grasp and adequate representation."[40] The derivative standing of humanly constructed spaces and places is thrown sharply into relief by this sense of natural spaces and places as, finally, harboring an immensity that lies beyond our control.

Notwithstanding this sense of nature as mysterious presence, when we consider all of the ways in which these kinds of places and spaces have been impacted, altered, or remade by our activity, human aspiration seems almost equal to this dimension of nature. Some—but not all—of these processes and products reshape and take their place as part of a *fūdo*. A newly created species of crop and a reservoir count as constituents of a *fūdo*; the installation of telephone poles and the erection of skyscrapers do not, even though they affect the space and scenery of a landscape. Here one may ask what makes the former "natural" (and so part of a *fūdo*) but renders the latter "artificial," if both are in some sense products of human intervention and effort. In the former case, the plant and the river are first simply and sheerly there as "given"; in selectively breeding the plant or damming a river we intrude upon something whose form is not primarily made by us and whose operations are not set in motion by us, something that sustains itself in its causal powers, and so appears, as one commentator puts it in elucidating the distinction between nature and artifact, as a "spontaneous nonhuman nature that is free to develop according to its own laws."[41] In this sheerly given self-unfolding of things, we find the second criterion that distinguishes nature from artifice in a given locale.

That which constitutes, belongs to, and occurs in the places and spaces of the natural world remains in these respects beyond our reach. And while the way in which nature transcends us in its scope and in its power enables us to differentiate the natural from the nonnatural, Watsuji wants to avoid an unqualified affirmation of this divide. This can be seen in his pointed avoidance of the modern Japanese term for nature, *shizen* 自然, to name what is covered by *fūdo*, since in its roughly century-old modern incarnation, *shizen* has been, and continues to be, used to translate the Western concept of nature as that which lies outside of and opposite the self—as opposed to culture. This is especially evident in the use of *shizen* to denote the nature investigated by science, since a withdrawal of the subject must be effected before such an object can appear. Watsuji is unwavering in his rejection of any notion of nature as separated from and opposed to human beings. Nature is not a background against which human beings act or a stage upon which human life is lived; it is a medium in which we are caught up and in which we have our being.

This latter sense of nature and of what is natural accords with the classical Japanese conception of nature as *shizen* before the term was used to translate the modern concept of nature into Japanese. In this older, premodern understanding of *shizen*, the human and the natural are not opposed to one another but are different profiles or moments of a common relational field. If *this* meaning of *shizen* were still the predominant one in Japanese, Watsuji would surely have embraced its use in characterizing this foundational dimension of *fūdo*. Indeed one way to understand Watsuji's elevation of *fūdo* to a philosophical concept is to view it as a modern attempt to recover part of the classical understanding of *shizen* by imbuing it with a certain intellectual rigor.

Shizen is the Japanese pronunciation of *ziran*, the Chinese term from which it is derived; it was introduced into Japan along with the influx of other elements of Sinitic culture in the seventh and eighth centuries.[42] In English *ziran* has been translated by Arthur Waley and others as *what-is-so-of-itself*, and already appears in the *Daodejing* to designate what unfolds of its own accord as opposed to the will and designs of the self. This unfolding, eternal flow of nature is a continuum in which all modes of being are organically connected such that human life too is part of this continuous transformation. Because we form one body with the whole in this way, nature is an all-enfolding unity, an all-encompassing harmony with nothing exterior to it.

Although the importation of the concept of *ziran* had a profound influence on Japanese thinking about nature, the indigeneous Japanese understanding of the natural world was in some respects not very far removed from these ideas. In ancient Japanese, the first sinograph in *ziran* (*zi* 自) was used both in the term *onozukara* 自ずから to indicate that which originates from itself, as well as in the term *mizukara* 自ら to refer to that which originates from oneself, or from the body. So while there was no uniform category for the totality of stars, mountains, rivers, and so on, no term with which to designate "nature in general" until the importation of the sinograph compound *ziran*, the term *onozukara* enabled the Japanese to refer to a natural phenomenon as an objective state that commences of itself without external intervention (which closely resembles the dimension of "nature" within a *fūdo* that I have argued for), in contrast to the term *mizukara*, which refers to a subjective state in which someone carries something out. Hubertus Tellenbach and Kimura Bin maintain, "That the Japanese believe they can express these seemingly autonomous terms by means of a single character points towards a deeper insight by which they apprehend *Onozukara* and *Mizukara*, nature and self, as originating from the same common ground," a ground that "binds the spontaneous processes in nature with the self-fulfilling events and activities in the course of my own self-development."[43] This means, Kimura says, that the inner origin and reality of a person is derived from nature: while the *mi* of *mizukara* signifies a body that delimits an ego boundary and distinguishes one's own being from others, *onozukara* as intrinsic nature emerges into the outer intersubjective reality of human life through the "exit" of this body. In the traditional Japanese concept of nature, self and nature are the subjective and objective aspects of a single flowing forth, a single coming into being from an original source.

This is, in fact, the *ultimate* sense of nature that stands behind Watsuji's concept of *fūdo*. Hence the distinction that we have made between the human (and hence artificial) and the natural in further specifying the natural basis of *fūdo* cannot be an unqualified one. The explanatory pattern here is one that we will see repeatedly: the difference between the two is constitutive of a higher unity. So while humans and nature do not compose a duality, they are also not identical with one another. Every complex whole is differentiated; nature as it appears in a *fūdo* and human artifacts as they appear with it name an identifiable difference, but not an absolute one. Hence this distinction is less like a dichotomy and more like a continuum. Yet coherent and experienceable realities can be recognized and distinguished from one another within such a continuous series (such as languages on a dialect chain) without positing their absolute difference. Even within the domain of "nature" that makes up the content of a *fūdo*, there are natural entities that have been excluded by this definition but that cannot actually be separated from a *fūdo*, such as the animals that plants attract with their brightly colored flowers or sweet-tasting pulp so that they are pollinated or so that their seeds are dispersed. Even in death such animals contribute organic matter to the soil without which plants could not grow. In short, without these animals, there could be no vegetation.[44] Notwithstanding these and other such points, something like a place, considered solely in terms of the landscape and climate in and through which a culture emerges, is a cogent reality that can be identified and experienced.

V. The Conflict of Interpretations: Determinism and the Politics of Nature

While *fūdo* cannot be equated with nature *simpliciter*, a certain sphere of nature, a world marked off from the human one, clearly lies at the root of this concept. This point has led a second group of commentators to treat the materiality of nature as the primary dimension of the concept of *fūdo*. Most prominent among those who hold this view are those critics who contend that the physicality of nature plays an outsize role in the concept of *fūdo*. This perception is reinforced by methodological shortcomings in the text of *Fūdo* itself. Although Watsuji declares at the outset of his study that we must not understand *fūdo* in terms of a natural environment that directly and causally determines human life, his approach throughout the rest of the book drifts precisely into a kind of determinism; much of the rest of the book is filled with observations about the myriad ways in which the local environmental features of a particular geographical region shape, and even produce, the character of the people who live there.

While we cannot follow Watsuji here and accept these claims as they stand, we also cannot deny that, on a general level, human beings and nature can and do mutually influence one another. Watsuji in fact offers wide-ranging descriptions of this phenomenon. He observes, for instance, that even something like the ways a culture is impacted by its having arisen in a densely populated area (here he probably means features such as a culture's level of sophistication, or customs that have arisen to reduce friction between people in crowded places) can itself sometimes be traced back to what he calls certain "geographical opportunities"—such as temperate climes, fertile plains, or resource-rich deltas—that allow many people to survive and flourish in a specific place.[45]

The problem with this line of thought is that Watsuji goes far beyond such general and empirical observations to intermittently espouse an out-of-date and now discredited geographical determinism in which the values, characteristics, outlook, and so on of different peoples and cultures are to be accounted for in terms of the features of the geoclimatic zones in which they live. To take just one example, he claims that the development of science is a direct result of the climate of Europe, which is mild compared to that of Japan. He cites as evidence his experience of the flooding of the Po River, in which a tranquil and almost leisurely flow of water quietly overran its banks. This contrasts strongly, he says, with the torrential flow the Japanese are used to associating with floods. Another instance of the gentle European climate is the force of the wind, which, generally speaking, he maintains, is slight. This results one another. This interaction involves the interconnection of one consciousness with another rather than a series of separate and individual mental acts executed in response to the mental acts of the other, as in the mutual adjustment of players in a chess game to the moves of one another. So, for example, my comportment and attitude in the family home subtly shifts when a guest arrives—the tone of that shift varying with, and even *as*, my awareness of the identity and disposition of the newcomer.

Even when consciousness is not explicitly directed toward anyone in particular, there is still a form of interaction here, however minimal. Watsuji's own example of this phenomenon is the experience of riding on a crowded train. Our being in the presence of one another codetermines the consciousness of all such that the passengers in the train possess a definite attitude toward one another as passengers. One can easily adduce further examples of similar kinds of experiences: my awareness of others on a tour bus, during a Christmas Eve service at Notre Dame de Paris, at a public event such as a street festival, or at a somber occasion such as a funeral will be determined by the consciousnesses of those around me.[11]

While mutual awareness shapes consciousness in ways that are not wholly in the control of the individual, an awareness of the emotional tenor of someone else's consciousness illustrates especially well the extent to which one consciousness can permeate another in interaction. While my moods and emotions would seem to be a paradigmatically private affair, Watsuji observes that many emotions, such as the concern of parents for a child, or grief at the death of a great leader, are by their very nature common or shared emotions. Not only can emotions and moods be shared, but they can often be contagious: your feelings can become mine. If I am tired or feeling down and I join a group of friends in high spirits at a party, their emotions can easily become my own, or, conversely, my buoyant mood can come to suddenly be colored by the atmosphere in the hospital room I have just entered. This kind of collapsing of the distinction between inner and outer in a shared consciousness need not be limited to intimate relationships. In a library full of students or in a town square during a crowded festival, my consciousness is penetrated and colored by the consciousness of those around me such that we come to share a mood, a spirit, a certain kind of awareness with specific contents and a particular contour.

Consciousness and its contents are in essence open to and permeated by the states of consciousness of others, a phenomenon Watsuji calls the "interpenetration of consciousnesses" (*ishiki no shintō* 意識の浸透):

> The conscious acts of the I are never determined by the I alone but are also determined by others. This does not mean there is a "reciprocal

exchange" of one-directional conscious acts back and forth between each side. Rather, there is only a single process that is determined by both sides. Thus in being-in-relation-to-others, each consciousness is able to *permeate* or *penetrate* [*shintō* 浸透] the consciousness of the other. When you become angry, my consciousness can come to be entirely colored by this anger, when I feel sorrow, your consciousness is also able to be influenced by this feeling. The consciousness of such a self can never be independent.[12]

This passage suggests that the "interpenetration of consciousnesses" culminates in all involved sharing the same contents of consciousness. But this is only one possible outcome, one found especially in phenomena such as moods. The interpenetration of consciousnesses takes other guises as well. It is possible for the contents of the consciousnesses of participants in an exchange not to be shared at all, and even for these to be opposed to one another (as in a heated argument). The mutual interpenetration of consciousnesses cannot simply be equated with shared understanding in the sense of agreement. Neither can it always be defined in terms of a shared understanding in the sense of a firm grasp on what each party to the exchange is thinking and feeling, since social life is also marked by misunderstandings such as the mistaken attribution of emotions felt or the mischaracterization of attitudes held. Notwithstanding this, in negative experiences of being together there is still a mutual interpenetration of consciousnesses. Even episodes of misunderstanding, if they are to be resolved, require a level of shared and mutual intelligibility which presupposes that the consciousness of the other is laid open and accessible to my own; that is, it presupposes that your consciousness and mine are interconnected.

Watsuji characterizes this interconnection as the "essential feature" (*honshitsu* 本質) of *aidagara*.[13] In my view, this is because the porosity or openness of one consciousness to another is an inescapable part of our existence as relational beings rather than a psychological condition that arises only in particular situations.[14] In *every* interaction the consciousness of each extends into and permeates the consciousnesses of all, since any interaction with others involves the conscious perception of them, regardless of what the activity is, who the participants are, and what kind of relationship they have with one another. Irrespective of whether an encounter is a casual and temporary or intimate and sustained exchange, and regardless of whether it is characterized primarily by physical exertion or by the barest form of perceptual awareness, the participants involved necessarily perceive and are aware of one another. The form of this awareness, whether loving, reserved, hostile, indifferent, fearful, politely friendly, and so on, is influenced and even determined to an extent by the conscious stance of each subject toward the other.

The reciprocal penetration of consciousnesses does not, however, exhaust the practical interconnection of acts. While it is true that every interaction includes the mutual awareness of the participants of one another in the inescapable interconnection of one consciousness with another, in interactions involving physical activities in addition to and beyond this shared train of consciousness, such as, to use Watsuji's examples, delivering a package to someone, cooking a meal together, or even rescuing someone from a burning house, a state of affairs also holds in which one connection is determined by both participants, since each act both governs and is governed by the corresponding act of the other person. The manner in which a package is handed to me will depend in part on how I am disposed to receive it; the way someone prepares a meal with me will depend in part on how dexterous my movements are. In saving someone from a fire, the question of whether I lead someone out by the hand or assist them by having them put their arm around my shoulder will be determined by their capacity to act in these ways.

The contention that physical interactions are also instances of the practical interconnection of acts requires a very different conception of bodily interaction than is customary. This means that the bodily and physical interaction of practical subjects cannot be accounted for, as is typical, from the standpoint of the autonomous individual actor whose existence can be separated out from the interactional exchange itself. From this standpoint, the to-and-fro of interaction transpires as a serially ordered succession of isolated actions and reactions that have their source in the subjective attitudes and intentions of independent and autonomous agents. For the practical subject, however, every interactional exchange unfolds in, and as, an interconnection (*renkan* 連関) of acts.

The continuously linked character of physical interactions is especially conspicuous in that most ordinary and most widespread form of interaction: speaking to one another. Although this activity would seem to be one that hardly qualifies as physical interaction, it might be argued that the sound of the voice is both the lightest and most potent form of touch; a few carefully chosen words, for example, can enliven or demoralize the person who hears them. This kind of contact, like other forms of physical exchange, resembles a smoothly connected train of interaction. Gadamer famously likens the back-and-forth of asking and answering, of speaking and listening in turn, to the playing of a game.[15]

But he maintains that we must not explain the concept of the game, as is customary, from the standpoint of the consciousness of the player. On the contrary, he contends that a game is a dynamic whole, sui generis, that embraces the subjectivity of the one who plays. The to-and-fro of the game thus does not have its source in the subjective attitudes and intentions of the players. Rather the game is genuinely under way when the players become absorbed in and are carried away by the to-and-fro of the game such that they lose the sense of themselves as intentional, independent, and autonomous agents separate from the game.

Like the moves in a game, every word in a dialogue "comes into play" within a definite context within which it is understood and spoken. In this "playing out" of a conversation, we risk words or hold onto them, provoke responses and respond ourselves, adapting ourselves to the moves of others in a game of give-and-take. There is also, as in all play, an element of chance, surprise, and accident, part of a buoyancy that elevates us above ourselves and carries us along as statement elicits counterstatement and plays the dialogue further.

The examples of engaging in conversation and playing a game also display a final structural characteristic integral to all interactions: one act is prescriptive for and so partially determines another. Both mental and physical acts are able to be prescriptive for others in this way because they bear a meaning that is expressed in and through the behavior, demeanor, gestures, facial expressions, words, and so on that arise between persons within a given exchange. These expressed meanings motivate, direct, and constrain the comportments each person brings to, and the actions they undertake within, an encounter. Consequently such actions do not simply issue forth from the isolated consciousness and will of an individual; they arise or occur together with the actions of others in a transactional relation that links one person to another; that is, they always take place within a nexus of action (*kōiteki renkan*).[16] For this reason, Watsuji maintains that expressive actions or expressions are constitutive moments of the practical interconnection of acts.[17]

II. Expression and Practical Understanding

This interconnection of acts is a practical one in two senses. First, the subject of the actions within this interconnection is a practical subject; that is, it is, as we have seen, an active and embodied subject rather than a disembodied observer or epistemological subject. Second, this subject and its expressive and meaning-laden acts are grasped and understood by others by means of what Watsuji calls "practical understanding" (*jis-senteki ryōkai* 実践的了解).

Watsuji calls this form of understanding "practical" to distinguish it from conceptually mediated modes of theoretical understanding. Practical understanding is anterior to theoretical understanding, and, unlike knowledge grasped through concepts, it is direct and immediate. Hence Watsuji compares practical understanding to something like instinct, a comparison that both captures and misses something at the same time. Like instinct, practical understanding is more akin to a tacit mode of awareness than a type of knowing that involves the explicit and rational comprehension of something; unlike instinct, practical understanding, as a self-aware form of relating to the intelligibility of the human world, unfolds as a form of consciousness and is articulated and developed in language.[18]

Watsuji illustrates the way practical understanding is operative in the practical interconnection of acts with the earlier example of the act of mutual looking. Looking always already involves a definite understanding of one's partner and their actions. All of the various modes of looking that were discussed presuppose this kind of understanding; without it, it would not be possible for one to, for example, look furtively at the expression on the other's face or drop one's glance or exchange knowing looks.[19]

These examples demonstrate that objects of practical understanding are other persons and their acts. These, moreover, are understood in a direct and immediate way. As Joel Krueger has shown, we have this kind of unmediated access to aspects of the minds and hence the subjective spheres of others because mental content for Watsuji is not restricted to internal and so purely private mental states, and therefore cannot be accounted for by them. Instead, in Watsuji's view the mind and thus subjectivity itself is partly expressed and externalized through bodily activity.[20] In order to see more clearly the basis of this claim we will first indicate how this understanding of subjectivity and mind as embodied and enacted is founded on Watsuji's understanding of the subject as a body-subject (*shutai* 主体), that is, as an embodied and active agent.

The term *shutai* is intended capture in a single concept the union of the mental and physical that lies at the center of human persons. Yuasa Yasuo observes that for Watsuji "from the outset, we are not to think of body apart from mind. In other words, the fundamental mode of being human must be grasped as the unity of mind-body or the 'oneness of body-mind' (*shinjin ichinyo* [身心一如]): this is Watsuji's claim."[21] In describing Watsuji's position with the term *shinjin ichinyo*, Yuasa links Watsuji's position to Buddhist and especially Zen Buddhist views of the relation between mind and body. Yet even if it is the case that Watsuji developed his notion of the body-subject by drawing on Buddhist metaphysics, he also offers phenomenological descriptions and deploys a variety of evidence to argue for this view on grounds that he characterizes as "the concrete facts of experience."[22] The position Watsuji wants to oppose, and that he contrasts with his own, is an understanding of the mind as a mental entity distinct from the body as a physical thing. He supplies a range of examples to show that we never experience the body of another person as a solely material object; we always encounter the body of another as presenting a union of the psychological and the physical.

Watsuji begins by conceding that in his earlier example of the patient on the operating table, the human body is encountered as a physical substance. But he reminds us that this arrangement is only provisional, and for the highly specialized purpose of medical care. Furthermore, this reduction of the body to its physical and organic dimensions is carried out for the sake of the person who *is* that body. This identity between the body and the person in all of their mental and psychological aspects can also be seen in a plethora of ordinary experiences: when I shake hands with a friend, this hand is not first given as a moving material substance which I then infer has been set in motion by my friend's mind. Rather, from the outset I shake hands with my friend himself. When I smile with pleasure, I display one of the vast number of bodily movements that are inseparable from mental and psychological states. When I gravitate toward a new friend, or when a husband and wife, or mother and infant, feel pulled toward one another, these instances of attraction cannot be accounted for in purely physical terms (else any other body that resembled the original closely enough would necessarily suffice to generate the attractive force); neither are these wholly mental and psychological experiences (else these relationships could flourish without embodied interaction). These cases of attraction are instead phenomena that display the inseparability of mind and body.

This example is related to another important difference between the body and entities that are purely physical. Unlike the latter, the human body cannot be what it is independently of others. As we have shown, for Watsuji to be a body is to possess capacities and features that are always already attuned to and directed towards others; these enable the body to bear and express a meaning for them that exceeds the merely organic. Indeed, it is only in the expression of this kind of social significance that the body is truly a human body. Moreover, this expressivity of the body is a capacity that is there from the beginning and that belongs naturally to it. This includes the body's capacity for vocalization and gesture, its ability to assume a variety of postures, its power to consciously and unconsciously transmit meaning through movement (e.g., "body language"), and so on. The meanings expressed in these ways connects us to others, drawing them to us (and us to them) and helping to establish our being in relation with them. Human being in relation with others, then, has its basis in the expressivity that arises out of our bodily existence.[23] In this regard the concrete, living body is a union point of the physical, psychological, and social.[24]

The unity of the psychological and the bodily that Watsuji argues for here enables us to see how the mental and the subjective can be externalized through bodily activity and so how it is possible to gain direct access to the subjectivity of others in practical understanding. Krueger makes explicit the way these two ideas are linked and shows their broader significance both for the way mind and subjectivity are understood as well as for accounts of how we understand others.

According to Krueger, whose discussion I will be recapitulating in what follows, Watsuji's view amounts to a rejection of the influential and widespread model of the mind in which "the subjectivity of another is wholly realized inside the head, hidden to everyone but the subject."[25] For Watsuji, the contents of the mind—and so an essential dimension of subjectivity itself—appear in the expressivity of bodily activities such as gesture, facial expression, vocalization, touch, gaze, posture, body language, and so forth. The perceptual availability of this mental content to others motivates the coordinated back-and-forth dialectic of transaction and exchange that Watsuji calls the practical interconnection of acts.

Although Watsuji undermines the primacy of a sharp distinction between an inner, subjective, and mental sphere versus an outer, objective, and purely material and physical domain, it remains true that some aspects of the mental (e.g., hidden motives, personal memories, thoughts that remain unvoiced) remain private and so transcendent to the perception and understanding of others. But such phenomena can remain shrouded in complete privacy only to the extent that they remain unexpressed. And while it is possible for us to keep such things concealed in our exchanges with others, what Watsuji wants us to see is that the very nature of interaction is such that *everything* subjective and mental cannot and does not remain so concealed; insofar as we act, we express a meaning that can be understood by others. This means that in order for the fluid continuity of transactions that we call interaction to be possible at all, we must be able to understand (or even misunderstand) others and their actions in order to respond or react in kind. The fact that understanding takes place here entails that some kind of meaning has been expressed, whether intentionally or unintentionally. But the expression of subjective meaning for Watsuji is not, as it is conceived of in some quarters, a process whereby the meanings held in the interior of consciousness are externally and objectively represented by physiological events such as the vibration of vocal chords or the movements and behavior of the bodily organism. On this reading, such publicly observable data would then be used by other participants in the interaction to draw inferences about the inner states of another person on the basis of their own experience of bringing inner meanings to external representation in the same fashion.

Watsuji rejects this view of expression. Subjective meaning is not mediated; it is understood and experienced directly in gestures, facial expressions, tone of voice, words: "Expressing is a putting something out, a disclosure between people, and is not simply an activity within pure consciousness. Consequently, the act of expression for us is something visible and tangible."[26] Krueger notes that Watsuji's arguments lean heavily on Scheler, and he directs our attention to a well-known passage in Scheler's *Nature of Sympathy* to foreground the connections between Watsuji's and Scheler's views: "For we certainly believe ourselves to be directly acquainted with another person's joy in his laughter, with his sorrow and pain in his tears, with his shame in his blushing, with his entreaty in his outstretched hands, with his love in his look of affection, with his rage in the gnashing of teeth, with his threats in the clenching of his fist, and with the tenor of his thoughts in the sound of his words. If anyone tells me that this is not 'perception,' for it cannot be so, in view of the fact that a perception is simply a 'complex of physical sensations,' and that there is certainly no sensation of another person's mind nor any stimulus from such a source, I would beg him to turn aside from such questionable theories and address himself to the phenomenological facts."[27]

That which is expressed—joy, sorrow, shame, threats, the tenor of thoughts—is not something distinct from the laughter, tears, blushes, curled fists, and tone of voice of the body. The contents of our minds are not restricted to an inaccessible inner domain. This means that they do not require a mediating mechanism such as analogical inference to be made known to others; once expressed, they can be immediately recognized and directly perceived by others, whose counter-expressive reactions and responses are shaped by the immediacy of this understanding. Moreover, because what comes to expression between one self and another is mental content, the mind, and hence an aspect of subjectivity itself, extends out into the shared space of face-to-face interaction.

For the practical subject, then, interactions with others form a moving stream of mental and physical acts that are carried along by a shared understanding (or even, at times, misunderstanding). This dynamic whole of interaction encompasses the subjectivity of the actor, who is taken up into this set of interlocking comportments and acts much as a pair of dancers is swept up into a ballroom dance.

III. Constitutive Sociality as Social Whole

If we now move in our analysis to the other sense in which sociality is constitutive for the self, we can see that our belonging to groups and bodies such as families, companies, or schools furnishes us with roles that help to constitute our identity in multiple respects.[28] First, the roles that are given through these wholes allow us to participate in and function as part of them, that is, as a wife in a family, a department head in a company, a priest in a church, a professor in a university, and so forth, just as a part in a machine receives its significance and function by being part of a larger entity. Moreover these roles depend on the roles and personas of others who also compose the group to be the roles that they are. Thus a priest depends on congregants to be a priest, students cannot be students without a teacher, doctors require patients, and so on.

Second, in enabling people to perform particular functions within a relationship, for example, as a teacher or a parent or a nurse, such roles help to give shape to the structure of agency. Thus even as these roles make possible an identity and a field of action that is entailed by this identity, they both constrain and give direction to our actions and possibilities. So, for example, being married makes it possible for me to be and to undertake the activities of a family man even as it precludes my being and doing so as a bachelor. Roles in relation, then, might best be understood as *enabling* constraints.

Fulfilling the functions of one's role in interacting with others also enables a person to be a certain way for them in ways of acting and speaking, and in attitude. This is because the roles that our relationships with others entail prescribe or determine attitudes, gestures, and ways of speaking appropriate to that role: a person's behavior and demeanor in the office cannot be identical to the attitude and actions they take up and engage in while at home with their children, for instance. Or, to use Watsuji's own example, the manner in which I express concern will vary according to my position in the family and the identity of the person I am engaging with; my approach to an interlocutor for whom I am a parent will differ in important ways from the way I address someone for whom I am a younger sibling. This observation goes beyond the familiar point that a person can be at least partly identified with her actions, with what she does, and shows that a person also comes to be who she is through the *way* she does what she does.

With this we arrive at a full conception of both senses in which the self is social for Watsuji: first, relations to others and to social wholes are constitutive of the human being as an embodied agent, one that occupies certain roles, belongs to specific groups, and is possessed of particular modes of awareness and affectivity. Second, the self that is so constituted overlaps, is continuous with, and extends into others in specific forms of consciousness and action in relational interactions that Watsuji calls the practical interconnection of acts.

The sociality of the self in this regard is, nevertheless, a condition that can be provisionally escaped through solitude or reversed by isolation. This marks an important structural difference between the manner in which the practical subject "stands out" in being among others and the way in which, as Heidegger says, Dasein *ek-sists* as "standing out, into and enduring, the openness of the there," such that "by its very nature, Dasein brings its there along with it."[29] One self does not belong to another in the same way in which the "there" contained in a world belongs to Dasein.[30] No matter the extent to which the interlocking character of interaction and the openness and permeability (even vulnerability) of one consciousness to another make it possible for me to share in the being of others, there is always an insuperable difference and distance between one self and another. To have and to be a self, in the minimal sense, is to occupy a first-person standpoint on the world about which it can be said that this perspective is *mine*. This property of "mine-ness" that is the basis of my first-person point of view is always distinct from the perspective that belongs to others, because as physically discrete and mobile, I am not and can never be another.

On the other hand, the interaction that takes place between such selves does not involve hermetically sealed and fully independent atoms facing one another. What the self is in the presence of other persons is not the same as what it is when alone. Something new and different emerges between these selves, a coproduction that encompasses and determines all participants. This enlargement of subjectivity, in which the self "stands outside" of itself by interacting with others—which Watsuji calls the practical interconnection of acts—is especially visible on public occasions in which we create something that exceeds and is bigger than any one individual, such as marriage or funeral ceremonies or mass sporting events. But selves are also immersed in one another through interaction in the turn-taking of conversation and the swirl of argument between friends, in the converging voices of a church choir, in the to-and-fro of jokes and laughter in a comedy club, in the momentarily shared awkwardness between strangers in an elevator.

This immersive contact and interaction with others is the initially given position and normal condition of the human being. Given this state of affairs, it is less the case that being-in-relation-to-others is an enlargement of subjectivity than it is that solitude or isolation is a contraction or shrinking of the self. Like the detached stance of the scientist, seclusion or separation from others is an artificial imposition and always only a temporary attainment. Watsuji thinks that this is shown first by the fact that solitude is achieved solely as "the negation of community," in that we posit ourselves as solitary by escaping or being separated from human relationships (such as those in the family or community) through the force of our own will or the will of another, or through what he evocatively calls "the workings of fate." Yet the relationships we leave behind are never thereby transformed into something to which we are indifferent. Nor does the need to be related to others ever disappear. The priest who has left his family of origin for the Church, for instance, only feels that much more keenly the desire to satisfy this longing for a relation to someone through the pursuit of a deeper mode of existence, one that finally takes the form of a relationship to the ultimate person, namely, God. Solitude is thus a deficient mode (*ketsujotai* 欠如態) of sociality. This, Watsuji says, is seen in the phenomenon of loneliness, which is the felt awareness of that deficiency.[31]

* * *

With this account of the practical subject as a being-in-relation-to-others that is robustly social and communal, Watsuji arrives at a very different conception of the self from that found in the notion of Dasein. The practical subject differs from Dasein first, to the extent that direct relational interaction is constitutive for it, and second, insofar as the kind of self it is that is so constituted is able to be continuous with and extend into others, who, in turn, are able to extend into and be continuous with it. This much is now clear.

Notwithstanding these very large differences, however, there is one facet of the practical subject that overlaps with Dasein: the practical subject, like Dasein, is also individuated. This means that even as we have our being in each other in all of the ways that have been inventoried, we are also capable of attaining a certain form of individuality, so that the "I" never fully disappears into the "we." Instead the singular character of the "I" emerges only in and through the "we" in which the I is embedded. To articulate this claim about human selfhood and to capture the hybrid strangeness of what has been uncovered here, Watsuji converts the Japanese terms for human being (*ningen* 人間) and human existence (*ningen sonzai* 人間存在) into philosophical concepts. An explanatory analysis of these notions in the following chapter will conclude our account of Watsuji's transformation of the Dasein pole of being-in-the-world. This, in turn, will open the way to a consideration of Watsuji's parallel appropriation and modification of the concept of *Welt* within this framework, and so to a consideration of the social, historical, and natural features of his conception of this structure.

5

The Hybrid Self: Oscillation and Dialectic

The previous chapter portrayed the extensive and dramatic changes that the concept of the practical subject as being-in-relation-to-others, or *aidagara*, brings to the notion of Dasein; its concluding section briefly indicated the way in which this constitutive mode of sociality also makes possible, rather than precludes, a fully individuated self. And while this aspect of the practical subject echoes the individuality at the core of Dasein, it does not mirror it, since the practical subject always arrives at its individuality only through its relational contact and interaction with others. The distance and difference between Dasein and the practical subject is captured most fully by Watsuji's conception of being human as an individual and collective way of being in which each mode of being depends upon and is irreducible to the other. Thus even as relational contact with others and with larger social structures individuates the self, these relational wholes depend at the same time upon the individuals who compose it to be what they are.

In what follows, I provide an explanatory account of this hybrid structure and show that the dialectical relation that underpins it describes the metaphysical structure of the human being itself. The mutual dependence of the individual and the relational whole on one another is best captured for Watsuji by the Buddhist metaphysics of nondualism, a philosophical standpoint that allows him to articulate the way the human being, in his words, is a dialectical unity in which the whole exists in the parts and the parts in the whole. This reconstructive analysis brings to a close our account of the way Watsuji remakes the "subject" position of the Dasein-world dyad; it also begins to pursue a direction indicated by the ontological structure of *ningen* itself by turning to consider the space that both subtends the relation between practical subjects and links them to a world and, ultimately, to a *fūdo*.

I. The Human Being as *Ningen*

Mine Hideki observes that for Watsuji, the confrontation with Heidegger meant putting into question the entire European tradition with respect to its understanding of the human being.[1] While Watsuji recognizes that thinkers such as Aristotle grasped the social nature of human existence as "being in a *polis*," he nonetheless detects a deeply flawed conception of the human being that runs, in one form or another, through the main channels of the tradition, one that is neatly encapsulated in Clifford Geertz's celebrated characterization and assessment of the Western concept of the person: "The Western conception of the person as a bounded, unique, more or less integrated motivational and cognitive universe; a dynamic center of awareness, emotion, judgment, and action organized into a distinctive whole and set contrastively both against other such wholes and against a social and natural background is, however incorrigible it may seem to us, a rather peculiar idea within the context of the world's cultures."[2]

Watsuji sets out to show that this whole conception of the human being is misguided and ought therefore to be jettisoned. In its place he proposes a radically different view of the human being as well as a new set of philosophical concepts to capture this understanding. Following his customary hermeneutic procedure, he converts the ordinary Japanese words for human being, *ningen* 人間, and human existence, *ningen sonzai* 人間存在, into philosophical concepts by descending into the layers of meaning he finds sedimented in them and returning with a new reading of these terms.

In Watsuji's view, excavating the original meanings attached to each of the sinographs in these two Japanese sinograph compounds can tells us something about the manner in which human beings exist. To begin with, our existence or being is expressed by the compound *sonzai* 存在, which means "existence" or "being." The first sinograph is *son* 存, which in the original Chinese meant "to preserve or sustain something over time and so retain it from being lost or destroyed."[3] This term is well-matched to the human condition, since the human being is more like a temporal event with a beginning, a developmental arc, and an end, than it is like an atemporal object or an entity that exists in a permanent way. For Watsuji, this means that the human being occurs and unfolds in interactions with others that are constitutive for it. Put in his terms, the practical subject sustains itself through time as a being-in-relation-to-others, such that "*sonzai* is the interconnection of the acts of *ningen* [*ningen no kōiteki renkan* 人間の行為的連関]."[4] The second sinograph in *sonzai* is *zai* 在, which means "dwelling or being in a place," both in a spatial and a social sense. Watsuji thinks that this is exemplified by phrases such as *zaitaku* (在宅, being at home), *zaishuku* (在宿, being in an inn), and *zaikyō* (在郷, being in a hometown). The human being, then, is not something that is objectively there; rather we *dwell* among others, who are the very setting of human life. The space and place of human existence is social.[5]

The organic connections between Watsuji's account of the characteristics of the human being and the layers of meaning unearthed in the term *sonzai* lead him to turn this ordinary Japanese term into a philosophical concept by restricting its use in his thought to refer to the being of the human being, much as Heidegger had reserved *Existenz* for the mode of being of Dasein. Thus he declares that "*sonzai* is neither the 'being' of an objective thing, nor is it the logical 'to be.'" Instead *sonzai* is the "dynamic interconnection of embodied subjects (*shutai no dōteki renkan* 主体の動的連関)," which is "neither an objective ontic relation between things, nor even a noematic relation of meaning."[6] Hence *sonzai* (being, existence) can be applied only to *ningen* (the human).

In turning to an analysis of the other sinograph in this compound, *ningen*, Watsuji notes that the word *ningen* first gained currency in classical Japanese literature and in Buddhist sutras to designate the public world and affairs of society (*yononaka* 世の中 and *seken* 世間) found between people (*hito no aida* 人の間) in and among which we are located. In Buddhism the abode of *ningen* is located between the realm of the beasts and the heavenly realm of enlightened beings; through a kind of shorthand, *ningen* eventually comes first to denote humankind and then, because human beings are involved in the process of transmigration, an individual human being.[7]

These developments are also reflected in the semantic composition of *ningen*. This is a compound term that consists of two sinographs, *nin/hito* 人, meaning "person" or, in certain contexts, "individual," and *gen/ken* 間, meaning an interval of space, a period of time, or a mode of relationship "between" things. This character can also be read as *aida* and appears in *aidagara* 間柄. *Gen/ken/aida* 間 points to the social space or place in which the self is located. Unlike the word *human being* (as well as terms such as *anthropos, homo, man,* or *Mensch*), the sinographs in *ningen* capture both the single parts (individuals) and the relations with others and with larger social wholes (families, organizations, societies, etc.) that make up the human being.

For Watsuji, the way in which the meaning of this term can encompass and alternate between both our social (*shakaiteki* 社会的) and our individual (*kojinteki* 個人的) natures shows us something about what human beings are, namely, beings that are individuated, yet at the same time that always exist in relation to specific others and to wider social structures.[8] Insofar as we exist in this way, we find ourselves linked in some form to specific others through unavoidable contact, association, and interactions with them; in our belonging from the outset to a family (or even to an orphanage) as well as to a society, we also discover ourselves as always already related to larger and more encompassing social structures—from ethnolinguistic groups to religious organizations, companies, institutions, and other social bodies. This relational contact with others and with larger social structures individuates the self while simultaneously revealing its ineluctably social nature.

II. Constitutive Sociality and the Achievement of Individuation

For Watsuji, sociality is constitutive for the self as a conscious and embodied agent, identified with the roles it takes on, and for the self in its singularity, in its capacity to be an individual. The self is still a relational self in coming to be an individual because it is only through relational association that we differentiate ourselves from others and from the groups within which we find ourselves to acquire a singular identity. Hence the relational contact of being-in-relation-to-others is a form of primordial sociality that is ineluctable, even in the moment at which the self achieves individuation.

One distinguishes oneself as an individual, according to Watsuji, by standing out or differing from the group to which one belongs. He terms this rejection of the wider social whole to which we belong—an event in which we negate its supremacy over us—a *movement of negation* (*hitei no undō* 否定の運動). Nonetheless, as Maraldo points out, Watsuji does not really address "the question of how individuals arise by 'negating the greater whole.' Is this simply a matter of someone rebelling against the common will of a family, community, society, or state?"[9] If the claim is that one comes into one's own in, for example, resisting or refusing the expectations or requirements of one's role in the family or by rebelling against the confines of a religious or political tradition to which one once belonged, then it is not clear how the movement of negation amounts to anything other than the initial stages of individuation. In truth, Watsuji's analysis of this movement is too thin and imprecise to sufficiently account for the complex role that social wholes play in individuation.[10] But perhaps this problem need not detain us; it may be sufficient simply to recognize the form of self-understanding that comes from breaking from intersubjectivity, and to see that some part of the activity of self-definition that is so central to becoming an individual always occurs in relation to groups of various sorts.

In addition to the constitutive nature of our relational contact with social wholes, it seems obvious that individuation is also tied to direct interaction with others, although Watsuji never really addresses this either. And this is true not only in the obvious sense in which one resolves not to be like *him*, but also insofar as one acquires a distinctive self through the "how" of how one interacts with others. We saw earlier that Watsuji had already given some attention to the particular way we interact with others through our public roles. Nonetheless this focus on the manner in which we discharge our roles only highlighted the formal aspects of the social self that are forged through interaction; it overlooks how the *style* of our interactions also helps to form a self that is far more distinctive and singular than the various personae that are expressed in our social roles. We need not only speak and act with others "as" a strict mother or genial uncle or concerned teacher—we can also adverbially modify our actions in ways that are not directly linked to our social roles and conduct ourselves in a fashion that expresses a specific manner of existence. In such instances, my transactions with others allow me to be a certain way for them not only in terms of what my formal roles prescribe but also in terms of *how* I do what I do with, for, or against them. Insofar as these adverbial modifications of actions and behavior express a singular way of being in speaking, walking, acting, and so forth, one might argue that they also amount to the enactment of a distinctive self.

III. Between Individual and Communal: Oscillation and Dialectic

While Watsuji acknowledges the way the self is established and exists as an individual, the manner in which the individual exists is not, as in the Western paradigm, as a self-subsisting and completely independent entity, since this is not possible for it. The self is individuated *only* in and through its contact and association with others and its initial participation in social wholes. That means that individuals depend on these forms of *aidagara* to be what they are, so that they are never exclusively independent—as in atomism. Hence the self is only an individual in the fullest sense insofar as it is also social. It exists as an individual in a limited way and depends for its existence on its relation to others and to social wholes.

But the dependence here runs both ways: social wholes, too, do not subsist or exist in themselves, as if each were a kind of entity possessing its own reality that could exist apart from the individual members that compose it. In order to exist, these wholes need individuals to commit themselves to them; each individual must give up some part of her own will and join with others to form a collective entity, overcoming their separate interests for the sake of the interests of the whole. A church, school, or company, for example, could not function and be what it is without this kind of commitment from the individuals who constitute it. Every whole also requires real individuals to freely shape and change it, otherwise they would be dead rather than the dynamic and living wholes that they are; one thinks here, for instance, of the range of active civic, religious, or governmental institutions found in any fully functioning society.

A group is thus always composed of individuals. At the same time, we have seen that individuation requires a relationship to a group. Watsuji observes that this dialectic is quintessentially embodied in the phenomenon of the taboo. The very existence of taboos demonstrates the way the group circumscribes and determines its members, while revealing at the same time the possibility and reality of individual self-assertion against the group and its norms. If this event were not a real possibility, there would be no need for the existence of taboos. This would be the case, if, for instance, the collection of individuals making up a group were like the collection of cells that compose an organism, existing as nothing more than elements of a larger whole. But since there are always taboo-like prohibitions in social life, the group never constitutes a whole of this kind; hence Watsuji rejects any attempt to characterize social existence in terms of organicism.[11]

Neither individuals nor wholes exist, then, as completely independent and self-subsisting realties; to use Watsuji's Buddhist-influenced terminology, both are "empty" of this kind of intrinsic nature. Instead each of these aspects of the being of the human being depends on the existence of the other, in nondual fashion, to be what they respectively are. We have spoken thus far in positive terms about this dual dependence, but Watsuji speaks far more often about this dependence in terms of the relation of "negation" that both of these poles have to one another. The individual "negates" a social whole in order to be what it is (e.g., by rebelling against or rejecting a group), and a social whole determines, subsumes, incorporates, or "negates" the individual in order for *it* to be what it is. This reciprocal negation is also another way of expressing the idea that neither the individual nor the social whole has or takes priority or precedence in existence: to reach the individual, the social whole must already be negated, and to arrive at the social whole, the individual, too, must already be negated.

Therefore, when Watsuji asserts that the human being is both individual and social, the terms *individual* and *social* do not name two different entities that exist in an absolutely independent way—as if he were simultaneously asserting the mutually exclusive claims of atomistic individualism and social organicism. Such individual and social modes of existence are abstractions from the dynamic and concrete reality of human being in the world. Rather than being purely and unconditionally individual or social, the self exists in the continual movement between these two poles; different situations and times will find the self moving closer to or further away from the individual and social poles that structure human existence—even as the human being never completely attains to either pole of this duality.[12]

This dynamic is regulated by an important ethical ideal that Watsuji formulates in two different ways. In the first place, he asserts that the ethical goal is to maintain a continual movement between individuality and sociality, such that coming to a standstill in one or the other would be an ethical failing. At other times, he maintains that after the self has negated both a particular social whole and its own individuality, the ethical imperative is for the self to return to the highest social totality, which is represented in the state. This formulation of the ethical ideal has generated a large amount of controversy, and rightly so. Some scholars have interpreted this idea as a call for the dissolution of the self in the state, a call that, given political circumstances of the era, would appear to be deeply troubling.

As Sevilla has shown, the publication history of *Rinrigaku* (*Ethics*) suggests a subtle move away from this elevation of the state to such an absolute moral position. Yet as far as I know, Watsuji never straightforwardly and unambiguously repudiates this version of his ethical ideal.[13] I suggest that the basis for a rejection of this version of the ethical ideal can be found in Watsuji's own philosophy, so that with regard to this ethical aim of subsuming the self in the state, we can, and should, read Watsuji against himself.

A number of scholars have shown that there are several reasons why a totalitarian vision of the state cannot be reconciled with the particulars of Watsuji's own account of the self. Couteau points out that totalitarianism could only result from the cessation of the constant movement of separation from, and immersion in, a social whole, that is, it could only arise from violating the first version of the ethical ideal formulated by Watsuji.[14] In a similar vein, Lafleur and Shields note that throughout *Rinrigaku*, Watsuji himself viewed one of his contributions as balancing out or giving the proper proportion to the excesses of Western thought, such that throughout the work we find an explicit commitment to balancing the temporal with the spatial and the individual with the social.

Hence it is clear that Watsuji's theory of the self is obviously intended to restore a "middle way" between the extremes of atomistic individualism and the kind of social organicism that underlies totalitarianism.[15] Finally, Kalmanson reminds us that the nondual metaphysics of dependent origination that underlies Watsuji's conceptions of the social and the individual means that both are "empty" such that there is no ultimate foundation which could support absolute totality at the social level.[16]

So while Watsuji's philosophy has been at times intensively criticized and even dismissed by those who see his metaphysics of the person and his ethics as either directly or indirectly providing a philosophical ground for totalitarianism, and although there are clear shortcomings and troubling statements from Watsuji on this topic, the issue is far from clear-cut; these commentators have shown that a careful reading of Watsuji indicates that his theory of the self is in fact inhospitable to totalitarianism.

The other version of Watsuji's ethical ideal for the self can also be understood as and is at times expressed in terms of the realization of an "absolute totality," but in a different sense. This totality is the relational ground that underlies the social and individual dimensions of human existence, and it is embraced or realized in the continual movement of the self between these dimensions.

This movement is in essence nothing less than the unfolding and development of ethical life; the social and the individual poles that structure our existence are sites of moral danger as well as of moral self-realization. Our interaction and association with the people around us can become in this regard opportunities to embrace our interconnectedness in solidarity with others. So for instance in our immersion in a particular social or political group, we may lose our sense of ourselves as a separate self or ego. Yet whatever social or political unity is achieved, however exemplary, can only be temporary since the authentic self does not remain permanently in the social dimension. An example of this kind of phenomenon might be the kind of unity that people experienced as participants in the South African struggle against apartheid. In these cases we find ourselves willing to respond to the claims that specific others and larger social entities make on us. In such experiences there can even be a nondual merging of self and other that enables me to identify with others as myself, an identification that serves as the ground of benevolence and compassion.

This drive toward sociality contrasts sharply with the way the self can and does assert itself against others or the group to which it belongs in the process of individuation. One can say that this too is a paradigmatically ethical moment, insofar as a weak sense of the self as individual puts one in danger of everything from falling into the mindless conventional-

ity of the crowd to developing a willingness to submit to powerful external forces, as for example the forces found in extremist political movements such as fascism. One might even go so far as to say that if a person
allows the social dimension of the self to overwhelm the individual one,
she is in danger of not having a self at all. This danger is underscored by
the drives and desires that sustain and strengthen the social dimension of
the self. Hence although we are "thrown" into standing relational contact
with others and with larger social wholes such as schools, companies, and
churches, we also at times embrace these, we have a drive toward sociality
that maintains, deepens, develops, and expands this contact; we desire to
join with and immerse and even lose ourselves among others. We experience at times a longing to be part of something larger, to subordinate
our individuality to a more encompassing whole.

Thus to take an ethical stand against the crowd and become who
one is requires a robust sense of oneself as an individual. But this mode
of selfhood entails its own moral risks: the many varieties of greed, self-
ishness, and narcissism can be seen as a form of stasis in which the movement of the self has stopped at the pole of individuality. The solitude
and self-assertion of the individual can be inadequate to situations that
call for solicitude and sympathy: a problem or situation in a marriage, or
in a company or temple to which we belong can require us to give up or
subordinate our own interests and desires to those of the group, to transcend our own point of view by taking up the standpoint of the whole.

Beneath this continual cycling between the poles of individuality
and totality, then, we find a resistance to the inertia of viewing one's identity wholly in terms of either of these dimensions of the self, a refusal to
give oneself over completely to either. Instead the ethical aim is for this
dynamic oscillation between individual and social dimensions to be directed by a sense of individuality that is open to our interconnectedness
with others.

IV. The Nondualism of Self and Other:
Not One, Not Two

The oscillation of the practical subject between immersion in social
wholes and emergence from them in individuation also has its basis in
and is expressive of what Watsuji understands as the nondual structure of
human existence. For Watsuji, human existence is nondual insofar as it
is a unitary whole composed of the difference and distance between one
self and another. Before we enter into the complexities of this position,

it is necessary to make several prefatory and qualifying observations. First, Watsuji's description of the connection between the metaphysical structure of nondualism and the basic movement underlying human life remains at a highly general level; this means that we will once again need to engage in some interpretive push and fill to coherently present this view. Second, his account is laced with jargon: there is talk of "the self-activity of absolute negativity" (*zettaiteki hiteisei no jikokatsudō* 絶対的否定性の自己活動), "the self-return of the Absolute" (*zettaisha no jikokanki* 絶対者の自己還帰), "the conversion or transformation from being to nothingness, and from nothingness to being" (*yū kara mu e, mu kara yū e no tenpen* 有から無へ、無から有への転変), and so on.[17] Watsuji explicitly draws on terminology derived from Buddhist philosophy, as well as the thought of Hegel, in order to situate the dialectical movement of the practical subject between individual and communal positions within the metaphysical structure of nondualism. Unfortunately these terms and phrases are often scattered throughout his discussion in ways that seem only to confuse or obscure the relevant issues. Moreover, as William LaFleur observes, the centerpiece of this apparatus does not even appear to be necessary. While he acknowledges the importance of the Buddhist idea of emptiness for Watsuji's philosophy, LaFleur maintains that, in his opinion

> the notion of "absolute negation" is not functionally significant in Watsuji's thought. This is not to deny that he ever uses such a term; it is merely to judge that it is never integrated well into the architecture of his philosophy. It is a term which, as others have noted, was probably borrowed from Nishida Kitarō, the doyen of the Kyoto school. It may, in fact, be precisely because this notion of "absolute negation" is never integrated fully into Watsuji's thought that his position is bound to remain somewhat ambiguous within the intellectual ambit of the Kyoto school. There is, I would suggest, a consistency on both sides: the Kyoto school "in the strict or narrow sense" makes much of absolute negation for the same reasons that it ultimately views religion as something which, while included in culture, also transcends it. Watsuji, by contrast, holds that religion is to be understood as a part of culture and, therefore, the need for an "absolute negation" in his philosophy would seem moot.[18]

LaFleur's contention is that Watsuji's thought has difficulty assimilating terms and structures from the religiously oriented philosophy of the Kyoto School because it is not itself grounded in the same kind of all-embracing religious commitments. This state of affairs may account

for the functional attenuation within his work of concepts such as absolute negation, but the problem here is not only that these terms lack
substantive utility. Another important reason why terms such as *absolute
negation* are "never integrated well into the architecture of his philosophy" is that Watsuji's confused and confusing attempt to identify the
movement of the self between individuation and community with the
metaphysical structure of the nondual whole of human existence *as such*
makes a muddle of this vocabulary.[19] His effort to directly correlate the
processes of individuation and communion with the multiplicity of the
one, that is, with the nondual totality, is so disjointed and so full of ambi-
guities that rather than simply repeat and endorse the account he gives,
I will attempt to reconstruct what, it seems to me, the proper relation
between these two structures is.

Although I will pass over much of Watsuji's needlessly technical
vocabulary in doing this, we will need to treat certain concepts from
Buddhist philosophy that bear on the hybrid composition of the human
being as *ningen.* The first and most important of these terms is probably the sinograph compound *jita funi* 自他不二, which refers to the way
human existence constitutes a unity insofar as each self is united with
every other in the totality of a nondual whole.[20] The literal translation
of *jita funi* is "self and other: not two." The first part of this compound
phrase indicates that self and other (*jita* 自他) are preserved as distinct
elements within the nondual (i.e., not two) whole. This is meant to convey the idea that human beings do not form a monolithic entity, a single
whole thing; they do not dissolve into one another without difference or
distinction, like drops in a human lake. Through my body I am physically
distinct from others and mobile. These features form the basis of my first-
person perspective on the world, which serves to further heighten my
sense of separation from others, insofar as this subjective viewpoint dif-
ferentiates me and the position I occupy from the perspectives of others
located in *their* positions. But all of these perspectives, finally, are encompassed by the standpoint of the human whole: I occupy a distinct and
individual subject position while also being an element within and aspect
of this whole.

Human beings compose in this regard a nondual whole that is plural and discrete. I suggest that the structure of differentiation within this
whole provides the basis for and drives the process of individuation that
constitutes the second phase or moment of the activity of *ningen.* Given
this claim, we can now understand this phase as the activity of convert-
ing or transforming the physical distinctness furnished by the body into
something singular in terms of the identity, psychology, personality, and
personal history of the self. As we have already shown, this process of

differentiation from others takes place through a movement of separation in relation to a group. Individuation is mediated by social wholes; human beings break away from one another through the group. These wholes take many forms and range from smaller groups, such as couples, families, teams, clubs, and congregations, to political, cultural, and regional wholes, which include communities and even nations.

The second half of the term *jita-funi* indicates that, at the same time, self and other are not two (*funi* 不二); that is, the difference between them is not absolute, nor is the separation between them total. Self and other, like everything else in the nondual whole, depend on one another to be what they are; neither exists in an absolutely independent way.

According to Watsuji, both the initial stage of the dialectic of *ningen*, in which we begin by discovering ourselves as always already belonging to an array of groups and social wholes, and the third phase, in which we return to these after breaking away, are likewise motivated by the underlying metaphysical structure of the human whole. We begin with others and rejoin them in a kind of echo and imperfect mirroring of the nondual totality of self and others that is both the true origin and proper and final destination of the self.[21] His exposition of the sense of origin here is somewhat thin and does not amount to much more than a paraphrase of the claim in Zen Buddhism that the nonduality that underlies self and other, as well as all things, is the ground from which we emerge. With this we almost reach the limits of what is available to and can be reached by conceptual thought. The focus of the rest of this discussion will be on Watsuji's contention that others are the rightful destination of the self, and that this is given finite expression in the return of the self to the group.

The unified whole of self and other, as our origin, is that which is most essentially and properly our own and not something alien to us. Our movement toward the other is driven by a desire to reach this original ground, one that is our natural place.[22] Because this activity moves in the direction of what is proper or normal, this end is a normative one. Watsuji declares, "The supreme value is absolute totality, and an aspiration (upward impulse or burning desire) for it is 'good' [*zen* 善]."[23] It is for this reason, Watsuji says, that across cultures and times, love of and devotion and service to others has been seen as "good." Here he identifies others in general with absolute totality, but in our desire for and movement toward unity with others we cannot, of course, unite with human beings as a whole (although it may perhaps be possible to carry out this movement psychologically and spiritually in forms of religious experience). What we unite with are communities, groups, and social wholes of all types and sizes—the human totality is mediated through these ensembles. Watsuji, however, speaks only of communities, but the unity achieved between one self and another is not a solely communal affair; we experience union with others on sports teams, in school clubs, in church services, in military training, at band practice, and in protest marches, in wartime, and during national tragedies. Episodes of being united with our local, regional, or national community would even appear to be far less frequent than other, more modest forms of social togetherness. Furthermore the scale of a community changes the nature of this experience; in uniting with a large community, we identify with others in a mostly indirect and symbolically mediated way, projecting our feelings onto a whole (such as an ethnic group or gender or nation) that can be fully present to us only in imagination.

No matter how deep-seated and thoroughgoing the sense of oneness or communion with others achieved in these experiences is, such experiences should not be taken to signify a mystical union in which the individual is immersed in the whole through an *actual* return to the nondual unity of self and other.[24] The kinds of communal unity experienced in the list above do not describe religious experiences. Nevertheless, to the extent that we are driven to unite with communities, groups, and other wholes by a desire for the other, this longing is a form of homesickness, and this movement a movement of return—even if it is never fully realized as such. We are driven back to others because they are the home ground of the self.

This movement does not simply repeat the unity with and immersion among others experienced before the self is individuated through a departure from a social whole such as a family or faith community. We come back to the social whole in a new way, and sometimes to a different group. Our way is new because if we have successfully appropriated our experiences of being immersed in a whole and separated from it in individuation, then we come to it in freedom, in, as Sevilla puts it, "freedom from both ego and herd."[25] We rejoin a whole having achieved individuation, and this makes possible, through the exercise of our freedom, what Sevilla terms "a formative determination by the individual of totality."[26] In this return, the individual is understood as that element in a particular social whole that shapes and even directs this whole as it unfolds in time. Because this movement of return to a whole is not a simple repetition of an original condition of union with others, Watsuji uses different terms to describe the first and the third stage of this movement. He calls the initial condition in which *ningen* begins a state of unity (*tōitsu* 統一) and the return to unity after separating (*bunri* 分離) from others a "joining together" (*ketsugō* 結合).[27]

Thus far we have shown how Watsuji calls upon the classical metaphysical concept of *jita funi* to assert that human beings as a whole constitute a composite unity. This made visible the underlying metaphysical structure that drives the continual to-and-fro movement of *ningen*, which, on my reading, is a finite expression of this structure. But this description did not do much more than state the sense in which we compose a whole and the respect in which we are also separate and plural; it did not resolve the essential tension between these claims. Since it is inconceivable for the forms of objectivism and dualism we have already surveyed for something to be in a state of both unity and division at the same time, it is apparent that the resolution of this difficulty must be uncovered through the metaphysics of nondualism. Hence Watsuji maintains that it is possible for us to be both divided into self and other even as we are one, insofar as unity and division are two profiles of the same structure, that is, insofar as they are aspects of the same nondual entity. But in presenting this view he does not do much more than recapitulate—in highly compressed and almost epigrammatic formulations—the line of reasoning found in a specific version of nondualism. The presupposition implicit here is that the nondual whole of human existence is a region located within a wider and more encompassing nondual totality, one whose underlying logic resolves the tension between unity and difference.

In more fully spelling this out, we must begin by recognizing that metaphysical nondualism is not a single doctrine with a uniform identity; hence it does not take a single form through the history of Buddhist philosophy. We will be concerned with the rendition of this position found in Mahāyāna thought, especially as set down by the great Buddhist philosopher Nāgārjuna (c. 150–250 CE). This is because Watsuji's own views most closely resemble Nāgārjuna's and appear to be drawn in large part from him.[28] Broadly speaking, this type of nondualism is a view about the way in which things exist. According to this viewpoint, careful observation of experience shows that it is not possible to clearly define the boundaries of individual entities in such a way that each thing could be grasped as what it is independently of anything else. This is because all things depend upon one another to be the particular things that they are, so that nothing exists in a self-subsistent manner. Nāgārjuna illustrates this idea with the example of the relation between pairs such as father and son, and fuel and fire. A father can be a father only by having a son, and a son can exist only in relation to a father. Neither of these can exist on its own—both exist only in relation to one another. Or again, fire cannot burn without fuel, and fuel can be what it is, namely, a flammable substance, only if fire exists.[29]

Because each thing causally depends upon something else in this way, nothing can be said to exist on its own, or to exist in an absolutely independent manner, that is, in a manner not produced or caused by its relation to something else. Buddhist philosophy expresses this lack of self-sufficient existence as the absence of a substantial or intrinsic nature in things, so that they are described as being "empty" of such a nature. And because all things in the world depend on other factors for their existence, all things are empty. The mutual relativity and hence emptiness of all things shows that existence is a unified, nondual whole: since one thing does not exist as absolutely independent of or separate from another, there are no absolutely independent subjects, nor is there a multiplicity of absolutely separate objects. Instead everything exists only in relation to everything else in a vast and causally interdependent totality.

Watsuji confines most discussions of nondualism within his philosophical texts proper to the relation between self and other. But the nonduality of self and other is only one aspect of a nondual totality that comprises self, other, and the world as a whole. Watsuji recognizes that these forms of nonduality are not different. Hence in *Ethics*, it can be seen that the emptiness that he contends is the "origin" (*honraisei* 本来性) out of which self and other both emerge is the same emptiness that the meditator breaks through to as the true reality (*shinsō* 真相) of the body in an event that discloses it as united to the emptiness of the world.[30]

While the nondual nature of existence unites all things in their emptiness, emptiness is not itself some metaphysical thing. It is not, for example, another, higher reality that would somehow lie behind the multiplicity of appearances. In his commentary on the dialectics of Nāgārjuna, Watsuji warns against conceptualizing or objectifying emptiness as this kind of transcendent ground on which self, other, and world can be founded.[31] This conception of emptiness as the ultimate reality results in a type of monism, since on this view the multiform phenomena of the world merge with one another in the undifferentiated unity of emptiness. But this unity or oneness of existence as empty cannot be the final truth, since, as Nāgārjuna observes, emptiness, like all other things, must itself be empty of intrinsic existence. The nondual emptiness of all things is not equivalent to the simple oneness of them. Yet a conception of things as truly differentiated returns us to a view of entities as existing in a self-sufficient and independent way, which denies the web of conditional relations through which everything exists.

The logic of nondualism transcends this binary disjunction between one and many by denying and affirming both disjuncts. The very fact that something exists means, as we have seen, that it depends on other things and conditions for its existence. For instance, a parasite requires the existence of a host organism in order to be a parasite, while the converse is also true. Parasite and host organism rely on each other, but in this reliance are also differentiated from each other in what they are. This holds for every such relation, so that from this perspective it can be asserted that things are many and not one. Yet insofar as things depend on one another to be what they are, they are "empty" of a self-subsistent nature; that is, they cannot be differentiated from one another as independently and separately existing entities. Because this is true of anything that exists, it can be said that things are not many insofar as they are one in their emptiness and mutual dependence on one another. Finally, the interdependence of all beings on one another for their existence reveals that emptiness is realized only when the multiplicity of phenomena exist. Emptiness as nothing is at the same time the fullness of beings. So although all things have their being in one another and hence compose a web of interlocking relations, they do not dissolve into an undifferentiated "oneness" in this whole. Experience by its very nature is differentiated: things in the world are distinct and differentiated while not existing in complete independence from one another.

The general configuration that emerges from the logic of nondualism can now be delineated. Two or more elements are understood as belonging together and as inseparable insofar as they depend on one another in helping to co-constitute each another; these elements thus do not exist as separate and independent entities disconnected from or alien to one another. Yet no element can be reduced to or absorbed by a single and uniform entity, whether this be another element in the relation or the system of elements as a whole. Each element remains distinct and differentiated. The configuration here, in sum, is a unity composed of difference.

Human existence—like any other system of elements embedded in and configured through the wider whole of the nondual totality of existence, is subject to the same logic. Like everything else, self and other are neither the same nor different. Hence in the formula *self and other, not two*, we are not forced to choose between either *self and other* (differentiation) or *not two* (oneness) but are able to affirm both together. Both are together in a unified whole of elements that can be distinguished and identified without standing apart and subsisting in and of themselves. Thus the simultaneous being-one-being-different of self and other is a continuity of discontinuities, that is, of differentiated things. This means that self and other are one in their "emptiness," and they are empty because they depend on each other to be what they are in all of the ways that were rehearsed in the previous chapter. But to rely on each other in this manner (and hence to be one in their "empty" identity), self and other must also be distinct and differentiated entities in order to be situated in a relation of dependence on one another. In this regard, relation requires differentiation. The terms of the relation cannot coincide with one another—they must be distinct; there must be some distance between them in order for them to be related to one another at all. On this view, the elements constitute the relation and the relation constitutes the elements: both are true at the same time.

This understanding of what is operative in the difference and distance between one self and another undermines the conventional view of the way selves are related to one another. The prevalent (and commonsense) view is that a relation with another person is a state of affairs that we choose or form or enter into. Yet the very idea of coming into relation with, or coming to be related to, another person presupposes a form of dualism: it assumes that the self is separate from others in such a way that connections to them are something that must issue from and be formed by it.

Although Watsuji rejects the ontological dualism of self and other, his reconception of this relation still requires that there be a certain kind of separation between the two. This is because in any relation between physical entities (such as the practical subject), there has to be a physical separation—in space—between one thing and another. But space is not, as the conventional view would have it, a fully separate and independent entity that appears between likewise fully separate and independent entities as mere background. Space is what makes this mode of relational unity possible; it holds together and separates at the same time, inasmuch as there must be a distinction in and through space between one thing and another that separates the things related.

The relational space between practical subjects in this regard separates a plurality of distinct selves that are connected insofar as they depend upon one another to be what they are. The relation between one self and another is thus not a relation between autonomous subjects that then come into contact with one another, but a configuration whose elements, as aspects of a single whole, are differentiated and distinct from one another in space without thereby being ontologically separate. Hence the difference between subjects in space is not an absolute opposition; the separation here is such that self and others are one in a unity composed of difference. The space between practical subjects, which Watsuji calls *subjective space* (*shutaiteki kūkan* 主体的空間), can thus be regarded as a region within the totality of the general spatiality that structures the nondual whole.

V. The Features of Subjective Space

Subjective space has four features that distinguish it from all other forms of spatiality. The first of these can be treated with some dispatch, since this is an iteration of a point that was made earlier in this study. The other three features of subjective space will require a more extensive discussion to elucidate.

Insofar as subjective space makes possible the separation and connection between one self and another, it is the ontological foundation of *ningen*. As such, this space is never simply an objective medium in which we are arrayed alongside other items. Nor is it even a space of possibilities for the practical subject, a neutral field in which any course of action might be taken or not, so that it becomes a merely contingent matter as to whether, for instance, we happen to find ourselves interacting with other people or primarily preoccupied with dealing with things. Instead, according to Watsuji, what unfolds first and foremost in this space is the movement of the self between individuation and communion with others. We come together through this space and experience the unity to be found, for example, in agreement, in a common purpose, in a shared mood, or in the ecstasy of the crowd, just as we move away from others through this space in the course of becoming an individual. Even when this movement is more psychological in character than literally physical, there must be a space between us through which we can face one other, and so through which this dynamic can transpire. This dynamic is neither contingent nor optional; it is based in and driven by the metaphysical structure of the nondual whole of human existence itself. The first characteristic that distinguishes subjective space from other forms of space is thus the permanent presence within it of the alternation between the demand for self-expression and self-assertion that characterizes the process of individuation, on the one hand, and the call to sociality, solidarity, and perhaps even communion, on the other.

This cycling of the self between the poles of individuality and community is supported by a material infrastructure that includes telephone lines, railroads, highways, bridges, airline routes, postal systems, the radio, newspapers, television, and now, of course, the internet. The particular configuration of these networks reflects and expresses the style and structure of our social existence, and the historical development of this infrastructure also reflects the historical development of a given society. So, for instance, it may be the case that all of the main roads in a given region converge on a city because it was once a capital, or that the streets in the next town over are disordered and crooked because they are laid out over paths once walked by cows, and so forth.

This array of transportation, telecommunications, and mass-media facilities, equipment, and networks crisscrosses and organizes subjective space, abolishing its distances and making it possible for people located far apart to interact with each other. Some of these technologies, such as highways and railroads, do this by allowing us to physically close the distance between parties with great rapidity. Other technologies, such as telephones, newspapers, television, and email service, are media; they mediate and almost instantly bridge this distance, so that we are able in a certain sense to be present to and in contact and association with others located at a great remove from us. This mode of being together takes the form of an awareness and an understanding that is shared with others. This is found in such phenomena as the widening of publicity about an event or the spread of news about an incident. Terms such as *widen* and *spread* indicate that an essential difference between something that is disclosed to an individual consciousness and something that is disclosed to the shared consciousness of the public is the way information and knowledge extend, through various media, across space. From this it can be seen, Watsuji believes, that the "public" is grounded in a space of relationality connected by communication and transportation networks.

This relational space is a part of subjective rather than objective space. This is because the space between things is not the same as the space between practical subjects who exist in and as a relation to others. The practical subject in its physical body is a thing, an object in-itself that is seen, but it is also a consciousness, a subject for-itself that sees, one that overlaps with and extends into other such subjects. So although the body as object is physically extended in space, this is only one dimension of the way the human being is spatially extended. The self also extends into the space between subjects in and through its connections and relations to other selves.

Watsuji calls this phenomenon subjective extendedness (*shutai-teki na hirogari* 主体的なひろがり).[32] Each of the modalities of being-in-relation-to-others is characterized by subjective extendedness: in direct interactional exchanges, so-called mental content, and so an aspect of subjectivity, is expressed and externally distributed in the shared space of face-to-face interaction. In inert and inactive forms of relational association, such as with extended family members who live in another city or with coworkers whose offices are on a different floor, we are present to others through the shared understanding of a mutual knowledge of one another—a condition maintained through regularly renewed interactions. Finally, in indirect and mediated forms of contact, such as communication by phone or email, we are able to be present to others without face-to-face interaction. All of these modes of being-in-relation-to-others are essentially made possible by the phenomenon of subjective extendedness, that is, by the capacity of the practical subject to be with and present to others by extending out beyond its actual physical position in space. In this regard, subjective space belongs to and is part of the very structure of the self. This is the second characteristic of subjective space.

The third feature of subjective space can be seen in another essential difference between the relational space between selves opened up by subjective extendedness and the objective space located between things: positions and relations in this space such as proximity and distance, being together and being apart, are determined by subjective factors such as the nature, tenor, and intensity of the connections between practical subjects, as much as they are by purely objective factors such as the physical location of these entities. The way practical subjects experience their physical positions relative to one another depends largely on the capacity of the practical subject to be "extended," as well as on the degree to which they are with and present to others.

The capacity of the practical subject to transcend its physical location and be present to others at a distance can be sharply reduced or even eliminated by physical barriers to subjective extendedness, such as those seen in emergency conditions. To find oneself physically cut off from communication with others is a form of being at a remove from them that can in many ways far exceed the actual physical distances involved. If these conditions become widespread, as when, to take Watsuji's example, an area of a country (especially if it is a region isolated by its geographical features) is cut off from the outside world due to war or to natural disasters such as earthquakes or floods, this becomes cause for tremendous anxiety on all sides. Rumors, speculation, and ill-informed opinions take the place of the normal flow of information conveyed through communication, news, and transportation. This infrastructure as a whole constitutes what Watsuji metaphorically calls the nervous system of a society; hence when these lines of communication and contact are weakened or collapse, society itself weakens and is in danger of collapsing.[33]

From the point of view of an objective and empirical spatiality, the physical distance between one person and another within the disaster zone, as well as the distance to the troubled area from outlying regions (and so the physical position of each subject in relation to the other), remains unchanged throughout these events. But relational configurations like near and far or together and apart are not—as they are in purely objective space—determined solely by the objective position of entities relative to one another. The distance between people separated by a catastrophe is determined as much by changes to the connections and relations between them brought about by this event as by the physical location of the participants.

The degree to which we are able to be with and present to others can be greatly affected not only by physical barriers such as those found in extreme situations but also by the way others are disposed to and respond to us. Watsuji illustrates this point with an example of the way "inside" and outside" and "near" and "far" can become psychological positions that the practical subject occupies in the relational space opened up by the kind of subjective extendedness that is the practical interconnection of acts:

> It's just that this "outside" of and in "opposition" to, however, are entirely different in meaning from those cases that deal with strictly natural objects. When your physical body is considered merely as a material object, it exists outside of and in opposition to me, in the same way that a natural object does. It is never united or one with me. But in this case I am merely the epistemological subject [*shukan* 主観] of observation and not the embodied subject [*shutai* 主体] of practical action. However, when I as the practical subject face you, you also face me in the same way as the practical subject. Your physical body exhibits your personality in all of its parts and thus draws out in its every motion that response or reaction that is my personality. It strengthens *opposition* through hostility, and *unity* through affection. It shows what it is to be *outside* through coldness, and what it means to be drawn *inside* through kindness. In this way, as that which constitutes the subjective interconnection of acts, you are able to exist outside of and in opposition to me. This kind of spatiality is not the same as the space in the world of nature. That is, it is not like a form of intuition; *it is a way of connecting multiple subjects to one another*. It is not a uniform and homogenous expanse, but a *dialectical one* in which relations such as far and near, or wide and narrow, are mutually transformed into one another.[34]

Watsuji attributes this mutual transformation in spatial relations, these changes in the degree and kind of being together, to the ever-present oscillating motion between the individual and communal moments in the life of the subject.[35] This movement can be physical, as for example when one joins a team or quits a political movement, but it need not be. Several people can live in the same house while inhabiting opposing psychological spaces. Two people can be miles apart but, in speaking on the telephone to one another, of one mind.

What moves us closer to or further away from others, then, are the actions we take in relation to one another, as well as the actions that are taken by others in relation to us, including the respective reactions or responses to our actions. The to-and-fro movement of human existence is composed, in short, of interactions. This is made possible, in turn, by the fact that the expressions (e.g., gestures, words, facial expressions, movements, posture, touch, vocalization) that fill this space of interaction can be understood and responded to because they have a certain meaning. The fourth and final characteristic of subjective spatiality, then, is that subjective space is a space of meaning.

***

Watsuji's conception of the human being as a hybrid, dynamic, and nondual entity—as well as his understanding of the practical subject as *aidagara*—underscore the degree to which his appropriation of the subject pole of the Dasein-world dyad is a transformation; it also reflects the myriad ways in which the self is, above all, a relational being. And while the emphasis thus far has been on the relation of the self to others, the closing portions of the description of *ningen* indicate that the self is linked to its surroundings, not only—as in the manner of Dasein— through its comportments but also insofar as subjective space is part of the relational structure of the practical subject itself.

This has significant philosophical consequences for the nature of the world that the practical subject is "in" and inseparable from—since ipso facto it must include this space between selves—as well as for the lifeworldly dimension of nature that is disclosed in and through such a world. The manner in which Watsuji takes up the world pole of Heidegger's dyad here also changes it, since incorporating this form of spatiality into the concept of world furnishes it with novel social and natural features that also belong, at the same time, to the very structure of the self. Inasmuch as the phenomenon of subjective space is perched between and belongs to the self, its world, and a *fūdo* all at once in this way, it is an essential dimension of the relational continuity between all of the entities in this configuration. A full examination of these issues uncovers a cavalcade of questions and problems that will require a separate chapter to address properly.

6

The Space of the Self: Between Culture and Nature

In the notion of subjective space Watsuji uncovers a phenomenon that links his concept of the practical subject as *aidagara* with his concept of a world as a social, historical, and natural structure. To account for the form of unity operative in these relations, Watsuji attempts to assimilate this configuration to a spatial scheme drawn largely from Heidegger's account of the existential spatiality of Dasein. But rather than simply recapitulate Heidegger's account, Watsuji distinguishes between public and private spheres within the existential spatiality of Dasein and shows that these forms of space are arrived at through a specific mode of representation and distanciation that draws on, and so presupposes, the interpersonal space located between practical subjects.[1] Watsuji folds each of these forms of space into what he takes to be the more fundamental phenomenon of subjective space, and identifies *this* space with the most basic or primary dimension of the space of a world. This means that the space opened up and defined by the relation between one self and another, one that belongs to the structure of the practical subject, belongs at the same time to a world. Subjective space functions in this way as an essential link between Watsuji's concept of the self as a being-in-relation-to-others and his notion of a world as a social, historical, and natural structure. Watsuji's conception of the subjective space of being-in-the-world is thus not Heidegger's—it is more fundamental, and, unlike the spatiality of Dasein, it is interpersonal.

Nonetheless these changes to Heidegger's construal of subjective space are still not sufficient to show how this phenomenon provides the relational and structural continuity that unites the practical subject to its socially, culturally, and naturally constituted world. My contention is that this difficulty can be overcome once we recognize that the structure of subjective space presupposes a physical dimension—one that Heidegger appears to deny to the existential spatiality of Dasein. Such a dimension is necessary insofar as the practical subject is not encased in and reducible to its physical body but exceeds it in extending into the space of interactions with others. Although space belongs in this way to the very structure of the practical subject, it also encompasses and contains both the other people and the tools and equipment that are part of a world. Subjective space can function as a receptacle of this kind, in turn, because it is always opened up and moored by a certain kind of place—one whose final ground is nature.

I. From Subjective Space to World Space

While Watsuji's notion of space is not Heidegger's, it shares much with his account. For both thinkers, what space is, is revealed by our phenomenological experience of it. For both, too, we encounter space just as we encounter everything else: in and through our being in a world. Thus Watsuji equates subjective spatiality, and Heidegger the spatiality of Dasein, with the existential spatiality of being-in-the-world. A primary difference between Heidegger and Watsuji here, however, is that the existential character of subjective space is disclosed first and foremost for Watsuji in the relation between one self and another, and so in the predominantly subjective rather than objective significance of the distances between practical subjects and their positions relative to one another. So, for instance, the proximity of participants in a protest march to one another is not the same kind of proximity as those moving through a crowded subway station at rush hour. The availability or accessibility of people at a customer's firm differs from those at my own worksite, even if (or perhaps because) I labor in the vast spaces of a maritime container terminal and my customer operates out of the densely packed offices of a small logistics consultancy. In these examples we are also able to see that the existential character of this intersubjective space arises only with and in a world.

The existential character of space is also revealed for Watsuji, as it is for Heidegger, in our capacity to comport ourselves with competence and familiarity toward things in our engagements with them. As a result, our involvements with these things are primarily experienced with respect to their practical, cognitive, and psychological availability (or lack thereof) rather than in terms of features that can be objectively mapped, such as their distance from a fixed point or their exact position in three-dimensional space. Moreover this way of experiencing space is tied, as Jeff Malpas puts it, "to the teleological ordering of equipment and project," so that this aspect of existential spatiality is also encountered only within a world.[2]

The space of the world is thus characterized for Watsuji by both the existential spatiality of Dasein's practical involvements as well as the subjective space of relational interaction and expression. Watsuji's contention is that this (inter)subjective space is more primary than the existential spatiality opened up by the equipmental and involvement wholes that ground Dasein's comportments and activities. By this he means that what we encounter first and foremost in our experience of spatiality is the relational space between selves rather than zones of practical intelligibility structured by the worldliness of the world. Watsuji goes beyond even this to claim, furthermore, that only *after* we become aware of these zones of practical space do we arrive at what is usually thought to be the principal and most prevalent experience of spatiality, namely, the consciousness of being oriented in space through the body.

Watsuji's ordering idea here is that the spatiality of being-in-the-world has more than one dimension, and that these are arranged in an experiential hierarchy that begins with the initial and basic experience of intersubjective space. His contention is that the subsequent awareness of each of the other dimensions of space arises only when this form of space is considered from the standpoint of the individual. As we shall see in what follows, each of the successive ways of encountering space is derived from some aspect of this individual standpoint.

The initial form of space derived from the space between selves is what Watsuji calls environmental space (*kankyōteki kūkan* 環境的空間). This mode of spatiality parallels and mostly overlaps with Heidegger's notion of existential spatiality, or Dasein's lived sense of space, which is underpinned by constellations of equipment. In his account of this spatiality, Heidegger observes that because Dasein is practically situated, each piece of equipment has its proper place: it *belongs* there or else it is encountered as just lying around—though this latter state of affairs must be distinguished from the random occurrence of something that contingently occupies a spatial position. The place of equipment is what makes it available to Dasein. Because the iron sits atop the ironing board and the table lamp is on the desk, they are ready-to-hand. The positions of such items are ordered by a larger context of practical significance, such as the space of a toolshed or a kitchen, which determines where a particular piece of equipment belongs and whether it is "in place" or "out of place." Dasein's orientation and directionality are also determined by these regions of equipmental space: "The 'above' is what is 'on the ceiling,' the 'below' is what is 'on the floor,' the 'behind' is what is 'at the door.' "[3] Finally, these regions refer to and are circumscribed by a particular whole of Dasein's everyday involvements, which, in turn, are defined in terms of these regions.

For Heidegger the existential spatiality of Dasein's practical involvements is the fundamental form of space, and the homogeneous space of an objectified nature is founded on it. Watsuji maintains that while the existential spatiality of Dasein constitutes in this regard a foundational form of "subjective" spatiality, it is an inadequate one, inasmuch as the encounter with this space of equipment arises from a more primordial kind of space that it presupposes and relies upon.

According to this argument, in order to uncover regions of practical significance, one must first suppose a concern with tools and equipment. Tools and equipment, in turn, are "at hand" for an individual. And one finds the individual only by abstracting it from its embeddedness in relations with others. The most fundamental form of space is thus the space of *aidagara*; we arrive at the spatiality of Dasein only by leaving behind the constitutive relationality of contact and interaction with others and taking up the standpoint of the individual and its concern with tools.[4]

A third kind of spatiality arises when the standpoint of the individual subject is considered wholly apart from its concern with equipment and tools; here we find the subject occupying a point of view that just "looks on" (*nagameru* ながめる) and out at things rather than occupying a perspective determined by the practical involvements of care (*Sorge*). This standpoint reveals a space occupied by objects that are devoid of tool-like characteristics, which Watsuji calls "the perspectival space of fixed positions" (*teii serareta enkinhōteki kūkan* 定位せられた遠近法的空間). Here we are dealing with the private or personal rather than the public dimension of environmental space; as Watsuji puts it, this space is environmental space with the ego or "I" at its center. The space of fixed positions is structured by the perspective of this ego center, and its positions are fixed in relation to it.[5]

Watsuji maintains that this personal spatiality of the embodied individual is also a derivative form of spatial awareness rather than one that is immediately given. This is rather puzzling and seems counterintuitive when one considers that what is given is given to the first-person standpoint, a standpoint that inheres in the world through the body. As Erin McCarthy points out, it is through the body that we first experience and understand space at all: "It is largely the body which enables us to understand spatiality—it is from the place/space of our embodied selves that we first experience spatiality or even begin to grasp it as a concept."[6] Because this space, as opened up by our body, is centered in each of us, the availability (e.g., near and far, accessible and inaccessible) and orientation (e.g., up and down, left and right) of things in it are tied to our personal perspective. Nonetheless Watsuji's claim is that inasmuch as this personal perspective is never that of an absolutely independent and self-contained individual, but always only part of the more encompassing and fundamental viewpoint of an I-in-relation-to-others, this kind of spatiality also ultimately presupposes and arises from the subjective spatiality of being-in-relation-to-others. Thus the experience of the bodily space of fixed positions, like the encounter with environmental space, is ultimately grounded in subjective space.

A fourth and final form of space, which Watsuji calls homogeneous space (*tōshitsuteki kūkan* 等質的空間), depends upon but does not, strictly speaking, belong to this hierarchy of the experiential dimensions of the spatiality of being-in-the-world. This is because while homogeneous space also originates with subjective space, it does not arise from it in the same manner. This form of spatiality is produced by objectifying the space between practical subjects. Hence unlike the other forms of space, homogeneous space is not and cannot be encountered or inhabited by the practical subject; it is not, therefore, part of the space of a world. Instead, as space that is represented rather than lived through, it is both everywhere and nowhere—a pure abstraction grasped by the disembodied and worldless epistemological subject.

As with each of the other forms of spatiality, homogeneous space also presupposes what was uncovered in its immediate predecessor. This means that homogeneous space can only be extracted from the space of fixed positions, just as the space of fixed positions arises from environmental space. Homogeneous space thus cannot be derived, *pace* Heidegger, directly from the equipmental spatiality of Dasein. Watsuji draws on the insights of Oskar Becker and Theodor Litt in concisely summarizing how the production of homogeneous space relies in this way on the intervening spatiality of fixed positions. Within the bodily spatiality of fixed positions a certain perspective and set of positions are established in relation to the ego at the center of this space, but this perspective, and these positions, come to be dislodged through a process of abstraction: through the reciprocal exchange of perspectives and the movements of a mobile and embodied "I," both the positions in this space and the perspective that structures it are seen to be relative rather than anchoring or centering this space. This then emancipates the individual subject from the standpoint of the "I" and leads to the postulation of a point of view from which it becomes possible to grasp (at least in cognition) homogeneous space.[7]

With this hierarchical reordering of the forms of space, Watsuji follows Heidegger in reversing the usual view in which subjective space presupposes and is derived from an absolute (i.e., infinite) and homogeneous space devoid of qualities. Because his notion of subjective space borrows so much from Heidegger, he also runs squarely into a problem that Heidegger's account generates but never resolves. Since this is a difficulty that hinders the identification of subjective space with the space of a world, it must be addressed if the concept of subjective space is to successfully function—as Watsuji appears to have intended—as an onto-logical bridge between the practical subject and its world.

The difficulty emerges in tandem with Heidegger's reappraisal of the ontological status of existential spatiality, or the lived experience of space. This form of space, which is always encountered within a world, was uncovered through the recuperation of ontological primacy of pre-objective being and the return to the standpoint of the lifeworld that was accomplished in *Being and Time*. Thus the space of being-in-the-world, rather than the homogeneous space of an objectified nature, constitutes the most fundamental and ontologically basic form of space.[8] Watsuji thus maintains with Heidegger that the objective expanse of space is dis-covered from within subjective human existence rather than constituting the objective setting that renders it possible.[9] Thus Dasein, as Heidegger says, does not occupy a position in space or "eat up" the kilometers in traversing stretches of it, nor is it found "within" it, as though space were a receptacle.[10] Nevertheless David Cerbone and Jeff Malpas have shown that this view cannot be reconciled with the corporeal nature of Dasein, with its practical engagement with the world, or with the fact that any equipmental array requires a spatially extended dimension in which each piece of equipment can be juxtaposed alongside other such pieces.[11]

Notwithstanding these difficulties, or the notoriously fraught and even confused character of Heidegger's discussion as a whole, Watsuji himself seems to simply endorse this aspect of Heidegger's conception, building atop it in developing his own notion of subjective space.[12] For Watsuji as for Heidegger, existential space is revealed by our concerns and involvements, so that space is something we are oriented toward rather than something that surrounds and contains us. The primary modifica-tion Watsuji makes to Dasein's mode of existential spatiality is the idea that the involvements on which this space are founded are now first and foremost with each other rather than with equipment.

This amendment still does not go far enough, however, since this kind of space can neither meet the objections raised by Cerbone and Malpas nor accommodate the subjective extendedness that is the essen-tial feature of the practical subject as *aidagara*. To be able to do both of these things, subjective space must also possess a physical dimension in which the equipmental network and embodied activity of the practi-cal subject can be located, and through which this subject can be exter-nalized and extended in its interactional exchanges with others in the practical interconnection of acts. The successful identification of Wat-suji's notion of subjective spatiality with the space of being-in-the-world thus requires a physical dimension, one that can function as a receptacle within which we find both ourselves and the assemblages of equipment that help to compose the internal structure of the world. This space, in turn, must be rooted in a particular kind of location or place if it is to be capable of surrounding and containing human beings and the objects produced by them in this way. It is this dimension of space that Watsuji appears to suppress in his account of the hierarchy of forms of space. As we move into the final stages of this study, it will become increasingly evident that he at the same time nevertheless tacitly relies upon this dimension of spatiality in depicting the phenomenon of *fūdo*.

While this aspect of space is physical, it is not, like homogeneous space, "objective" in an absolute sense; insofar as it is experienced and lived through, it possesses existential features, namely, features that are in some sense subject-related and so "subjective." Because the spatiality of containment is composed of a mixture of physical and existential characteristics, a complete account of this modality of space must extend to a consideration of its existential character, or the way it is experienced. Since, as Heidegger had shown, something can be an intelligible object of experience only on the basis of its belonging to a world, the physical aspect of space is always experienced in and through a world. The spatiality of containment is encountered as part of a world insofar as it is shows up as an environment in which the other people who share our world, the human constructions that order it, and the natural setting that encompasses it can appear. This spatial environment, moreover, is never experienced as a neutral or blankly featureless receptacle; it always has a certain quality or sense, a particular kind of intelligibility and atmosphere, which is tied to my encounter with these three elements that are always part of any world.

Because Watsuji has difficulty in unambiguously incorporating the spatiality of containment into his overall account of subjective space, he also has trouble recognizing the existential feature of physical spatiality that we have uncovered here. Since his limited remarks on this topic are not sufficient to complete our account of the physico-existential dimension of subjective space, in what follows we set out more fully what the existential side of this dimension involves.

II. World Space and Social Tenor

Our lived sense of space as physical medium is an experience of its having a certain quality and a particular atmosphere. This sense of space arises from the interpretive encounter of the practical subject with specific elements of a world, namely, the expressions of the other human beings in it,

130

the meanings contained by the human artifacts that belong to it, and the intelligible aspects of the nature that supports and comprehends it—all of which refer to, rely upon, and are possible only on the basis of a world.

The differences between Watsuji's concept of world and Heidegger's are, as this inventory of elements indicates, acute and emphatic, but Watsuji nonetheless also praises Heidegger for first uncovering in an exemplary way the subjective significance (*shutaiteki na igi* 主体的な意義) of the phenomenon of world.[13] Hence his interpretive reconstruction of the concept of world both embraces and diverges from Heidegger's. For Watsuji as for Heidegger, a world is a structure of meaning connected by a network of roles, equipment, comportments, and practices. But as the presence of equipment in this list suggests, a world must contain at least some material components to which someone must be related in order to find herself "in" a world at all. Watsuji's conception of the way in which a world is always woven out of physical and material elements in addition to nonmaterial ones is considerably more extensive and far-reaching than this: a world relies on equipment, but it also requires, for Watsuji, the presence of other people and their natural surroundings. Watsuji thus defines *world* as the historical, climatic, and social structure of human existence (*ningen sonzai no rekishiteki, fūdoteki, shakaiteki na kōzō* 人間存在の歴史的・風土的・社会的な構造).[14]

Hence in the course of setting forth our account of the lived and experiential sense of the social, artifactual, and natural dimensions of the physical spatiality of containment, we will also need to give an explanatory description of the elements in Watsuji's concept of world that correspond to these aspects of this space. The first of these dimensions is our lived experience of the physical space in which others are encountered. This experience is tied to the expressive space of meaning opened up between practical subjects. Just as we are able, in the space of interaction, to understand and respond to the expressions of others because they bear a particular meaning, the atmosphere of this space also has certain intelligibility, a certain character and quality, that arises with and in the continuity between expressive act and practical understanding. The meanings that emerge here all run together; thus when I am angry with my friend, not only is the anger on my brow, it is also in the air between us. This is true of every space in which interaction takes place; it helps to explain, for example, the dreary atmosphere of an academic conference, the animated one of a classroom discussion, the lively one of a children's birthday party, and the cozy one of a family home during a holiday meal.

The atmosphere of all such interactions is also determined by the degree to which we have a shared understanding of the meanings expressed in these kinds of spaces. Consider a successful comedian on stage in a foreign country whose jokes disappear, one after another, into a remorselessly oppressive silence. On the one hand, the usually merry, even at times exuberant atmosphere of the comedy club back home is nowhere to be found due to the lack of a shared recognition of what counts as amusing; on the other hand, the understanding that the members of the audience share with one another—which is so at odds with the comedian's sensibility—is precisely what leads to this excruciatingly awkward exchange.

A shared understanding of this kind, or the lack of one, is determined largely on the basis of a shared background composed of values, ideas, and norms—as is so clearly in evidence in something like divergent senses of the comic; it is also constituted by a shared grasp of roles, equipment, and practices. The atmosphere came to be so uncomfortable because the event was understood by all to be a stand-up comedy performance, the raised wooden floor a stage, the person on it a comedian, and the others in the seats encircling it his audience.

In sum, what is "in the air" between us depends on the extent to which my actions and expressions are intelligible to others, and theirs to me; this mutual intelligibility, in turn, depends upon the shared understanding that is a condition of being in a world together. So the atmosphere of the space between people on a cruise ship, or around a bonfire at a festival, or between the staff and residents of a retirement home, or between the priest and worshippers in a temple, for example, will depend on how the words, gestures, and actions of the participants fit into a whole context, one that is framed and provided with scaffolding by the roles the participants understand themselves to be occupying, the practice they are engaged in, the tools they use, and the networks of referential and involvement totalities within which they operate.

Nevertheless, even when, as travelers, immigrants, or exchange students, we leave our world behind, we never simply interact with others in a void; on the contrary, the types of interactions that occur here only dramatize the essential role that a world plays in what does and does not emerge in the atmosphere between people. Without the shared array of implicit and explicit understandings that form the backbone of a world, the space between people takes on a different kind of atmosphere. When I fail to register the shock on my Japanese host mother's face as I enter my host sister's school building with my shoes on, the atmosphere quickly becomes one of confusion mixed with consternation. Or the delight that the visitor takes in certain quotidian practices and behaviors in a foreign country, on the one side, and the bemusement of the natives at this response, on the other, join together as a shared atmosphere of goodwill and light amusement. Or again, as the visitor struggles to communicate and connect with those he meets in this new country, he can't help but notice how *thin* this space between himself and other people can feel. Yet the depth, intensity, and complexity of this space seem to be instantaneously restored to the visitor who encounters his fellow countrymen abroad.

This final example does more than any other to illustrate Watsuji's contention that a world is also composed of others. There is an initial hurdle, however, to understanding this claim, one that can be formulated as a question: How can I be both in a world *and* be an element that composes a world? The answer to this would seem to be that I can be so because being and acting in the world entail that insofar as I am there in the world attending to my concerns, I am there in the world as the concern of others; in this sense I am part of their world, and they are part of mine. Heidegger, Watsuji says, misses this phenomenon, which is obscured for him by an almost too ardent focus on the relation between Dasein and its equipment.

Perhaps in order to show that his own view of these matters is no mere idiosyncrasy on his part, Watsuji makes approving reference to Löwith's contention that the German word *Welt* implies a human element. He cites Löwith's examples of this kind of usage in German, but these meanings are also present in English, since, as Gadamer notes in making the same point, the English word *world* has Germanic roots: "Just think of the English 'world'—here the root '*wer*' is contained in it: '*weralt*.' Consider also '*Wergeld*' and '*Werwolf*.' All of these words contain "*wer*' (who), i.e. human beings. In short, the world is a human world. This is the original meaning in the Germanic and Indo-European languages."[15] This explains why Löwith's examples of this form of usage are directly translatable into English: "a man of the world," "accustomed to, or inexperienced in, the ways of the world," "escaping from the world," "the world of women"—all of these uses of *world* point to a definite realm of society. For Watsuji they also indicate that the concept of world must include the world of social relations, such that "an analysis of *In-der-Welt-sein* must be an analysis of communal life."[16]

Watsuji represents these differences between his own and Heidegger's conception of world by translating Heidegger's notion of *Welt* with the ordinary Japanese term *seken* 世間, which denotes the world in the sense of the public, society in general, or that domain of human affairs about which one can be knowledgeable, or "worldly." But because *seken* is intended to both translate and amplify the philosophical concept of *Welt*, it also bears a philosophical meaning that extends beyond its connotations in ordinary Japanese. Thus insofar as Watsuji builds the human being into his concept of world, *seken* must accommodate the particular features that characterize *ningen*. Hence Maraldo helpfully observes:

> The actual world is an extension of subjectivity (*shutaiteki ni hirogatta mono*) in his sense of that term. . . . The world *seken* does not stand opposed to people as something that transcends them because it already contains the Between (*gen*) that is constitutive of being human (*ningen*). Nor does this world *seken* for Watsuji demarcate the human from the non-human. It is only a slight stretch for Watsuji to interpret *seken* or *yo no naka* as a space spread out between individuals (*hito*) and whatever is taken as other to them. A world construed as objective nature independent of humans would be an abstraction, just as the individual subject is an abstraction from our existence as *ningen*. On the other hand, the world cannot be read as a social construction in which objects or phenomena are rendered dependent on the conceptualization and social practices of distinct groups of people, because the world *seken* counts as the actual space or interval (*ma*) of the interactions that constitute us.[17]

This analysis indicates that the presence of others in the composition of a world accounts in important respects for its character as a setting that is neither fully external to human subjectivity nor merely a product of it. This is because the space of a world is composed, in part, of the space between (*ma* 間) us, which is both empirical and existential. But it is also because the temporal intervals (*ma* 間) that separate us, like the spatial ones, are both given and lived through.

Our experience of the temporal structure of the world is shaped by the presence of others in it because insofar as a world is constituted, in part, by the subjective extendedness (*shutaiteki na hirogari*) of *ningen* (i.e., the way the self extends into the space between practical subjects in and through a nexus of interaction), this interconnection is a continually changing and dynamic structure.[18] To be in a world, then, is to be "in" a spatiotemporal whole that is both empirically given and existentially lived through. Watsuji attempts to capture the manner in which the spatial and temporal nature of a world is tied to our relations with others by translating *In-der-Welt-sein* with the Japanese term *yononaka* 世の中. In Japanese, *yo* 世 can mean both "a society" and "a generation" (*sedai* 世代). *Yo* indicates in this regard something that human beings cross through in both time and space. To be "in" or "within" (*naka* 中) a *yo* is really to be among people; this can be expressed quite literally with the sinograph 仲, which is also pronounced *naka*. Thus Watsuji notes that the peculiar spatiality of human relations finds expression in ordinary Japanese phrases such as *fūfu no naka* 夫婦の仲 (the relationship of husband and wife) and *nakatagai suru* 仲違いする (to fall out with, be estranged from). The spatiality of such relationships is not like the static space found between objects like a couch and a table; one person is related to another through the living, and so temporal, dynamic of association, interaction, and exchange that characterizes what Watsuji has called the practical interconnection of acts.

III. World Space and Artifactual Aura

As all of the foregoing examples demonstrate, being in the presence of others, and having them in one's own, always charges the space between people with a certain quality and texture, which arises from what is expressed and understood between people—whether this is built upon a shared horizon of meaning or whether the chain of expression and understanding is diminished or altered by the lack of such a horizon.

The meanings expressed and understood in the space of interaction, however, are fleeting; moods and atmospheres dissipate with the last exchange in an interaction or at the close of an event. Yet there *is* a sense in which subjective space harbors meaning—and so its attendant atmosphere—of a more permanent sort. To uncover this phenomenon we will need to bring together a range of ideas that are present in Watsuji's reflections on human culture and supplement them with our own observations and examples. And while we were able to treat the phenomenon of transitory meaning with some concision, the other, more permanent form of meaning will require a somewhat more elaborate analysis to spell out.

This form of meaning is derived from the intelligibility of human artifacts—a term we use here to designate any man-made object, from personal items used to decorate the body such as pieces of jewelry, to monumental structures such as skyscrapers and stadia. And just as a certain atmosphere arises with and in the continuity between expressive act and practical understanding, it also arises with and in the continuity between the meanings expressed in human artifacts, and an understanding that is interpretive rather than practical.

Hence Watsuji contends that artifacts are *expressions*; they express a meaning that is understood. This can be seen in the fact that we encounter and treat them not as mere objects but *as* something or other: "We treat the 'things' found in our surroundings as a desk, as a room, or as a house."[19] The meanings expressed in human artifacts differ in multiple ways from those expressed by other subjects. These differences also account for why the form of understanding involved here is interpretive rather that practical. The meaning or significance of entities such as tools, infrastructure, products, dwellings, and the like are already expressed in and as the entity itself; these meanings do not take the form of the unfolding expressions of a conscious agent, that is, of a practical subject who intends something. Thus the understanding here is not the practical understanding (*jissenteki ryōkai*) of acts in interaction but the interpretive understanding of artifacts in a cultural world. What is expressed, then, is not persons and their intentions but the elements of a form of life and, through these, *ningen sonzai* itself.

Watsuji makes these points using as examples the ordinary items encountered in everyday life:

> For example, we already experience as "goods" the things we buy daily. However, these goods are neither simply object-like things nor economic concepts. Rather, they are something which, as clothing, food, and shelter, express these respective moments [*keiki* 契機] of human existence and which are treated as foodstuff, beverages, clothes, furniture, etc. and sold in their respective stores or departments. More specifically, food is characterized as a daily household necessity, an object of consumption in a restaurant, or something given as a gift, or something to celebrate an occasion, and so on. In the same way, clothing is sold as ceremonial clothing, visiting clothes, daily clothes, uniforms, children's clothes, baby clothes, and so on. Furniture, too, gives expression to all of the ways we live. There are thus no goods in which *ningen sonzai* is not expressed.[20]

For Watsuji, all human artifacts are an expression of *ningen sonzai*. Yet it is not self-evident from this term (nor from the way Watsuji uses it) what it is exactly that comes to expression in these artifacts. The semantically ambiguous character of the term *ningen sonzai* has led commentators to translate it at certain points as *human existence* and at others as *human being*. Watsuji himself seems to use this term in both of these senses, albeit at different times. In this case, however, he speaks as if *both* human existence and the human being come to expression in our artifacts. Hence in the preceding passage, he shows that the meanings embodied by manmade goods range across multiple dimensions of human life, including the various forms of need, work, and pleasure that appear in the activities of feeding and protecting our bodies; in this regard, they express human existence. At the same time, Watsuji also contends that expressions in and as artifacts are the self-externalization of human beings, that is, of us ourselves (*soto ni deta wareware jishin de aru* 外に出た我々自身である).[21] In this regard, they express the being of the human being, the *sonzai* of *ningen*. And because we have our being (*sonzai*) in being-in-relation-to-others (*aidagara*), this will mean that artifacts also express forms of *aidagara*. Thus, for example, what is expressed in equipment like transport, communication, and information facilities and infrastructure such as roads, telephones, radios, mailboxes, is never only their significance as equipment, but also the being-in-relation-to-others of the practical subject. They point to and are a concrete and material embodiment of a structure of relationality in which practical subjects regularly connect with and separate from one another.[22]

Watsuji's other examples are, to varying degrees, less persuasive and more difficult to parse. He says that other kinds of tools, too, express—in addition to their practical significance—this aspect of the being of *ningen*: "In reality, we already stand in a being-in-relation-to-others when we discover tools. Without living in a family, there is no interaction with furniture; without laboring in a society, one does not come into possession of a hammer. Tools are therefore already an expression of *aidagara*, and not just something 'ready-to-hand' for me."[23] But it is not evident from this example precisely which aspect of being-in-relation-to-others comes to expression in the furniture or the hammer. Watsuji has not shown that the social significance of these kinds of tools in particular extends beyond their reference to other users, producers, possessors, or sellers of them. These meanings relate us to others *through* the tool (e.g., my furniture refers to the salesperson who sold it to me). Because this is a point that, as Watsuji acknowledges, Heidegger had already made, the referential significance of such tools is as compatible with the way an atomized Dasein is related to others as it is with the being-in-relation-to-others of the practical subject.[24]

Watsuji's thesis fares somewhat better in a final example that illustrates the way daily life, crammed with human artifacts, is brimming with expression and understanding. He asks us to consider the simple experience of waking up and eating breakfast in the morning. The room in which the Japanese person awakens (now with less and less frequency) is covered with straw tatami mats and equipped with wooden sliding doors covered with cloth or paper (*fusuma*). Someone from a different culture will awaken in a room with a wooden floor that has a door that can be locked. The shape and style of such a room is the expression of the various historical, climatic, and geographical constraints (*rekishiteki fūdoteki shoseiyaku* 歴史的風土的諸制約) of a particular society. At the breakfast table, too, these conditions frequently appear in the type of utensils used, the form of the dining table, and the way the food is prepared.

Watsuji maintains that in addition to such factors, the furnishings, food, and houses that are part of our lives also express culturally inflected forms of *aidagara*. We have already indicated some reasons to be skeptical about the contention that tools such as hammers and equipment such as furniture can express *aidagara*, and Watsuji does not provide anything further in his analysis here that would change this judgment. Food, on the other hand, is something more straightforwardly communal. The flavors of breakfast, whether this is hot rice porridge garnished with peanuts, eggs, and pork, or pancakes topped with strawberries, or grilled fish accompanied by sides of soy soup, fermented soybeans, and pickles, are a result of the use of certain ingredients and preparation methods. As such, these flavors do not express my individual inclinations and tastes; they express a shared palate and a communal set of preferences, and hence my being-in-relation to a concrete and historical community. This aspect of what is expressed in food can be seen in the longing among expatriates, immigrants, or refugees for "our" food, for the flavors of home, a feeling whose intensity explains the inevitable establishment of restaurants, grocery stores, delis, bakeries, and so on that serve these communities when they reach a certain size.

Just as it takes a little reflection to see how our culturally embedded being-in-relation-to-others comes to expression in food, it requires a certain amount of comparative analysis to uncover the way houses are also cultural expressions of *aidagara*. A house, Watsuji says, is not simply a collection of lumber and building materials; it is a dwelling that expresses *ningen sonzai*. The structure of the house expresses the way human beings exist in relation to a family. The living room, bedroom, guest room, kitchen, and foyer each reveal aspects of our shared and communal activities and relations in the family. Each morning we wake up in the bedroom rather than the kitchen or hallway. Consequently, waking up already exhibits an understanding of what is expressed in and as a house, and does not happen without it.[25]

The precise contours of what is understood in this regard will vary with the society to which one belongs. The features and design of the traditional Japanese home express a different form of being-in-relation-to-others than those of the typical Western home. Watsuji draws our attention in particular to the manner in which the spaces of a Japanese home are lightly partitioned by opaque screens (*fusuma*) and wooden grids covered with translucent paper (*shōji*). Both slide open and closed on wooden tracks, so that while each member of the family may have his or her own room, these sliding screens can be freely opened and closed by others. This function also allows rooms in the home to be dynamically reconfigured, giving the impression that the distinctions between individual chambers are fluid rather than permanent. According to Watsuji, these features of the Japanese home reflect the weak sense of individuality, the collective orientation, and the internal fusion that mark family relations in Japanese culture. One finds evidence of this everywhere in Japanese society; to take just one example: it is perfectly normal for a father to resign from his job to atone for a serious crime (such as murder) committed by his adult child—and the converse is even, at times, possible: an adult child whose career is damaged or ended by a serious crime committed by a parent.[26]

Watsuji observes that Western houses, by contrast, are partitioned into individual and independent rooms set off from each other by thick walls and sturdy doors. These are usually secured by lock and key, so that only key holders can freely gain access. This construction stresses division and individuality and reflects the Western will to autonomy and separation even within the family.[27] In expressing the forms that *aidagara* takes among a group of people, man-made artifacts express their form of life. Such are the results, Watsuji notes, when you merely consider the facts of getting up in the morning and eating breakfast. Thus it is quite clear that our everyday life is in reality an immense sea of expressions.

Considerations of this kind show that the *sonzai* of *ningen*, the being of the human being as being-in-relation-to-others, is constituted differently in different cultures, and that this is reflected in the artifacts that surround us. They also demonstrate (as seen in the examples of tools such as hammers, utensils, and tables) that while artifacts can give concrete and material expression to *aidagara*, they do not always do so. Yet all artifacts are *always* intelligible; they always embody some meaning or other: either they represent human needs and values in being understood "as" something or other and so in this way express human existence, or they articulate in addition to this a particular mode of being-in-relation-to-others, and hence express the being of the human being.

Both of these forms of artifactual intelligibility have a role in constituting the atmosphere of subjective space. We will assess each in turn, beginning with the examples of the forms of being-in-relation-to-others that are embodied in a people's cuisine and style of house construction. There is little doubt that the atmosphere of a place is directly shaped by both of these things. The atmosphere of certain neighborhoods in Taipei, Jakarta, and New York, for instance, is composed to some extent by street food stall vendors and the smells, colors, and textures of the food on offer, the dishes it is served in, and the equipment used to cook and display it. The stately atmosphere of a historic neighborhood may derive, in part, from the considerable number of sprawling old multiroom homes that fill it, designed for an era when extended families and multiple generations lived under a single roof. Another street nearby might have a very different atmosphere, dominated by massive hive-like apartment buildings filled with studios and units designed for singles, young couples, and young nuclear families.

Atmospheres are also shaped by the understanding of artifacts "as" something or other, since this can govern how I experience the space around or inside of something. So, for example, in an antique shop or one specializing in crystal tableware, I move more gingerly than otherwise; I move through the space in a church, library, or archive more respectfully than in a gymnasium—there I can be rowdier, more physical, my movements freer; the way I walk as I return to my seat with a tray of food in a university cafeteria or fast-food restaurant will differ from how I comport myself in returning to the table from the restroom at a Michelin-starred restaurant in Paris.

But the way we experience the space that surrounds or is enclosed by artifacts is also determined by a meaning that is related to but differs in kind from the conceptual representation of something *as* an x or y. As Hubert Dreyfus—drawing on Heidegger and Merleau-Ponty—has done much to show, reflection on skillful perception and action uncovers this form of nonconceptual meaning, since our successful coping with the world presupposes that things can be perceived as relevant for our goals, interests, and activities; that is, it presupposes that things exhibit what Charles Taylor calls a practical intelligibility.[28] The practical intelligibility of things is the significance they have for our actions. Dreyfus, borrowing a concept from J. J. Gibson, suggests that we understand this significance in terms of what things afford and do not afford.[29] Affordances solicit or motivate one to act in certain ways and discourage one from acting in others: a doorknob affords turning but not pulling, a chair affords sitting but not squatting, the space between the sofa and the desk affords passing gingerly, but not running, and so on. These examples show that this aspect of the space opened up by artifacts overlaps with but is not identical to what Watsuji calls the space of equipment. The perception of affordances also affects the way I experience the atmosphere of certain kinds of spaces. Thus the aisle of an airplane, a warren of alleys in Venice, or the space inside a vehicular mountain tunnel is encountered as cramped or confining because the narrow range of what these structures afford and do not afford dictates the kind and degree of movement one can make within them.

If our analysis moves to other, much larger constructions, we can see that certain structures are so vast that the vocabulary of affordances is no longer sufficient to take their practical measure. These artifacts no longer offer meanings legible to my body, instructions that would help it to get an "optimal grip" on the world, as Dreyfus puts it.[30] Here the imperatives of practical intelligibility give way to something else: it is not my actions that are determined, but my mood and sense of things, which are likely to be shared with others who occupy the same space. Consider the space of a city plaza adorned with statues and anchored by a fountain or the stands at a baseball stadium or inside a skyscraper canyon in Manhattan. The spaces opened up by these artifactual structures can be experienced as freeing or lonely or oppressive; a sense of isolation or grandeur or openness is derived from and arises with factors such as their size and structural layout, their shape, and the type and density of the materials out of which they are made. Because these structures configure space in a way that is different from and on a scale that is far greater than other artifacts, the atmospheres and spaces of meaning attached to them extend far beyond the personal space of the embodied standpoint and reach into the public space of the group or the crowd. The subjective space of a world thus encompasses both the personal and interpersonal regions of space, and a space that is in principle able to be encountered and experienced by anyone, namely, the shared and common space of the public.

IV. World Space and the Atmosphere of Nature

Up to this point we have examined the atmosphere of interactions and the atmosphere that is attached to human constructions. The separation of these two phenomena was somewhat artificial and undertaken for the purposes of analysis only. We find much more frequently that these atmospheres mutually influence and interlace with one another. So, for example, the spaces and attendant atmosphere of any structure within or around which people interact can often become a factor in the tone that emerges in these exchanges. The tenor and style of the very same interaction may vary according to whether you and I are in a hockey arena or in a nursing home, in a car or in a temple, in an office in a skyscraper or in an office in a trailer. The atmosphere of such structures, in turn, can be influenced by the kinds of things that are being expressed and understood; the ambience of the space of a once-grand ballroom can differ considerably depending on if, on a summer evening, the space is filled with the sounds of an international ballroom dance competition, or if, one late winter afternoon, it offers a glimpse of two aging dance hall employees in whispered conversation in a dark corner, their figures seemingly swallowed up by the cavernous expanse of the empty dance floor. Or, to take another example, the atmosphere of a visit to the doctor may vary depending on whether this takes place in an imposing city hospital or in the far more modest confines of a small rural clinic.

Although each type of atmosphere can be a principal component in the look and feel of the other, there are also cases in which this presence is negligible, and the air of a particular interaction or specific construction remains largely unaffected by the additional circumstance of being joined with the other kind of atmosphere. The air of immensity of the Great Pyramid of Khufu at Giza remains untouched by the dispute unfolding at its base between my friends and their guide over the itinerary for tomorrow. The general tone of their discussion, in turn, is unconnected to the aura of the massive structure looming over them. There is, however, a third type of atmosphere that is always a factor in both interpersonal and artifactual ones. This is the atmosphere furnished by nature. Thus a brilliantly clear sky, vast and boundless, will set off the pyramid to great effect; the tone of the argument with the guide can subtly shift depending on whether it takes place in the blazing heat of noon or during the cooler evening hours.

The physical atmosphere of nature—the air we breathe and the space through which we move—functions as the ever-present medium in and through which interpersonal and artifactual atmospheres appear. Though this atmosphere is a physical medium, it is not a purely empty space, without qualities or features. As J. J. Gibson observes, "We could not conceive of empty space unless we could see the ground under our feet and the sky above." Empty space is "a ghost, a myth, a fiction for geometers."[31] Watsuji repeatedly draws our attention to the array of concrete and sensuous qualities that animate the atmosphere of any *fūdo*. In his explanation of the differences between the natural features of central and northern Europe and Japan, for example, he provides a close description of the role humidity plays in the composition of the atmosphere: "Humidity again brings a marked difference to the tone and feeling of the atmosphere. In Japan the abundant changes in the light and shade of the atmosphere which results in the morning mist, the evening fog, or the spring haze which we ordinarily encounter serves an important function; on the one hand, it provides a sense of the season or of time or a sense of calm or freshness, and, on the other, it is the source of the appeal of the light and shade of the landscape itself."[32]

Atmospheres differ in tone or feeling, and this is partly because atmospheric space is always a certain temperature, always has a dew point, always has or lacks light, is always apprehended in a certain season, and so on. Because such atmospheric conditions, or what we can call *weather*, are always with us, even when we are not interacting with others and not in the presence of human constructions, we are nevertheless always in an atmosphere of one kind or another.

The permanent presence of weather means that even those human constructions that are explicitly designed to insulate us from the extremes of weather never provide a complete escape from what is exterior to them. While adjustments to the temperature and humidity of an interior space can be made with the proper equipment, we are always enveloped in other elements of the natural atmosphere, such as its barometric pressure, the amount and type of lighting available, and the full ambience of the seasonal moment (as is attested to by syndromes such as seasonal affective disorder). This suggests that buildings are largely permeable points of transition between an inside and an outside rather than chambers that fully seal off an indoor space from an outdoor one. Consider what comes in through or is visible at the windows of most buildings: the sound of birdsong or thunder, the evening bronze of a sunset, the aural and visual drama of a typhoon or hurricane, the dreariness of another day of drizzle and fog, the beginning of another bright, expansive, and sunlit summer day.

While buildings are vehicles through which we experience much of the climate, weather itself is a condition for the possibility of almost any experience whatsoever.[33] So although we can perceive certain elements of this atmosphere, above all, we perceive *with* and *through* atmospheric conditions such as lighting, mist, moonlight, humidity, heat, and shadows—both indoors and out. The polished stone floor of a *pendopo* (the covered pavilion at the entrance to a traditional Javanese house), for instance, looks inviting and cool in the tropical heat, but the same structure has a very different aura when it has been removed to the somberly lit and temperature-controlled spaces of a museum. Thus what appears in experience is conditioned not only, as Merleau-Ponty and other phenomenologists have taught us, by the immanent structures of subjectivity, but also by phenomena and states of affairs that transcend us. Watsuji makes the same point by observing the way, for instance, we find ourselves in a delighted mood or in a somewhat melancholy one in and through the spring wind that scatters flower blossoms.[34] As I stand in or walk through this wind, what comes into view—the laughter of children playing under a tree, a young couple on a date, the front gates of my old elementary school, and the concession stands that have been erected for next week's spring festival—takes on the appearance it does, in part, because of this perceptual frame.

In these examples we have an illustration of how the atmosphere of social and artifactual space is layered upon, intermingles with, and is shaped by the weather. But the converse is also true. What is expressed in interaction and by artifacts can also help determine the way particular atmospheric conditions show up. It is a matter of great consequence for the atmosphere of a particular beach, for instance, whether the human constructions that are placed on or located around it are bright beach balls and gaily painted lifeguard towers, or whether they are offshore oil rigs. The chill in the autumn air will feel very different for someone running across the school playground with friends after a long summer at home than it will for someone hearing for the first time about her best friend's diagnosis of bone cancer.

Phenomenological descriptions of weather showcase especially well the sense in which the act of perceiving is never a neutral encounter with something existing in-itself, which perception merely registers. Insofar as the conditions of the physical atmosphere enter into perceptual experience, they are never simply given, there to be taken by an "objective" observer. Instead, just as with everything encountered in experience, they appear through the interpretive understanding of the practical subject. And what is understood is never intelligible in isolation; the sense of a thing can emerge only in relation to a wider horizon of meaning. We make sense of weather, just as we do the actions of people with whom we interact and the artifacts that we use, on the basis of the background structure of meaning that constitutes a world. Hence it will be Japanese rather than Americans who feel wistful strolling through a spring wind that scatters the cherry blossoms; it will be American adults rather than Japanese adults who feel so in the crisp air of early fall, as the school year gets under way in earnest.

The interpretation of the atmospheric conditions of nature, then, parallels the way in which the acts of other people and the meanings embodied by artifacts are understood. But a decisive difference also emerges here. The air of an interaction and the aura surrounding a human construction arise with and in the interpretation of meanings that are a direct or indirect consequence of *human expression*. But the physical atmosphere of nature does not arise at all—or, at least, not in this way; it is always present. And the intelligibility that is the object of the understanding in this case belongs to and is furnished by this atmosphere itself. The physical atmosphere of nature, in short, constitutes the empirical dimension of subjective space. Moreover, because this space surrounds and contains both the practical subjects and the cultural artifacts that belong to a world, the forms of existential spatiality that stem from our interpretive encounters with interactions and artifacts are founded in it. Physical space, in turn, is able to receive and support these entities and phenomena because it is itself located in a place that serves as its ground.

To grasp the relationship between space and place here, we can follow Malpas's suggestion that the difference between space and place "is perhaps most succinctly expressed in terms of the idea of place as that which, through the boundary or limit that belongs to it, also opens up a space—place is thus tied to boundary . . . and space to the openness within the boundary."[35] There are as many kinds of places as the kinds of spaces they open, from cathedrals to nightclubs to wooded grasslands and limestone caves. The physical spatiality of containment, however, can only be opened by and anchored in a place that precedes and outstrips the places furnished by human constructions, and so one that these constructions do not and cannot themselves provide—since, as stipulated, this space surrounds and contains such artifacts. This place, which always extends beyond any artifactual location constructed upon it, constitutes the most comprehensive setting of all: that of nature. But we never, of course, encounter nature as a whole—only nature as it is present here, in and as *this* place: a location in a tropical river valley, a boreal forest, an arid plateau, a temperate savanna, and so forth. In sum, human beings and the artifacts they manufacture are surrounded by and found within a physical space because they are ultimately located in the particular and concrete places of nature.

The relation between the physical spaces and places of the natural world is not like that between one object and another; space is not located in or on a place, as if the two were distinct and fully separable entities. Each is tied to and conditions the other. The particular features that are part of a place shape the space that is inescapably linked to it. The open sky of a desert, for instance, is not the open sky of a prairie; a thunderstorm on land is different in important respects from one at sea. The atmosphere of nature is always joined to and impacted by a broader natural setting such as foothills or canyons, a river delta or scrubland, since the boundaries that delineate a place also at the same time open up a region of physical space.

Just as the various features of a natural locale shape its atmosphere, atmospheric conditions also mold the natural characteristics of a place. As the anthropologist Tim Ingold has argued, such places can never really be divorced from the spaces they are tied to:

> Rainfall can turn a ploughed field into a sea of mud, frost can shatter solid rocks, lightning can ignite forest fires on land parched by summer heat, and the wind can whip sand into dunes, snow into drifts, and the water of lakes and oceans into waves. As Richard Nelson puts it, in his study of how Koyukon people in Alaska perceive their surroundings, "weather is the hammer and the land is the anvil." . . . Yet the more one

reads into the land, the more difficult it becomes to ascertain with any certainty where the substance ends and the medium begins. For it is precisely through the *binding* of medium and substance that wind and weather leave their mark in the land. Thus the land itself no longer appears as an interface separating the two, but as a vaguely defined zone of admixture and intermingling.[36]

The space and place of a natural locale, then, together compose a unitary and inseparable whole. This is why we experience such a setting as a single, undivided scene, one that encompasses all of the visible geospheric elements in a particular locale. Such a locale presents itself in our experience as a vast in-itself that transcends us in its inexhaustibility and in its ability to enrich us. While the intelligible character of each such setting is in this regard already given in ways that direct and constrain our perceptions, the nature we encounter is never a bare given, simply "there" to be registered by an objective gaze. We make sense of this kind of intelligible whole against a background of values and practices, and this also determines how a natural locale shows up for us. Thus, for example, the manner in which the prairies of the American Midwest appeared to the nomadic and equestrian people known as the Plains Indians will have differed in significant ways from what was encountered by white Americans, whose primary interests included settlement, ranching, and the construction of railroads.

Watsuji employs the concept of *fūdo* to disclose this unitary whole of a natural and cultural setting. A primary reason why we have left this term untranslated is because of its capacity to capture and express the configuration of related elements in this whole. So, for instance, the way the spaces and places of the natural world belong to and determine one another in constituting a single phenomenon cannot be rendered with the words *climate* or *milieu*, both of which are widely used to translate *fūdo* into English and French. And the sense in which a natural locale transcends us in its givenness even as it is immanent to the interpretive frame of a world prompted the English-language translator of *Fūdo* to give a later edition of this text the title *Climate and Culture*. But this pair of words also has the unfortunate effect of suggesting that the relevant domain of culture is separate from nature rather than an essential dimension of it. Culture is an essential dimension of nature inasmuch as a *fūdo* always appears in and through the horizon of a world, a world, moreover, that it also helps, in turn, to constitute. Thus a world is always characterized by specific climatic and topographical regions, and these always have certain types of plants and trees and kinds of soil and are always populated by particular insects and animals; a world, in sum, is always located in and carved out of the places and spaces of nature.

This will mean that in a *fūdo* we do not encounter nature wholly untouched. *Fūdo* includes "objective" features such as geography and climate, but the "trail of the human serpent is over all," to borrow an expression from James: Watsuji draws our attention to the damning of rivers, forests shaped by the planting and harvesting of trees, the draining of marshes, the reclamation of coastal areas from the sea, the flourishing and spread of certain species of plants and animals through the development of crops and the domestication of animals, the creation of huge swaths of pastureland for these animals, and so forth.[37] This reshaping and modification of the natural world by human activity makes possible certain practices (e.g., rice cultivation, river rafting, gardening) and undermines others (e.g., the gathering of medicinal herbs in a primeval forest). And this, in turn, opens up new possibilities for what can come to be disclosed in a world (e.g., dairy farms, gardens, rivers for whitewater rafting) and eliminates others (e.g., sacred waterfalls, the forest as the abode of the gods). It is *this* face that large swaths of nature show us in the unveiling of its appearances through a world.

***

In opening up a physical dimension in Watsuji's conception of subjective space, we have presented, in the social space of interaction and the artifactual space of things, on the one side, and the natural space of weather, on the other, an interpretation of world that in its composition is both intersubjective and coextensive with any number of natural locales. Yet while there is a recognition here of the necessarily physical and material aspects of a world that had been suppressed in Heidegger's account, the world as *seken* is still, above all, a structure toward which we are oriented rather than an objective environment by which we are surrounded or in which we find ourselves.

Finally, insofar as this examination of space has also unearthed an essential plane on and through which self and other, world and nature, come together and cohere with one another, we have been led back to one of the central concerns of this study, namely, the question of the relation between the self and *fūdo*. A *fūdo* is always linked to the self in some fashion and so never reducible to, or simply identifiable with, an objective natural environment. And to the extent that the conception of the self that Watsuji calls upon here is decisive for the character of this relation, our somewhat lengthy detour through the concepts of the practical subject, *aidagara*, and *ningen sonzai* was an indispensable step in bringing this out. Thus this extended analysis of the self revealed that one of the principal ways the self is related to and continuous with a *fūdo* is in its distinctive spatial structure. In the next chapter, we survey the other major way the self is linked to *fūdo*: in and through the phenomenon of world and the activities of self-understanding and disclosure that accompany it, each belongs to and depends upon the other to be what it is.

7

Self, World, and *Fūdo*: Continuity and Belonging

The closing stages of the previous chapter were given over to establishing the contention that *fūdo* is structurally continuous with the self, and part of its world, in and through the phenomenon of subjective space. With this idea we have begun to make good on the promissory note issued in the first chapter, namely, to show that in the concept of *fūdo*, self and nature compose a relational whole, and that this idea has important philosophical consequences for our ordinary conceptions of the self, on the one hand, and the natural world, on the other. Watsuji insists upon this continuity of the self with a *fūdo*, however, without ever really giving a systematic explanation of the nature and status of the unity at work here. This shortcoming can be corrected by indicating more fully than Watsuji himself did the profound and extensive consequences of the claim that subjective space connects *fūdo* with the structure of the self through the phenomenon of world. Because this contention allows Watsuji to understand the phenomenon of *fūdo* as the "place" of a world—one that the Heidegger of *Being and Time* had largely overlooked—he is able to build upon the relational dependence that holds between Dasein and world to support his claim that self and nature are continuous with, and belong to, one another.

On the one side, the self depends on what is disclosed as *fūdo* (as it does other elements of what are disclosed in a world) to understand and interpret itself, and so to be any kind of self at all.[1] On the other side, just as with other features of a world, a *fūdo* is disclosed through our language, affectivity, and practices, and hence in this sense can be said to "depend" on us to be what it is. Self and *fūdo* constitute, belong to, and are continuous with one another in these ways.

Watsuji nonetheless does not simply recapitulate the forms of self-understanding and disclosure that were established by Heidegger in *Being and Time*; he modifies and expands each so that they are equal to his relational conceptions of the self as *aidagara* and nature as *fūdo*. And while the incorporation of *fūdo* into the structure of a world alters the notion of self-understanding in numerous ways, Watsuji reserves the most extensive change for the concept of disclosure. He contends that the disclosive capacities of practical, emotional, and linguistic comportments are shared such that when we are together with others, our experience of nature is at its core a single experience with a shared subject of experience, and not something that occurs separately in the heads of multiple individuals isolated from one another by the capsule of consciousness. Though this notion of shared comportments is new, Watsuji's concept of disclosure inherits and relies upon the form of continuity operative in the relation between Dasein and world.

I. World, *Fūdo*, and Self-Understanding

Linking *fūdo* to Heidegger's concept of world-disclosure has profound consequences both for how we view the appearances of nature and for how we understand ourselves. The latter connection can be seen in Heidegger's declaration early in *Being and Time* that Dasein is a self-disclosing which is at the same time the opening up of a world. Thus insofar as a *fūdo* is a feature of world, it is disclosed by the self; at the same time, a *fūdo* is also a place where the self is disclosed. It is this second aspect of the "worldly" character of *fūdo* that Watsuji expresses in the claim that we "apprehend" ourselves in *fūdo*. This notion is broader than Heidegger's conception of self-understanding, and both encompasses and enriches it.

Watsuji begins with a basic mode of self-awareness that he calls "self-apprehension" (*jiko o miidasu* 自己を見いだす).[2] Although self-apprehension is more "primordial" than forms of reflective self-awareness, he maintains that it is nevertheless still mediated—above all through *fūdo*. So, for instance, when I come to be aware of myself as being cold, this mode of self-apprehension is not the awareness of the self as a subject (*shukan* 主観) of a single sensation, but of the self as embodied and embedded in a wider context of geoclimatic conditions. Coldness comes, for example, as a relief in the sudden downpour of rain on a searing hot summer day, or it appears as an enlivening spring wind whose mildness contrasts with the much colder winter that has just drawn to a close. In each of these scenarios, I find myself relieved or enlivened in and through a coldness that stands in comparative or contrastive relation to other atmospheric phenomena. The cold is never experienced in isolation, but always as connected to other meteorological elements such as wind, rain, snow, sunshine, and so forth. In this respect, cold is only an aspect of our experience of the broader phenomenon of weather. And weather itself is experienced only in relation to the soil and to the topographic and scenic features of a given area of land. So in my awareness of myself as cold, I am at the same time—even if at times only indirectly or implicitly—aware of myself as situated in and conditioned by a *fūdo*.[3]

Moreover an awareness of myself as being cold or feeling wistful or desiring to go on a picnic is never solely an awareness of the self as an individual. Instead this form of self-apprehension reveals the self as an individual and as an interactional being-in-relation-to-others. It is my individual body that feels chilly and my individual consciousness that is permeated by wistfulness, but the self never achieves a pure or complete and autonomous individuality; in my coldness I reach for warmer clothes that refer to and are made possible by a whole world of factories, stores, and styles. Or the chill prompts me to remind my children not to forget their gloves and hats as they depart for school. My wistful mood, too, is not idiosyncratic and singular but belongs to, and is made possible by, a certain cultural vocabulary, and is even at times imposed on me by a *fūdo* that others live in and share, something that can be seen in the exchange of small talk about the weather with the others with whom we come into contact. So the experience of a *fūdo* is simultaneously an experience of responses, desires, attitudes, meanings, and possibilities for action that relate to the self as an individual and refer beyond this individuality to others, disclosing me to myself as an individuated being who always exists in relation to others.

A decisive difference with Heidegger becomes apparent here: the self-apprehension of *ningen*, unlike the self-understanding of Dasein, reveals the dual nature of the self as both individual and social. Yet despite what he takes to be a very substantial difference in this regard, Watsuji develops his concept of self-apprehension by building on the essential unity between self-understanding and the understanding of a world that Heidegger had first discovered and elucidated. Thus self-apprehension may start with an individual self-awareness that emerges in the sensations, feelings, and responses to a *fūdo* and expand to include a recognition of the self as a being that is always situated in relation to others, but it does not end there. What began as a primordial form of self-awareness develops for Watsuji into the self's taking itself to "be" a certain way in something like self-understanding or self-interpretation.

For Watsuji as for Heidegger, this form of self-understanding is interwoven with and inseparable from an understanding of a world. This connection between world and self-understanding comes out most clearly in Heidegger's discussion of the equipment and tools we use in order to act. Tools are not normally encountered as bare objects laid out before a theoretical gaze (which is the mode of being that Heidegger calls *vorhanden*), but are present to us as "handy" (*zuhanden*). Handiness—just as with everything that appears in a world—is never disclosed in isolation; it is uncovered through an interconnected totality of tasks, purposes, roles, other equipment, relations, situations, and ultimate ends that involve, refer to, and are relevant for one another. So, for example, the being of a pencil is its usefulness (its "handiness") for writing, drawing, or marking; we can make sense of the pencil in this way in part because it is used in conjunction with a larger equipmental whole (*Zeugganzes*) of other useful things such as paper, lead, erasers, lamps, desks, and pencil sharpeners. A pencil always "refers" to these other useful things (which refer to it and to one another) and so belongs and fits into an equipmental nexus structured by this network of referential totality (*Verweisungsganzheit*). In this regard, a useful thing such as a pencil cannot show itself by itself, but can only make an appearance insofar as it is part of these equipmental and referential wholes that precede it. The pencil also only makes sense because it bears upon and is relevant to use in an activity that takes place in a specific context or setting, such as taking an essay exam in a classroom. These activities are intelligible, in turn, only because they always already belong to a whole network of such related and relevant activities and involvements (*Bewandtnisganzheit*), such as the activities of turning in, reading, and grading essays. Finally, our use of equipment in an activity makes sense because the activity has a point or purpose, which itself constitutes a link in a chain or hierarchy of purposes. So I write an essay in order to pass a licensing exam, which is aimed at in order to obtain a teaching certificate, which is required in order to teach middle school, which allows me to understand and interpret myself as a schoolteacher. Thus we use this equipment, take up these purposes and activities, and relate to these wholes all for the ultimate sake of the final end of a self-interpretation that informs and orders all such activity.[4]

According to Watsuji, Heidegger's account seems to mostly overlook the multiplicity of ways in which the totality of equipment, the range of available self-interpretations, and even the very being of Dasein itself is determined by and depends upon the natural setting that environs any group of people. This is, in the main, a consequence of his failure to recognize in an explicit and sustained manner the sense in which nature constitutes a dimension of world. For Watsuji this oversight can be traced back to a basic flaw in Heidegger's existential analytic of Dasein, namely, his near-blindness to the way the places and spaces of the natural world are part of the structure of human existence. In his later work Heidegger meditates upon the ontological significance of these places and spaces, but he never really develops, as Watsuji does, an account of the way the specific locale we find ourselves in is constitutive of the self, even as this is also determined or shaped by this self.

Notwithstanding these considerations, even in *Being and Time* Heidegger does not completely neglect the question of the relation between nature and world. Moreover, as Bruce Foltz observes, in this text as well as in Heidegger's other early work there is already "a fundamental rethinking of nature and of our relation to it. . . . Indeed, one of the most radical features of Heidegger's interpretation of nature is a virtual reversal of the priorities generally granted both to the different ways in which we encounter nature and to the various aspects of nature itself."[5]

This reordering is a reversal of the traditional ontological primacy of the theoretical over the practical and aesthetic relation to nature in the metaphysics of objective presence. This turnabout is founded on Heidegger's claim that, as with anything that appears in human experience, "nature is itself a being which is encountered within the world and is discoverable on various paths and stages."[6] Heidegger distinguishes three senses in which nature can be encountered by us in a world. Nature is first and foremost disclosed as close at hand (*zuhanden*) and as bearing upon our concerns through our involvement with it; as such, it is never first encountered as a neutral presence, blankly there, but always already bears a meaning for us. Heidegger describes how, in this regard, the south wind is taken by the farmer as a sign of rain, observing that this way of taking the wind "is not a kind of bonus attached to something already objectively present, that is, the movement of the wind and a certain geographical direction. As this mere occurrence which is meteorologically accessible, the south wind is *never initially* objectively present which sometimes takes on the function of omen. Rather, the farmer's circumspection first discovers the south wind in its being by taking the lay of the land into account."[7] And just as for the farmer the south wind is a harbinger of rain and never merely an objectively present meteorological occurrence, other entities in nature are disclosed in the same manner to the same kind of pretheoretical and prereflective coping, and so "discovered in their being" and not uncovered as neutral objects in themselves: the forest is a source of timber, the mountain a rock quarry, the wind is wind in the sails. Or again, natural entities are the steel, metal, iron, stone, and wood out of which tools such as hammer, tong, and nails are made.[8]

Natural phenomena are disclosed as useful for and relevant to our individual tasks and projects through the practical comportments and equipment that we take up in connection with these activities, but nature is also discovered as having a bearing on "the public world" in addition to "the domestic world of the workshop."[9] The former is constituted, in part, by the broader referential significance of the tools, equipment, and cultural objects that are immediately at hand in something like a workshop, since at this level these things have a shared meaning that both refers to and is available to everyone. Heidegger maintains that along with this public world, the surrounding world of nature (*die Umweltnatur*) is uncovered by and accessible to everyone. Nature in this instance is what more fully and explicitly constrains and directs us and our equipment as we deal with things and pursue our tasks. Thus nature is taken into account by our paths, streets, buildings, and bridges, and by equipment such as covered railroad platforms, which take bad weather into consideration, and public lighting systems, which take darkness into account. While the surrounding world of nature can in this way pose an obstacle or threat to our projects, its regularity and predictability also help to make them possible. Our clocks, for instance, take the position of the sun into account in functioning as the tools they are.[10]

The second way we can encounter nature is disclosed by inspection rather than engaged concern and involvement, and is thus a form of knowing that requires a certain de-worlding (*Entweltlichung*) of the world. Here we "abstract from nature's kind of being as handiness" and "discover and define it in its pure objective presence."[11] In its most sophisticated incarnation, the detached gaze recontextualizes such occurrent and present-at-hand (*vorhanden*) beings as objects of scientific investigation, and so beings unrelated to the self-understanding for the sake of which Dasein takes up its specific goals, tasks, and projects.

Heidegger warns that in this form of the discovery of nature, nature as what "stirs and strives," as what overcomes and enthralls us, remains hidden: "The botanist's plants are not the flowers of the hedgerow, the 'source' which the geographer establishes for a river is not the 'springhead in the dale.'"[12] Nature in this sense clearly seems to be related to what Heidegger refers to at an earlier point in this text as the Romantic concept of nature. Here nature is encountered in our experience as something like an aesthetic phenomenon.

Nature, in sum, appears in the world as that into which we are thrown and which we must take into account, or as that which is useful, or even as what assails and entrances us. It appears, too, on the edge of a world (so to speak) as objectively present. Yet as intriguing and important for Watsuji's own thinking as these remarks on nature must have been, they serve only to indicate various aspects of the lifeworldy dimension of nature and are too sparse and uneven to establish the phenomenon of nature as an essential component of the concept of world.

Heidegger comes closest to this understanding of the relation between nature and world in his contention that the surrounding world of nature, like everything else we encounter within a world, is historical. This is because history for the Heidegger of *Being and Time* is the "occurrence" (*Geschehen*) or temporal unfurling of being-in-the-world, such that "*things at hand and objectively present have always already been included in the history of the world.* Tools and works, for example, have their 'fates'; buildings and institutions have their history. And even nature is historical. It is *not* historical when we speak about 'natural history,' but nature is historical as a countryside, as areas that have been inhabited or exploited, as battlefields and cultic sites. These innerworldly beings as such *are* historical, and their history does not signify something 'external' that simply accompanies the 'inner' history of the 'soul.'"[13] The historicity of nature is not derived from the scientific discipline of natural history, nor does it arise from the projection of the collective memory of a people onto an otherwise neutral substrate that would be what nature "really" is; rather the suggestion is that nature is taken up into history as the site of the historical unfolding of being-in-the-world, which implies that the spaces and places of the natural world are disclosed in a multiplicity of ways across different eras. But this is all too brief, and not explicitly pursued by Heidegger here. Moreover, while that part of nature that is "historical ground" is the surrounding world of nature (*die Umweltnatur*), for Heidegger *Umweltnatur* is coextensive with the modality of the world constituted by the public sphere rather than with the "world" in the relevant sense, namely, the whole of the world as held together by the structure of worldliness.[14]

Heidegger thus never manages to formulate a conception of nature as part of the structure of the world in the way Watsuji does. Hence whereas Heidegger understands that natural entities can be useful, Watsuji sees them as part of the internal structure of world. He notes, for example, that we make use of climate as another kind of tool, utilizing wind to fill the sails or climatic conditions to grow rice. And where Heidegger perceived that tools and equipment such as lighting and platform shelters are constructed to cope with the vicissitudes of nature, Watsuji understands that nature is at the very ground of the network of referential totality. He observes that while the teleological ordering of equipment is grounded on a self-understanding that is tied to role and project, it is also founded on the natural setting that is part of a world. Thus a fan may be used in my taking up an identity as a repairman or as a factory worker on an assembly line, but it is also used to combat heat; clothes and houses may be used to signal a particular kind of identity, such as that of an upper-middle-class professional, but they are also worn and built for protection against the elements. In sum, tools and equipment are manufactured and used both to interpret and define a self, as well as to respond to the nature that environs us.[15] Finally, while Heidegger sees that nature is also discovered in the materiality of tools, Watsuji shows that the forms that such tools, equipment, and other cultural objects take, as well as their purposes, are intimately linked to available materials, weather conditions, local terrain, and the like: ski slopes, trawlers, *dishdashas* (robes), levees, pirogues (canoes), gold mines, and conical hats emerge from and are tied to specific places. These, in turn, are indispensable elements in certain kinds of roles and projects that enable me to interpret myself as, for example, a mining company president, a *dishdasha* tailor, or a shrimp fisherman.

Watsuji also extends the notion of self-understanding beyond the defined roles and the projects they entail to include both the internal and external dimensions of one's whole way of being in such a world. Thus I come to see myself as someone who has certain tastes and preferences that are tied quite directly to a specific *fūdo*, such as a preference for bright colors or for raw fish or certain spices or an aversion to extremely cold weather, someone with a certain sensibility and an imagination populated by one set of images rather than another.[16] Externally the self is able to see itself in everything from leisure activities and customs to lifestyles and forms of food preparation. Who we understand ourselves to be is expressed in types of clothing, styles of cuisine, forms of worship, architectural styles, forms of art, modes of agricultural cultivation, and so forth; all of these things, in turn, are shaped, and at times even determined by, the *fūdo* of a particular land. What all of these examples show is that *fūdo* is in an important way constitutive of the self; I identify with and understand myself through the coal mining industry I work in, the weekend white-water rafting trips I take, the *dishdasha* I wear, or the food I love, all of which are themselves responses to a specific *fūdo*.

II. Watsuji's Hermeneutics and the Ontological Difference

While the self can be what it is only through its living in, incorporating, and giving expression to a *fūdo*—all of which make possible an essential form of self-understanding, a particular *fūdo* can be what *it* is only through its being opened up and *disclosed* by the self. Although this constitutive reciprocity neatly connects self to *fūdo*, the second half of this relation, namely, the dependence of *fūdo* upon the self to be fully what it is in the event of disclosure, remains largely implicit—even latent—in Watsuji's thinking. This idea must therefore be unearthed and established in a reconstructive analysis.

Because the notion of disclosure that we are attempting to excavate here depends on the distinction Heidegger makes between an entity and its being, we must first address H. P. Liederbach's charge that in developing his own hermeneutic theory in writings after *Fūdo*, Watsuji thoroughly misunderstood the ontological difference.[17] In Liederbach's view, Watsuji appears not to have grasped the meaning and import of this distinction, and decouples the hermeneutics of existence from fundamental ontology—an approach that also allows him to avoid making the question of being into a problem to be treated by hermeneutical philosophy.

These developments mostly appear in Watsuji's 1934 study, *Ethics as the Study of the Human* (*Ningen no gaku toshite no rinrigaku* 人間の学としての倫理学), a brief one-volume precursor to the much larger *Ethics*).[18] In this text Watsuji's chief criticism is that in subordinating the analysis of Dasein to the question of being, Heidegger had blocked the methodological approach to a proper analysis of existence, inasmuch as it was no longer possible for him take ordinary reality itself as his point of departure.[19] This is because his phenomenology pursues what, on the whole, does not show itself at all, something that lies hidden, or shows itself only in a disguised way: the phenomenon or the *being* of beings that lies behind the appearances. Watsuji sees his own task as that of securing a proper ground for a philosophical inquiry into existence by returning to everyday experience as the starting point of such an examination. According to Liederbach, Watsuji does this by detaching the analytic of Dasein from the question of being and from phenomenology, and so proceeding directly to the human being as *ningen sonzai*. Watsuji should thus not be regarded as just another interpreter of Heidegger, who, despite certain criticisms, adheres to his fundamental ontological claim. Rather Liederbach contends that Watsuji asks after nothing less than the appropriateness of fundamental ontology for a description of being-in-the-world.

If, as Liederbach puts it, for Watsuji Heidegger's fundamental ontology introduces a plane of abstraction that prevents us from arriving at a proper description of Dasein in its everyday concreteness, then a different mode of access to Dasein must be sought. Through a philological investigation into the Japanese language, Watsuji uncovers in this regard what he takes to be a decisive indication about the proper approach to Dasein. He examines—in an investigation we shall shortly set out more fully—the connections between the Japanese terms that denote *to exist*, *to be*, and *to have*, and unexpectedly discovers a certain kinship attested to in these expressions: that something "is" means that it can ultimately be understood only in relation to Dasein's "having" it. This means that such beings are not sheerly "there," unmitigatedly present in and to a world; they depend in some way for their appearance on something else. The Japanese language, then, would seem to be particularly suited to articulating the way the beings that populate a world are ultimately grounded in and arise from the kind of being that has its being "in" a "world."

Watsuji subscribes to the structural logic underlying the double of phenomenon and appearance set down by Heidegger in order to capture this feature of the beings encountered in a world. For Heidegger, the difference between phenomenon and appearance corresponds methodologically to the ontological difference between being and beings. Thus he says that appearing "is possible only *on the basis of* a *self-showing* of something. But this, the self-showing that makes appearing possible, is not appearing itself. Appearing is a *making itself known* through something that shows itself."[20] What makes itself known is the phenomenon, which, as the *being* of beings, is "something that does *not* show itself initially and for the most part, something that is *concealed*, in contrast to what initially and for the most part does show itself. But at the same time it is something that essentially belongs to what initially and for the most part shows itself, indeed in such a way that it constitutes its meaning and ground.* *Truth of being."[21]

In this duality of phenomenon (being) and appearance (beings), the phenomenon of being remains concealed behind the beings through which it appears. As Watsuji observes, this means that being manifests itself only in something other than itself. Hence, as the "other" of being, the appearances are not being itself but a manifestation or expression of it.[22] For this reason, Watsuji calls these appearances "expressions" (*hyōgen* 表現). Hiroshima Kojima adds with regard to this point, "To let something manifest itself in what is other (as other) is called 'interpretation.' "[23] But for Watsuji what is interpreted in these expressions is not the phenomenon of being; these appearances, as the beings that compose a world, are expressions of the Dasein in which they have their ground. Hence he says that such expressions are "saturated with understanding"; that is, the practical understanding of being-in-relation-to-others is reflected in them.[24] Watsuji thus adopts the formal structure of the double of phenomenon and appearance, while at the same time displacing the phenomenon of being in favor of the being of Dasein (*Existenz*), or what he also calls the *sonzai* of *ningen*.

And just as for the Heidegger of *Being and Time* we must pass through the appearances, and so behind beings to gain sight of being, Watsuji, Liederbach says, expects to gain access to the *Existenz* of Dasein through an analysis of expressions. Thus Watsuji declares that "the subjective existence of ningen can only be approached through its expressions (i.e., phenomena)."[25] Earlier we saw the way Watsuji understood the content of interactions, as well as cultural artifacts, as expressions of *aidagara*, but here we also find that expressions are, as Dilthey had shown, objectifications of the existence of the human being as a whole. Such objectifications include tools, equipment, gestures, language, behavior, products, social systems, customs, and entire forms of life.[26] Being-in-the-world, for Watsuji, Liederbach observes, means being in the midst of such expressions. What is seen or shown in these expressions are the various modes of Dasein's being in being-in-relation-to-others, and so all that this entails.[27]

From this series of developments Liederbach draws the conclusion that for Watsuji, world and Dasein as being-in-the-world are not revealed in the transcendence of beings by their being, but in the immanence of Dasein as being-in-relation. So Liederbach maintains that while in Watsuji's view Heidegger was close to the possibility of an appropriate hermeneutic explication of Dasein as being-in-the-world, the transcendental-philosophical question of being prevented Heidegger from taking the last step from hermeneutic phenomenology to a hermeneutics of existence that operates without transcendental-philosophical presuppositions.[28] In order to "free himself" from Heidegger's phenomenology, then, Watsuji reconceptualizes the phenomenon of being and turns to the task of clarifying the structure of the existence of Dasein by means of its expressions.[29] For Liederbach, these moves signal that Watsuji has abandoned the transcendental sphere and the attendant ontological difference that is opened by this domain.

It is difficult to dispute Liederbach's reading of these developments, since Watsuji's own remarks often seem to support his assessment. Nonetheless there are several items that must be reckoned with before embracing what is, in essence, a very strong claim indeed, namely, that after *Fūdo* Watsuji's thinking decisively and fundamentally diverges from Heidegger's. We might begin by noting that in spite of the frequently critical tenor of the comments that Watsuji directs toward Heidegger's phenomenology, they never contain an explicit renunciation of the idea of the ontological difference. As Liederbach himself acknowledges, Watsuji maintains that his aim is only to reinterpret Heidegger's question concerning Dasein. And while for Watsuji this necessitates a reversal of the relation between the analytic of Dasein and fundamental ontology, so that the question of being is to be subordinated to the elucidation of the structures of Dasein, it does not necessarily entail that the question is to be rejected outright. Rather, as Liederbach concedes, in Watsuji's view it is only when Dasein is clarified in its double structure of individual and social that the question of being gets a solid foundation.[30]

Notwithstanding the somewhat misleading character of his presentation of the differences between his hermeneutics and Heidegger's phenomenology, then, I propose that we take Watsuji at his word when he declares that he is restricting himself in this particular undertaking to clarifying the being of Dasein as being-in-relation-to-others. As Kojima remarks, "Heidegger's original intention may be made clearer, says Watsuji, through such a hermeneutical transformation of his concept of phenomenon, while, on the other hand, the necessity of a phenomenological reduction that guides our eyes from beings to Being is still to be affirmed."[31] There is, moreover, a dearth of the kind of scholarly opinion that might substantiate the claim that Watsuji abandons Heidegger's project and basic orientation. Instead the consensus appears to be summed up by Mine Hideki's assessment that Watsuji's basic philosophical method is a makeover of Heidegger's fundamental ontology.[32]

III. Disclosure: Human Being as Human Having

This view is further buttressed by a reconsideration of the sense and scope of what is covered in the claim that things "are" because human beings "have" them. While Watsuji seems in places to equate the beings that human beings "have" with expressions (or what Dilthey calls objectifications of lived experience) such as speech, writing, works of art, physical gestures, and observable deeds, at other times he also includes within this inventory phenomena that belong to the natural world, as we shall shortly see.[33] This suggests that as ambiguous and even as confused as Watsuji's hermeneutic theory may be, his philosophical position does not amount merely to a return to an earlier stage of the history of hermeneutics, one whose theory of interpretation would be revised so that the knowledge gained from human objectifications includes both an understanding of the sociohistorical world of specific individuals, as well as a conception of the multiplicity of ways the human being is an interactional being-in-relation-to-others. Instead the appearance of natural entities in the catalogue of those beings that are constitutively tied to human existence entails that such beings cannot be wholly identifiable with or reducible to objectified expressions of this existence.

A further consideration in support of this point can be found in Watsuji's discussion of the relation between human "having" and human existence itself. As Watsuji reminds us, the relation between being and having is founded on human existence: "There 'are' things [*jibutsu ga aru* 事物がある] because they are 'had' [*motsu* 有つ] by human beings, hence they are based on human existence."[34] Given that this is the case, how are we to understand the existence of the human being? In answering this Watsuji does not shy away from what is implied by the logic operative here: "If this 'there is' [*ga aru* がある] is taken as indicating that something is 'had' by the human being, how ought a state of affairs in which 'there are human beings' be understood? The human being itself cannot be 'had' by anything except human beings."[35]

Watsuji turns again to etymology for evidence for this contention, an approach that receives some justification from his conception of language as disclosive—albeit one that is implicitly held and so never adequately expressed.[36] He maintains that the term used in Japanese to denote human existence, *sonzai* 存在, signifies precisely the idea that the human being possesses itself. At present, he notes, the sinograph *son* 存 appears most frequently with this meaning in the expression *zonjite orimasu* 存じております (I [humbly] know, or am aware of, or acquainted or familiar with), which connotes that one keeps or holds something in one's mind or heart (*kokoro* 心). As he points out, this meaning of *son* is extremely old. Already in the *Mengzi* one finds the line "That by which humans differ from animals is slight. The masses abandon it; the gentleman preserves it."[37] The difference between human and animal lies in the possession of the capacity for humaneness (仁) and a sense of what is right (義), both of which belong to the heart-mind (心). Watsuji notes here that Zhu Xi emphasizes that this holding is a conscious holding, inasmuch as ordinary people do not know this and lose it, whereas the gentleman knows this and maintains it. This suggests that *son* is a subjective act that concerns the self. In other words, the *existence* (*sonzai*) of the human being is a conscious self-possession rather than a condition of blankly being there.

This line of interpretation finds further confirmation in a second passage in the *Mengzi*: "Confucius said, 'Hold fast to it and you will preserve it; let it go and it will vanish; when it comes and where it goes, no one knows.' Was it not the heart-mind that he meant?"[38] The "holding fast" in the heart-mind, Watsuji argues, is actually the process of the conscious having and so holding onto the self indicated in the sinograph *son* 存. That this having is not merely a consisting or a sheer thing-like persisting, but a holding and a survival, can be seen in such usages of *son* as *zonjō* 存生 (being alive, survival, life), *zonmei* 存命 (being alive; also used to refer to the life of a person *after* death), and *seizon* 生存 (to live, keeping or staying alive, to survive). Because the holding of human life is a retaining against forgetting, loss, and death, *son* indicates persistence over time; the existing of the subject, unlike the existence of the object, thus has a particular kind of temporal significance.

If *son* emphasizes the temporal dimension of existence, the *zai* 在 of *sonzai* 存在 indicates the temporal unfolding of this existence "in" a particular place—one that includes, but is not reducible to, a purely spatial location, since we find ourselves "in" interactional relation to others and "in" a world in the sense of a *Welt* or *seken*. Hence, Watsuji says, we are not in a place in the same manner that, for example, a rock is on a mountain, that is, merely occupying a position on it; if a person is on a mountain, he is there in such a way that he came to and can leave it, but a rock cannot come to or leave a mountain in this sense. In this regard, the negative expression *fuzai* 不在 does not mean that one is nowhere (since no such person could exist), but merely that one is not "at" a certain place. To be at a place is to dwell or inhabit or be present in it; it is to be there consciously. When one relates the dwelling among others in a shared world expressed in *zai* to the idea that *son* is "a self-conscious possession" (*jikakuteki ni motsu koto* 自覚的に有つこと), then it can be said that *sonzai* is nothing other than "self-conscious being-in-the-world" (*jikakuteki ni yo no naka ni aru koto* 自覚的に世の中にあること).[39]

This foray into philology indicates that human "having" includes not only expressions as objectifications of life but also the existence of the human being itself. These considerations suggest that there are actually two distinct ways to construe the connection that Watsuji draws between the existence of things and the concept of human "having" or possession. In the first, the contention that something "is" because we "have" it means that certain beings appear as objectifications of human life, or "expressions" of lived experience that are founded on and emerge from our being. In the second sense, to say that something "is" because we "have" it such that it is an "expression" of human existence is to say that the objectivity of objects is always contaminated with (and made possible by) the subjectivity of subjects. More specifically, an entity is what it is because we are "there" for and present to it; we have it in, or it enters into, our awareness. Hence to say, as Watsuji does, that the human being has or possesses itself is just to say that it is *self-conscious*. Watsuji himself is not careful to distinguish between these different uses of the equation of being with having; some of the confusion in his account appears to stem from a kind of crisscrossing movement between the two senses of this relation.

My contention is that human possession or having in the second sense, of human beholding and presence to things, can be identified with our capacity to disclose the things of the world. This openness to being is an openness that we *are* rather than one that we *have*. As Heidegger remarks, "With the existence of Dasein, insofar and as soon as Dasein exists, something occurs, has begun to have a history, something startling, namely, that being happens for another being and can happen for another, without the subject explicitly having this in mind."[40] In this regard, we can understand Watsuji's assertion that Dasein is at the ground of appearances to also mean that beings are *disclosed* by and to Dasein in virtue of its very existence.

Watsuji himself, however, never seems to have comfortably assimilated this concept of disclosure into his work. This is partly a consequence of his periodic and clumsy attempts to force Heidegger's thought within the framework of Husserl's phenomenology. Liederbach points out, for instance, that as a moment of disclosedness the meaning of understanding is not, as Watsuji seems at times to believe, a transcendental constitutional power.[41] A similar kind of confusion can also be seen in Watsuji's criticisms of phenomenology, which are often made in close proximity to explicit discussions of Heidegger's work, but usually rely on a certain reading of Husserl's phenomenology. One of the most significant instances of this occurs in an important moment in which Watsuji recognizes that beings become manifest in such a way that they are neither purely transcendent nor immanent to consciousness, even as he seems to accuse Heidegger of understanding such appearances as phenomena of consciousness:

> Therefore all phenomena are unconsciously treated as expressions of human existence. For example, what stretches before one is "fields," and the rising sun there at daybreak is "that which is to be worshiped." These are not merely to be viewed as transcendent beings. For this reason the exclusion of transcendent beings is probably not possible without at the same time excluding human existence. Consequently, *the reduction to pure consciousness can not be carried out here.* Phenomena are always placed between one person and another, and in one sense or another express our relational existence. They cannot be only immanent to consciousness. This is true for all things considered external, such as gestures, actions, words, houses, villages, fields, mountains, rivers, etc.[42]

While a certain kind of confusion appears to reign here, we should also note that these lines were written in 1934, a scant seven years after the publication of *Sein und Zeit*. Given that Heidegger's work was not well understood in the West at this time, Watsuji's own misreading of these issues should not surprise. Despite his intended criticism of Heidegger, however, Watsuji equates—perhaps without fully realizing it—his concept of the "expression of human existence" with the phenomenon of disclosure. A primary difference between these concepts is that insofar as "phenomena are always placed between one person and another," disclosure is not a process in which the individual is caught up; it is an event that both takes up and is taken up by the I-as-we and we-as-I of *ningen sonzai.*

Although in this passage the phenomenon of disclosure is not well foregrounded, at other places in *Ethics as the Study of the Human* Watsuji is quite unambiguous; at one point he makes the striking claim that "the way of being of things and notions as what they are is actually determined by human acts."[43] Nevertheless he never furnishes a general account of the phenomenon of disclosure; the closest thing to such an explanation occurs in a pair of remarks on language located, respectively, in *Ethics as the Study of the Human* and in the essay "The Question of the Japanese Language and Philosophy."[44] In these texts he maintains that the human capacity to open up and determine the way of being of entities is described by and can be expressed through particular grammatical features of the Japanese language. However, the plausibility of these assertions about the ontological significance of specific parts of speech in Japanese will not be our primary concern; instead we will recapitulate this account in order to show that the larger philosophical point that Watsuji wishes to establish amounts to a claim about the human capacity to disclose the world.

The philosophical view that emerges through this investigation into language is summed up by Watsuji in the idea that "the being of a thing" (*mono no yū* 物の有) emerges from human existence.[45] He begins his account by showing how this condition is reflected in certain peculiarities of the Japanese term *aru* ある, which, he observes, means "to exist" or, as a copula that connects subject and complement, "to be," as in the sentence "The sky is blue." In the former instance, the verb *aru* takes the particle *ga* to form *ga aru* がある, which means "there is" something, and hence is used to indicate the existence of a thing. This can be seen in the statement "There is a rock," *iwa ga aru* 岩がある. When, in the latter instance, the verb *aru* is used as a copula, it takes the particle *de* to form *de aru,* である. In this case, *de aru* predicates something of a thing in expressing something about the thing, as in the statement "S is P": "The rock is big," *ōki na iwa de aru* 大きな岩である.

Watsuji observes that if we follow what is indicated in ordinary usage, we find that *ga aru* is more fundamental than *de aru,* and that *de aru* is a determination of *ga aru* as being one way or another. When one says, for example, "There is a mountain," *yama ga aru* 山がある, this can refer to a mountain that reaches a high altitude or one that is modest in height. But when one says "This mountain is a high mountain," *kono yama wa takai yama de aru* この山は高い山である, the way the mountain exists is determined as "being high" by the copula *de aru* である. From this it can be seen that the existential "there is" of *ga aru* is more basic than the copular "is" of *de aru*, which expresses a mode of being or feature of the entity that exists by linking a descriptive complement or predicate such as "blue" or "high" to it.

But more fundamental than even the existential "there is" of *ga aru* is the human existence that is its primordial ground. This state of affairs is captured in a second meaning the term *aru* 有る can have, namely, "to have" or "to possess." In these instances, this sinograph is pronounced *yū* 有 and occurs as a compound term, as in *yūi* 有意, "meaningful or significant" (having meaning or significance), *yūshi* 有志, "voluntary" (possessing intention), *yūtoku* 有徳, "virtuous" (possessing virtue). Watsuji notes here that the sinograph 有 means "to have" with the same intensity that it means "there is." This is shown quite clearly in other examples. A capable person (*yūi no shi* 有為の士) is someone who is capable and at the same time someone who possesses competence; a profitable business (*yūri naru jigyō* 有利なる事業) is a business that is profitable and at the same time a business that possesses profitability. These things are, they exist, but at the same time they are possessed. *Yū* suggests an interpretation in which "to have" refers both to things that exist and to things that are possessed. Understood in this way, it can be said that "there is" a thing (*mono ga aru* ものが有る) means that something is had (*motsu* 有). The meaning of "to be" in the sense of "exist" is commutative with that of "to have." And because something can be "had" in the relevant sense only by a human being, it can be said that every being that "is" is "had" by a human being. Every statement that affirms the existence of the being of a thing necessarily and at the same time implies that the being of the thing is "had" by the human being. Being is linked in this way to human existence.

This means that the existential "there is" of *ga aru* actually indicates that there "is" something insofar as a human being "has" it; the manner in which she has it is then expressed by the copular "is" of *de aru*, which, as we saw, is a further determination of the "there is" of *ga aru*. Thus Watsuji maintains that in the case of our saying that "there is a planted tree in the garden [*niwa ni wa ueki ga aru* 庭には植木がある]; it is a beautiful tree [*utsukushii ki de aru* 美しい木である]," using the word *beautiful* determines the way we "have" the tree in the garden, namely, beautifully, or in a way that is cherishing and admiring.[46] When understood in this manner, he says, it can be seen that both *ga aru* and *de aru* belong to human existence. Lest we draw the conclusion that the kinds of entities that depend on human existence for their being are artifacts (such as gardens) we ourselves have made, we should note that Watsuji also makes these claims about natural entities that are in no way a product of or shaped by human artifice. He asserts, for example, that "because human beings have the wind, there is the wind [*kaze ga aru* 風がある]. Because human beings can have the wind as calmly felt, the wind is calm [*kaze ga shizuka de aru* 風が静かである]."⁴⁷ Furthermore,

> this can even be said about such things as the most distant stars. It may seem strange that a star can be the possession of a human being. But as Feuerbach had already declared, the fact that *there are stars* is a state of affairs that occurs only when humans have [*motsu* 有つ] stars. There are no stars for animals. Or again, the fact that there are stars as distant astronomical objects is also a state of affairs that occurs for the first time only when human beings have [*motsu* 有つ] such astronomical objects; there were no such celestial objects in ancient times.⁴⁸

This talk of "having" trees, wind, and stars, and having them in particular ways, that is, as beautiful, as calm, and as astronomical objects, cannot be squared with the construal of such beings as "expressions" of human existence in the manner in which artifacts, deeds, languages, and cultural structures count as such expressions. Instead we have to see that Watsuji uses the term *have* in these instances in a way that roughly corresponds to Heidegger's usage. As Daniel Dahlstrom writes, "Heidegger chooses locutions such as 'having' (*haben*), 'comporting' (*verhalten*), or 'understanding' (*verstehen*) in order to emphasize that that original, unthematic 'having' or 'comporting' is for the most part not some sort of deliberate, meditative act of knowing something. Instead those locutions signify any way—theoretical, practical, playful, devotional, tender, and so on—in which a human being might relate to something, whether himself, another, a natural object, an artifact, an artwork, a mathematical formula, a scientific hypothesis, a dream, and so on."⁴⁹ And for Heidegger as for Watsuji, the mode of being of an entity is closely tied to the way we "have" it. Thus the revelation that the basic human relation to things extends far beyond the act of cognizing them has ontological as well as epistemological significance, since, as Dahlstrom puts it, "the determination of the object (in what sense it is) must emerge from the manner in which one originally 'has' it, that is to say, the manner in which it originally becomes accessible (*wie der Gegenstand ursprünglich zugänglich wird*)."⁵⁰

IV. Disclosure and Perceptual Experience

The overlap and parallels between Heidegger's and Watsuji's conceptions of the ontological relation between "having" and "being" indicate that

Watsuji had a robust, if undeveloped, sense of the difference between an entity and its being, even if he did not openly thematize—much less launch a philosophical inquiry into—the ontological difference, that is, the metaphysical differentiation of being from beings. Given these intersecting philosophical foundations, our reconstruction of the notion of disclosure in Watsuji will draw heavily on Heidegger's conception without, however, claiming to faithfully reproduce it, since Watsuji parts ways with Heidegger on a range of issues that bear directly on the question of how we ought to understand this phenomenon.

We begin by noting that the foregoing train of ideas are connected by—and graduated according to—a single larger idea that underlies all of them, namely, that perceptual consciousness, in its nature and its structure, makes manifest or reveals, that is, *discloses*, the appearances. In order to bring into view the singular character of this conception of perceptual experience, we can briefly contrast it with the understanding of perception as a causal process in which things from the outside world impress themselves on the senses. On this view, perceiving subject and perceived object are exterior to one another in a relation set *in* the world as in a box, so that consciousness becomes, as Merleau-Ponty puts it, "a province of this world," and perceptual experience becomes an event in it.[51] The perceptual event that takes place in this container, moreover, is defined in mechanistic, causal, and materialist terms, so that perception is seen as a process in which physico-chemical stimuli are received by the physical system of the human organism. Even so, when we perceive, we perceive not isolated sensations but whole things. Materialist, causal, and mechanistic thinking explains this as a simultaneous experiencing of all of the atomic sensations that form a thing. We are then able to build up the thing out of these discrete sense impressions, first, because proximities and likenesses (including similarity to past shapes) cause them to be associated together, and second, because there is a stable relation between thing and percept, "a point by point correspondence and constant connection between the stimulus and the elementary perception."[52]

Watsuji rejects this account of perception because, as he observes, a "pure sensation" is never given phenomenologically. To make this point, he asks us to imagine a person looking at a wall in her study. In order to reach the isolated sense impressions underlying this experience, an atomistic theory of sensation must posit a primordial form of perceptual consciousness in which we do not yet see the wall *as* a wall but only as a mere visual sensation of some stretch of color. But, as Watsuji points out, we never actually have, and do not upon inspection discover, a discrete sensation in our perceptions. Perceptions—even the simplest ones—are always of whole forms in particular contexts. It is not the case that we begin from visual or tactile sensations and later unify them under some description. From the outset we are conscious of the wall *as* a wall, we treat the desk in an unmediated way *as* a desk by writing upon it, and so forth. The reduction of perception to sensations can be accomplished only by taking up a specifically artificial and abstract psychological standpoint.[53] In sum, close attention to perception reveals that in our perceptual hold upon things, we do not construct the perceived object from out of a collection of sensations; we perceive meaningful wholes.

These wholes, as meaningful, appear to perception *as* something or other; hence Watsuji also calls the appearances "expressions." And because "being expressed is essentially synonymous with being understood," expressions, that is, appearances, are always already understood *as* X or Y.[54] This understanding, moreover, is prereflective and immediate: "Although we are unaware of it, we routinely deal with all things as expressions. An article of black clothing with gold buttons is a *uniform*, and a room in which there are rows of desks is a *classroom*. Without resorting to judgment or inference, we deal with uniforms and classrooms directly."[55] Perceiving is thus no merely passive, mechanical, and reproductive registration of objects; it involves the ascription of content to one's perceptions, so that we necessarily see the thing as a unitary object under some description. There is thus no "pure" reception of things in perception; perception is always interpretive. Watsuji is careful to note that this does *not* mean we initially encounter a pure and purportedly neutral percept that is then given a subsequent interpretation that varies with differences in language and culture. Interpretation is not a secondary addition, a garment that is used to clothe a naked experience: the phenomena we encounter are perceived according to a certain interpretation from the beginning. He rejects the idea that there could ever be a bare or meaningless perceptual experience of a reality that is then overlaid with signification. So that for Watsuji as for Heidegger, we do not hear pure sounds or have neutral perceptions, but hear the noise, to use Heidegger's example from *Being and Time*, of a car engine or the north wind, and perceive and participate in an always already interpreted scene of meaningful things and events that perception "shows" to us as the things they are.

Watsuji references Gabriel Tarde rather than Heidegger in contending that this is in part because we always already perceive things through a certain interpretation given by our native language and the common sense and scientific theories of the age in which we live, all of which give a certain shape to our awareness of things from the outset and function as prisms through which we perceive the world.[56] And this is just to say that what we see things as, that is, the way things appear to the subject of perception, is determined by the manner in which we "have" or comport ourselves toward an entity—which discloses the way it exists, or its mode of being.

V. Shared Intentionality as Disclosive Comportment

Watsuji makes use of Tarde's examples of language, common sense, and scientific practices in order to highlight the intersubjective nature of our comportment toward things. Because such modes are always shared and social, he calls this relational stance "shared intentionality," or *kyōdōshikō* 共同志向. Watsuji maintains that he is able to uncover the true character of intentionality because, unlike Husserl and Heidegger, he begins from an understanding of the subject of intentionality as an embodied "I" embedded in relation to others:

> To grasp the human as this kind of being-in-relation-to-others [*aida-gara*] throws a new light on the relation between "I" and "thing" in intentionality. The human being becomes "I" within being-in-relation-to-others. The "I" expresses being-in-relation-to-others in its individuality. Consequently, the relation between "I" and "thing" is in truth the relation between "I in being-in-relation-to-others" and "thing." The I which intends things is the "I which is a being-in-relation-to-others," not the "I in isolation." If so, intentionality is originally a shared intentionality [*kyōdōshikō*] and this shared intentionality is in the I, and becomes the intentionality of the I. Phenomenology, which problematizes the consciousness of the individual, probably cannot accept this.[57]

Because the subject that is found in the intentional relation is constitutively related to others before it is intentionally related to things, Watsuji sets out to replace the intentional stances of a fully individuated consciousness with a conception of shared or collective intentionality that corresponds to this very different understanding of the subject. But what he offers by way of explanation of this form of intentionality does not amount to much more than the enigmatic assertion that insofar as all things are found in the intentional relation, they can be found from the outset in the being-in-relation-to-others of the human being. Moreover, for reasons that remain unclear, in his writings after *Ethics as the Study of the Human*, Watsuji ceases using the term *kyōdōshikō* altogether.

We are thus faced with the task of trying to arrive at an understanding of a philosophical concept that, while highly suggestive, is also relatively indeterminate. I propose that we approach this notion by returning to and rehearsing the singular qualities of *aidagara*, since it is evident that the distinction between the traditional model of intentionality and Watsuji's concept of shared intentionality originates in the difference between a conception of the subject as an individual consciousness enclosed upon itself, and a conception of the subject as an interactional being-in-relation-to-others.

For all of the many ways in which Husserl's concept of transcendental consciousness and Heidegger's notion of Dasein amount to a wholly new dispensation for thinking about the subject, and for all of the openness of each of these forms of subjectivity to the world, both the transcendental subject and Dasein, like earlier conceptions of consciousness in the history of Western philosophy, remain constitutively separated from others. For the relational and interactional model of practical subjectivity that is *aidagara*, however, how I am in the world and how I experience it, is tied directly to the presence of others. We have seen that one consciousness is entwined with another in interaction, and that the porosity of consciousness and its contents means that each flows into the other like a converging series of activities and events. This "penetration" of one consciousness by another does not mean that the internal contents of the consciousness of others are externally mediated by expressions and gestures, and so arrived at inferentially; nor, at the other extreme, does it mean that I fuse with the consciousness of the other, which becomes transparently a part of my own, so that together we would constitute a superpersonal subject. In the practical interconnection of acts, consciousness and its contents are neither fully transparent to nor fully sealed off from that of the others we interact with. Instead one consciousness is open to and overlaps in certain respects with another, so that we undergo the same experience in its most significant external and internal features, as when one person feels ashamed and blushes before another, or when a group of people laugh together at the same thing.

The "subject" of such experiences, then, is a self that enters into and is continuous with others who correspond with and relate to it in the same way. It is this "I-as-we and we-as-I" that is the subject of what Watsuji calls shared intentionality. Intentionality is not shared because each of us separately and individually takes up an identical intentional stance; rather an intentional comportment is a single and unitary phenomenon shared across the area in which one consciousness extends into another. This phenomenon can be found, for example, in something like the emotional atmosphere of a crowd. The mood that has established itself (excitement at a concert, anger at a protest march, a feeling of reverence inside a great cathedral) is not in the crowd, separately contained in each individual member; rather the crowd is *in* a mood.

Before proceeding further in this direction, we should note that the notion of shared intentionality is another important instance in which Watsuji continues to use the terminology of Husserl to address themes and phenomena that are better handled by terms and concepts taken from Heidegger's thought. As we pointed out in the third chapter, given the kinds of commitments and overall orientation of Watsuji's philosophy, it seems more appropriate to speak of comportments rather than of intentional stances; in what follows, then, we will refer to shared intentionality as *shared comportment*. Watsuji considers three such shared comportments in relation to the phenomenon of *fūdo*: practically disposed, affectively oriented, and linguistically structured comportments.

Watsuji does not develop an account of practical comportment at any length, either in *Ethics as the Study of the Human* or later in *Ethics*. One reason for this, presumably, is that he did not have to. Heidegger had already shown that practical understanding is not simply one of the possible activities we can engage in or avoid at will, but that it is, on the contrary, our very mode of being. We exist as understanding and interpreting beings such that understanding is our very way of being in the world. Nevertheless Watsuji is oddly unforthcoming even about his own notion of shared or collective practical comportments, offering only the barest indication of what this phenomenon might come to. Our task here as elsewhere will hence be one of speculative reconstruction.

The most obvious candidate for shared practical comportment is the background of competence and familiarity and the suite of skills that enable members in a group to synchronize their activity, such as the members of a marching band, a cheerleading squad, or a synchronized swimming team. The significance of and the way the amount and kind of space on the road, the border between the field and the sidelines, or the distance to the bottom of the pool, appears to the members of these groups is determined largely by shared practical comportments. These examples also allow us to see by comparison that more commonplace activities, which merely require coordination rather than synchronization, are identically structured by the same kinds of shared practical comportments that enable participants to encounter the same entities in the same way. One thinks here of things such as a team playing football or a troupe performing in a ballet or the kitchen staff of a restaurant cooking orders during the dinner rush. In each of these cases, what shows up as of value or interest in the field or stage or kitchen, and what these settings afford and do not afford with respect to the goals of the group, will depend on the kind of practical comportments that are held in common.

Watsuji is concerned above all with those practical comportments in this category that are directed toward the natural rather than the human world. He observes, for example, that the sun appears as something divine to those who comport themselves with reverence toward it, and that it appears as a natural celestial object to those who adopt a scientific attitude toward it. Moreover such comportments compose practices that shape and even determine the perceptual experience of the members of a given society:

> In societies in which sun worship was practiced, each individual perceived the sun as something divine. For that common sense which is affected by natural science, the sun is perceived as a celestial body. In either case, the sun is perceived in such a way from the start; it is not the case that the same sun is perceived differently according to differences in judgment or modes of inference. Those who worship the sun did not have the mere sensation of sunlight. From childhood a form of social consciousness is instilled in people long before they acquire the capacity to judge or infer for themselves.[58]

People from different cultures do not arrive at different interpretive understandings of the same things through divergent judgments or differing processes of inference; the interpretation is there from the outset and is one that the person is immersed in from birth. This means that the individual does not simply generate, from her own person, the intentional comportments that open up the meanings of things. Instead practical comportments are originally collective and social; they help to constitute the practices that belong to the structure of an already established world.

The sociality of practical comportments does not entail that everyone in a given culture has a uniform experience of the natural world, since within any culture assorted practices—even those directed at the same segment of nature—congregate around differing interests, goals, desires, and values. Theodore Schatzki claims that in this regard, even something like a landscape is plural. He takes as his example the horse farm landscape of the Kentucky Bluegrass. This landscape shows up as one type of geographical expanse from among other possible ones in this region by figuring in certain practices and not others. Moreover such practices also uncover different faces of the horse farm landscape itself, depending on whether they are, for example, training practices, tourist practices, city-county planning practices, historical preservation practices, transportation practices, or fox hunting practices:

In each of these, the world around is encountered and acted amid as a different array of places, paths, and regions. This means that members of different groups such as farm owners, managers, construction workers, trainers, groomers, tourists, planners, preservationists, and hunters, as well as members of such groups as Latinos and poor whites, live through different landscapes. Although these different groups and practices might exist and be carried out in the same portion of the world, the landscapes they live through or are performed amid vary. In addition, an individual person lives through and encounters as many different landscapes in a given portion of the world as there are practices he participates in there. Landscapes are relative, not to individuals or groups, but to practices.[59]

Within a single culture, different groups can gather around the same portion of the natural world and undergo very different experiences of it. Nonetheless the content of what is uncovered by any group that shares a practice will have a substantial degree of uniformity, and this makes possible the coordination, communication, and repetition within a practice that is necessary to sustain it and to enable other members of the culture to join it.

In learning how to participate in these practices, I first take up, with others, the practical comportments that are part of the structure of a particular activity. Some of these shared comportments involve jointly choreographed actions, such as when I join and learn from a group of farmhands harvesting crops, or a crew sailing a ship together, or a team of miners cutting into a coal seam. The way we encounter the field, sea, or mountain is the same; the appearance that each of these entities takes on for us is part of a single, joint experience made possible by our shared practical comportments toward each of these things. But there are also other comportments that can be shared in this way that are less directly dependent on this kind of coordination, such as the practical skills needed to hunt or fish, ski or scuba dive, or carry out speleological or botanical research. Here too, in each of these cases, the places and spaces of the natural world are opened up in the same way and show the same face to the I-as-we and we-as-I in a single experience structured by a shared comportment. We begin the process of acquiring comportments, then, largely with ones that are shared, since in learning about such skills and forms of competence and involvement from others, we must join with and be among them in interaction and imitation as we face the things of our world together. It is only after a range of practical comportments become part of my repertoire and come to form my habitual core that I find that my solo encounters with the natural world can also be enriched by these capacities.

Like his description of our shared practical comportments, Watsuji's treatment of our linguistically structured comportments evokes themes in Heidegger's phenomenology rather than Husserl's. Language, Watsuji says, expresses in order to display or show something.[60] He does not really attempt to unwind the skein of issues and themes that are coiled within this understanding of language, but it is clear enough that for him language is disclosive; that is, it is a mode of revealing, of making present, manifest, or evident. This conception of language stands in sharp contrast to the conventional picture of language as a kind of instrument for signifying things—a system of signs to which we attach particular meanings in order to refer to reality. But using language is not like using a tool that one picks up and then lays aside when one is finished with it, as if the self were confronted with a world standing outside of language that was somehow already known to it and to which, when necessary, it applied the appropriate words. This understanding of language most fully emerges in tandem with the representationalist epistemology of early modernity and the objectivist ontology that underlay it. Heidegger's critique of subject-object dualism had, of course, already shown how representationalism falls short as a theory of perception and knowledge, which, in turn, casts grave doubt on the view of language as referential and instrumental. This is not to suggest, however, that language does not sometimes function referentially—that is, refer to things in the world, represent them, and communicate information; it is only to say that this function does not characterize what is essential about it, inasmuch as language is first and foremost that which makes manifest.

Because language encompasses the *activities* of speaking and listening, reading and writing, as well as a *structure* of sedimented meanings, the capacity of language to disclose the world functions across multiple activities, forms, and structures. An initial distinction between types of disclosure can be made between the way language discloses by making something present to perception and the way it makes something present to the imagination. We will concentrate on the former mode rather than the latter, since we are concerned above all with the relation between language and *fūdo*.

What language presents to perception can be further divided between that which is displayed through the activity of speaking and that which is made manifest solely by virtue of my *capacity* to speak a particular

174

174

language. In the former case, something is brought to light through the words that are spoken by one person to another or others. So, for example, a speaker with a keen ethical or aesthetic sensibility, or someone from a different culture, can bring out aspects of a situation, activity, thing, or person for his listeners that had been overlooked, or even completely change the way something is understood and perceived by redescribing it in a new and different way.

In the latter case, the language I speak is a medium in which I live and in which an understanding of the world is deposited and maintained. Language in this sense, as sedimented structure, silently fuses with perception and is always already at work in shaping it. Perception, to borrow another expression from James, is "shot through" with conception. This makes possible a certain form of consciousness and quality of awareness in which things can be present to us *as* what they are—not because I have a voice inside my head naming the things I see, but because my very ability to see something *as* something is made possible by my possession of this ability to speak a language. While his exposition of this issue remains minimal, Watsuji does link linguistic disclosure directly to our experience of nature: "As Tarde has said, we do not arrive at the consciousness of even natural phenomena by beginning with sensations. Instead, we already perceive natural phenomena through a specific interpretation from the outset. Generally, we directly perceive phenomena as already *named by our native language*, as, for instance, *yoake* [dawn], *taiyō* [the sun], *seiten* [clear or fair skies], *ame* [rain], *kaze* [wind], *yūgure* [dusk, sundown], *yoru* [night], and so forth. In the perception of these phenomena, we are already conscious of the same shared matters."[61] These examples show the way an awareness of something is an awareness of it "as" something, so that it is already understood and interpreted in an understanding determined by language. But the point Watsuji wishes to make is not only that we *see* what we *say*; it is also that insofar as my capacity to speak a particular language is shared with the others with whom I interact, this language makes possible a shared comportment toward things.

What is shared with others as language is not a common set of sign tools but a vast sea of words and expressions in which we find ourselves immersed and which reflect an encounter with the way things appear to a people from a first-personal, involved standpoint. As Humboldt had shown, every language is an all-embracing medium for its speaker and, as such, a totality within which there resides a characteristic worldview. This standpoint is oriented and formed by the collective historical experience that is sedimented in each language, so that at its center there stands a particular interpretation of the lifeworld that is embodied in its words and expressions.

Gadamer has shown that this sense of what is shared in a common language can be foregrounded by reflecting on the experience of learning our native language. Learning to speak is less about learning how to follow the rules for using a system of signs than it is about learning to see the world as it is presented by one's language. This relationship between word and world can also be seen in the experience of becoming fluent in a foreign language; a true command of another language requires an understanding of what it is to view the world through the eyes of that language. To speak a language, then, is to participate in it by conforming our thinking and speaking to what has been said and handed down in it.[62] Language in this respect is a disclosive medium that allows us to be "there" together with others and present in the same way to the meanings offered to us by things.

While Watsuji does not explicitly draw on, or even address, Humboldt's views, his etymological interpretations of what he takes to be philosophically significant concepts in the Japanese language rely on an understanding of language as a structure of sedimented meanings whose content both discloses the world and furnishes us with a standpoint on it. This seems to be the reason he maintains that language unfolds on the basis of a mutual understanding between each other about the world and the thing being discussed; the stillness that precedes and follows such exchanges, he contends, is really the manifestation of a silent and shared understanding of that which all regard as self-evident about each of these things. This, he says, is what makes it possible for us to finish each other's sentences, to leave things half or completely unsaid, or to anticipate what is going to come next in a train of words we hear—as well as to be surprised when something thought to have been shared is found, through an unexpected statement, not to have been so.[63]

A common language thus carries and discloses a shared interpretation of the world, one that is both tacit and evoked each time we speak to one another. Because words derive their meaning from their relation to the totality of a language, to express what we mean is also at the same time to begin to summon our broadest and most basic sense of things. This is because, as Gadamer explains, when we speak, "every word breaks forth as if from a center [*Mitte*] and is related to a whole, through which alone it is a word. Every word causes the whole of the language to which it belongs to resonate [*antönen*] and the whole world-view that underlies it to appear."[64] For speakers of the same language, the to-and-fro of even the simplest conversational exchange about what we behold together not only reveals a shared sense of the thing about which we speak; it also makes visible a shared view of the world within which the thing has its place.

Consider, for instance, the following scene: Somewhere in the Great Plains a group of nineteenth-century American pioneers repair a wagon; the most seasoned among them offers advice to the others so that the vehicle will be equipped to handle the terrain and change in weather they know lie ahead. The leader of the group, pointing to a small body of water just visible on the horizon, tells the rest that they will begin to encounter these conditions just after they ford that river. After a few weeks of this, he says, they will arrive at the final leg of their journey on the Oregon Trail. As the group considers the seemingly endless prairies that stretch before them, the conversation turns to rumors about an acquaintance of the men who fled his gambling debts and was now a prosperous saloon owner somewhere in the Oregon Territory. This conversation discloses what must be heeded in fixing the wagon, but it also reveals a shared understanding of the frontier as, among other things, a place holding out the promise of opportunity (in the rich new lands of the western coast) and freedom (in the possibility of being a different person, wholly divorced from who one has been, for a new group of people). By appearing in this way, the western expanse of the open plains takes its place among the contents of a common world. Much of this, of course, remains implicit and unspoken, even as it is visible to all.

In fine, the words we speak to one another both uncover the thing spoken about and evoke a shared horizon—more sensed than fully articulated—whose limits determine the boundaries of what is intelligible. But these experiences are not simply something held separately in each individual mind; rather *we* are placed in front of the same matter and in the same world together through the shared medium of a common language. To speak, then, is to set up a shared comportment toward the thing being discussed and the world as a whole, making it possible for there to be a single experience whose subject is us.

Like our practical stances and skills and our linguistically structured comportments, our emotions can also uncover or reveal the world and its objects. It is not difficult to see there are at least some aspects of the world that are revealed only by the exercise of a sensibility that is affective as well as cognitive. For example, it seems doubtful that a situation could be understood as repugnant by a pure cognition free of any affective element, because one needs to also *feel* that a situation is repugnant in order to grasp its repugnance. Or again, there are certainly people who are emotionally insensitive enough that they cannot sense when someone they are talking to is in pain or distress or, less dramatically, merely uncomfortable. In both cases, a knowledge of how things stand in the

world requires the exercise of a particular kind of sensitivity, a sensitivity
to what is repugnant in the first example, and to other people's emotions
in the second.

While Watsuji understands emotions and moods to be disclosive in
this manner, he also uncovers the way in which emotional dispositions
are culturally formed and so first emerge as shared comportments. To
establish this point, he invokes the classical Japanese example of certain
encounters with nature as an experience of *mono no aware* 物の哀れ.[65] This
term, which belongs to the traditional vocabulary of Japanese aesthetics,
names a feeling that is at one and the same time the feeling of pathos
caused by the transience of beautiful things and a longing—triggered by
this encounter—for the absolute:

> The continual sound of insects on a moonlit autumn night is familiar
> to Japanese as a typical scene that evokes the feeling of *mono no aware*
> 物の哀れ. No matter how far astronomical and biological knowledge
> advance, they can never grasp the source of *mono no aware*. From long
> ago our ancestors were overcome by the feeling of the *infinite* in this
> scene; they expressed in poetry their experience in it of the deep
> bottom of human existence, of coming into contact with a bottom-
> less bottom. Because of this, that mode of feeling became, as it were, a
> frame through which to contemplate the moonlit night. However, this
> is not to say that each person only experiences this pathos within their
> consciousness. The moonlit autumn night itself appears as a landscape
> tinged with pathos. That is, the existence of the noematic [*taishōteki*
> 対象的] contents of the landscape itself is based on the formative
> capacity of human emotions.[66]

If we recall the way the objectifying perspective of the natural sciences
loses sight of certain dimensions of meaning, we will be able to see that
the phenomenon of *mono no aware* is not fully accessible to and cannot
be accounted for by these disciplines. This standpoint locates such feelings inside the head of each individual, and so conceives of emotions as
psychological states that are relative to each subject. Watsuji's claim, in
contrast, is that the scene itself is pervaded by a quality that is revealed
by the emotion or mood that is simultaneously a response to it. Moreover
this mode of affectivity through which such qualities make their appearance is shared rather than private. That is, these feelings are not simply
in us; we are in them, as in a shared medium. This mood or emotion
arises between us, acting, I suggest, as a single shared comportment that
discloses the same scene to a collective subject of experience, namely,
an *I-as-we* and *we-as-I* in which one consciousness overlaps with another.

This commonality of feeling is articulated in language—above all in a shared literary and poetic tradition. The link between linguistic articulation and shared feeling helps to explain instances like the one above in which certain affective comportments are taken up by the members of a particular culture. In this regard, the shared emotional comportments that make possible the common and public character of an affective experience are constituents of what Watsuji calls cultural commonality, or *bunkateki kyōdō* 文化的共同. With this term he includes, in a kind of seamlessly articulated whole, all of the cultural expressions of a communal and shared existence that awaken in us a consciousness of our common life together; cultural commonality is in this respect equivalent to a kind of mental or spiritual commonality. The constituents of this whole encompass everything from the same language, religion, and cuisine, to the same architectural styles and ways of cultivating the land.[67] And because cultural commonality also includes shared comportments such as emotions, it includes a common experience of the natural world that arises from and is grounded in these comportments.

This point can be seen in the earlier example of *mono no aware*: "In this case cultural commonality is not only that each person embraces the same feeling of pathos in their heart, but the very fact that this scene of a pathos-filled moonlit night itself *appears before each person*. Hence the *contents of this cultural commonality* are nothing other than this moonlit evening scene itself. In this sense the entire scenery of nature becomes the contents of cultural commonality."[68] Watsuji's contention is that the "entire scenery of nature" has a certain look to it; that is, it takes on a certain appearance for a culture through, most importantly, practices (such as sun worship), articulation in language (such as literary and poetic expression), and the emotional responses that are shared across a community. This relationship between culture and the disclosure of nature means that similar features of the natural world can take on very different appearances for different groups of people, as the geographer Yi-Fu Tuan has noted in speaking about the geography of the American West: "Americans have learned to accept the open plains of the West as a symbol of opportunity and freedom, but to the Russian peasants boundless space used to have the opposite meaning. It connoted despair rather than opportunity; it inhibited rather than encouraged action. It spoke of man's paltriness as against the immensity and indifference of nature. Immensity oppressed."[69] Our encounter with nature is in this sense always filtered through culture, but this experience is not the outcome of projection or construction; rather, as we shall see, the intelligibility of nature, like the whole content of human experience, is mediated by shared practical, linguistic, and affective comportments, such that we can say, borrowing an expression from Berque, that cultures are "the faults through which nature surges."[70]

Berque's remark also underlines the way shared comportments operate together to disclose the natural world. While our separate accounts of the dimensions or levels of perceptual experience opened by each form of intentional directedness enabled us to get an analytical purchase on the distinctive functions and types of shared comportments, this division itself is usually not reflected in the way the things of nature are revealed to perception. Take, for example, the perception of cherry trees in Japanese culture. Because the practice of picnicking beneath cherry trees at night is part of this culture, and because, coupled with a wistful mood, the presence of friends, and a perfect spring evening, someone can say, "Why don't we go view the night blossoms?" ("Yozakura o mi ni ikimasenka?"), the cherry trees in full bloom at the park show up as the scaffolding for a certain form of sociality, their dying blossoms as objects of aesthetic contemplation that make visible the connection between beauty and brevity.

***

In this reconstruction of self-understanding and disclosure as forms of continuity and belonging together that underwrite the unitary whole of self and *fūdo*, we uncovered how these modes of activity reshape the way we conceive of the self, on the one side, and the way we understand our experience of nature, on the other. For the modern ontological topos and its conception of the self as an individual atom, the location in which the self finds itself is a merely contingent affair, since what the self *is* must be distinguished from the place in which it is located; it remains the same entity in all the places and spaces of the world. But we have seen that insofar as a *fūdo* is part of and disclosed through a world through which the self understands and interprets itself, who we can be depends directly upon where we are. At the same time, what a *fūdo* can be—how it can appear—depends in part upon the comportments that *we* bring to it; in this respect, a *fūdo* depends upon the self to be what it is in and through the process of disclosure.

The mutual dependence of self and *fūdo* upon one another in these reconceptions of self and nature means that the identification of what is purely subjective or objective in this relational totality is something that is arrived at only through a later process of abstraction; what is given originally is an intertwining and unity in which culture and nature are encountered as a tightly interwoven texture. Yet the close identification of self and nature with one another allows for the troubling possibility that in this unity, one side will engulf the other. On the one hand, the way that our sensibility and self-understanding rely so heavily upon the *fūdo* in which we are emplaced would appear to reduce the self to its natural setting. On the other hand, inasmuch as the face nature shows us depends upon the manner in which it comes to presentation in a particular culture, we are confronted with the opposite kind of peril, namely, the reduction of what appears as nature to what is supplied by the self.

The continuity between self and nature in *fūdo*, then, houses a structural tension—but it is not one that is meant to be resolved. The objectivity of nature and the subjectivity of the self are irreducible to one another, even as this dualism is overcome: this is an inherent part of what is novel in and essential to *fūdo* as a philosophical concept. We turn in the final chapter to a discussion of the complexities raised by this question of how two things can be distinct but not truly separate, or together as one, but not one and the same.

8

Self in Nature, Nature in the Lifeworld

Throughout this study, each chapter has trailed into the next; this momentum has established that the self that has its being in the lifeworldly dimension of nature must be understood as a relational existence that opens on to other selves that also open on to it. This whole structure of being-in-relation-to-others, in turn, opens out onto a *fūdo*, or natural world that is part of, and disclosed through, a culturally and historically mediated human world by means of which the self understands and interprets itself.

In this happy convergence of self and other, culture and nature, we appear to have surmounted various dualisms and divisions and arrived, by a steady climb, at the sunlit peaks of all that was promised in the concept of *fūdo*. Yet a final set of obstacles remain, ones that originate with the very notions of self-understanding and disclosure that have brought us to this point and that undermine the idea that subjective and objective elements form an indivisible unity within a *fūdo*. These difficulties pull against one another: on the one side, the extensive dependence of the internal and external dimensions of our capacity to be in a world (i.e., our self-interpretations and sensibility) on a *fūdo* allows for the possibility that in the concept of *fūdo* the subjectivity of the self is simply swallowed up by the objectivity of nature. On the other side, inasmuch as the appearances of nature are always mediated by the practical, linguistic, and affective comportments that belong to a culture, we face a suspicion of a different kind: that the concept of *fūdo* captures only cultural forms of displaying nature rather than nature itself, in its objectivity and transcendence.

In what follows I suggest possible strategies for coming to grips with both of these difficulties, primarily by working out more fully what is at times only implicit or too thinly drawn by Watsuji himself. In the first case, the unity of a self with its *fūdo* poses the question of how transcendence, the distance and difference that make possible freedom and individuation, can be rigorously and convincingly accounted for if the self is so completely identified with its insertion into nature. I maintain that the capacity of the human being to transcend its *fūdo* is grounded primarily in Watsuji's understanding of spatiality as united to temporality, and that this becomes manifest in the phenomenon of human historicity. Watsuji comes to this conception of spatiotemporal unity, moreover, through a critical transformation of the notions of spatiality and temporality in *Being and Time*.

In the second case, the specter of subjectivism hovers over what is disclosed as nature; if the contents of our lived experience of nature are always given to perception through our interpretive construals, then it would seem that what we encounter in this experience is not nature itself, but culture. A close examination of the structure of our experience of nature, however—one that probes the very ground of this experience— will open up a way of thinking about the relation between nature and culture that moves us beyond this impasse and takes us to a far more radical conception of the shape of this experience.

I. Spatiotemporal Unity and the Structure of Human Existence

While the preponderance of Watsuji's account of the relation between self and nature in *fūdo* spells out the ways the self has its being in the places and spaces of the natural world, his intention was not, of course, to reduce the self to a mere expression and function of the *fūdo* in which it is emplaced. But his robust sense of the human being as embedded in and emerging from the depths of a particular region of nature leads him at times—notwithstanding his own insistence to the contrary—to give too much weight to the way a *fūdo* is determinative for the self. This becomes apparent, for example, in his dubious analysis of the manner in which various national characters are shaped and almost even created by particular geographical conditions. Although a substantial portion of the text of *Fūdo* after the first chapter is devoted to illustrating this point, we will pass over these descriptions, not only because they are fruitless but also because, taken in its full measure, Watsuji's vision is of a self that is both free and limited, determining and determined, in relation to the natural world in which it has its ground.

For Watsuji, freedom from nature appears in and as history. But this movement of transcendence is both constrained and made possible by our inherence in a *fūdo*, so that nature and history are in dialectical tension with one another. To grasp this relation, we have to place this dialectic in a wider explanatory perspective and approach this question—as Watsuji himself does—from the unitary whole of human existence. Watsuji shows in this regard how the individual and social dimensions of the human being come together with the temporal and spatial structure of human life to compose a totality. Hence the spatiotemporal unity that characterizes the structure of human existence entails that the self is never reducible to the spaces and places of the natural world that are constitutive for it, since these are always also at the same time sites through which the self temporally transcends the determination of nature through human historicity. In order to grasp this notion of transcendence, we will trace a trajectory that begins with Watsuji's conception of spatiotemporal unity, which trades, in turn, on the unity of the individual and social moments of human existence, and bottoms out in the dialectical unity of historicity and *fūdosei*.

On Watsuji's view, temporality and spatiality are coextensive and always show up together as an inseparable whole. He articulates this unity against the background of Heidegger's conception (in *Being and Time*) of temporality and spatiality as distinct and separable. He takes this approach because while his overall philosophical approach here can be classified as Heideggerean, hewing too closely to the concepts of time and space that Heidegger lays out in *Being and Time* muddies and eventually blocks the path to a clear understanding of the notion of *fūdo*. Watsuji's critique of Heidegger, then, is a prelude to the announcement of his own position.

This critique offers a corrective to what Watsuji views as Heidegger's artificial separation of spatiality and temporality, which is a consequence of his truncated conception of the spatial and temporal structure of human existence. His charge is that Heidegger grasps this structure solely from the standpoint of the individual, so that the ontologically fundamental or founding form of spatiality amounts to the bounded and lived space of action of the individual's being-in-the-world and the foundational form of temporality, namely, originary temporality, to the possibilities into which the individual projects itself; when this projection is authentic, temporality becomes manifest above all in the individual's awareness of its own being-toward-death (*Sein zum Tode*).[1]

Moreover, because temporality is apprehended from the horizon of the individual, it founds spatiality. Existential spatiality, it will be recalled, is the lived experience of being in space. And to be in space is to be oriented, that is, to be able to intuit directions such as left-right and ahead-behind in relation to one's body, to have a sense of what is near and far, to be able to make sense of regions that contextualize equipment and organize activities, and, drawing on all of these, to be directed toward, draw near, and act upon the objects of one's concern. But this kind of orientation is impossible without a prior orientation that emerges from the temporality of the individual. As Malpas puts the point, "Orientation is first and foremost a matter of being oriented toward that which one can be—toward a possibility of one's own—and this is always an orientation that calls upon temporality."[2] This is because to be oriented within the space of a world, I must make sense of equipment, roles, tasks, objects, spaces, and places. And these show up as significant for me first and foremost in terms of their purposes and mine—both immediate and ultimate: what, for example, a particular tool is used for, what this task is for the sake of, and what the specific self-understanding is which is the end that both of these serve. Thus the intelligibility of all of these things depends on my seeing them in terms of their possibilities: what can be—which also requires the retention of what has been—but what is not yet. And this, of course, is a temporal orientation toward things.

Arisaka points out that the founding-founded relation of temporality and spatiality presupposes that space and time are at some level separate and separable from one another: "In order to establish that temporality founds spatiality, he [Heidegger] would have to show that spatiality and temporality must be distinguished in such a way that temporality not only shares a content with spatiality but also has additional content as well. In other words, they must be truly distinct and not just analytically distinguishable."[3] She argues that Heidegger does not succeed in separating out temporality from spatiality in the requisite manner; Watsuji views this attempt and its failure as a consequence of the way Heidegger conceives of Dasein wholly in terms of its individuality. Watsuji himself, on the other hand, reaches tirelessly for a double vision of the structure of human existence that sees two realities at once: the individual and the social. This leads him to both expand and wed Heidegger's conceptions of spatiality and temporality to one another:

> Temporality not linked to spatiality is not yet true temporality. Heidegger did not go beyond this point because his Dasein was ultimately an individual. He treated human existence [*ningen sonzai*] merely as the existence of an individual. From the standpoint of the dual individual and social structure of human existence, the individual is only an abstract aspect of this structure. Hence when human existence is grasped in terms of its concrete duality, temporality comes into line and is coextensive with spatiality. We can then reveal, for the first time, the truth of historicity [*rekishisei* 歴史性], which never appears fully and concretely in Heidegger. In doing so, it will become evident how historicity and *fūdosei* [the lived experience of nature] are coextensive as well.[4]

Because the individual and the social are two moments of the same structure, Watsuji's conceptions of spatiality and temporality take into account, as Heidegger's do not, the social dimension of human existence. Thus, as we have shown, the existential spatiality of Dasein becomes subjective space, namely, the interpersonal space of being-in-the-world that is both anchored in nature and belongs to the structure of *ningen* as being-in-relation-to-others. The allegation that Heidegger does not incorporate sociality into his understanding of temporality, however, is more difficult to establish. Watsuji observes that to follow the logic of the temporality of the individual through to the end is to be taken, as Heidegger shows, to death as the end of Dasein. But temporality does not only reveal the finitude of human existence; the social dimension of temporality also confirms something that transcends the finitude of the individual:

> The twofold character of human existence as finite and infinite also becomes clear here. Individuals [*hito* 人] die, the linkage between them [*hito no aida* 人の間] changes, and yet, unceasingly, while dying and changing, individuals live and the linkage between them continues. This linkage continues in this ceaselessly *ending*, without *ceasing*. That which, from the standpoint of the individual, is "being-toward-death" [*shi e no sonzai* 死への存在], is from the point of view of society, "being-toward-life" [*sei e no sonzai* 生への存在]. Hence human existence is individual and social.[5]

The social dimension of *ningen* is both spatial and temporal, and its temporality enables the collective being of the human being to transcend the finitude of the human being as individual substance. There is something almost like consolation in this vision of the chain of human lives; it is not merely that human lives follow and are followed by others in turn, but that in this understanding of human temporality, the continuity of the being of the human being is disclosed.

   Notwithstanding this, Heidegger himself certainly carries his analysis of temporality into the social domain (and thus beyond the notion of a temporality that stretches between the birth and death of the individual) in his depiction of Dasein's condition of being thrown into a historical moment represented by a heritage that it must take up and make its own. The difference between Heidegger and Watsuji on this point is that because for Watsuji spatiality is part of the very structure of *ningen*, the temporality of the human being is inseparable from this social, cultural, and natural spatiality—and hence from the places in nature that are joined to, open up, and anchor such spaces. And so Watsuji, too, speaks about the social dimension of human temporality in terms of its historicity, but the collection of related events that make up the past must always unfold in and through a particular *fūdo*, so that history can be what it is only in taking place through nature. This is the "the truth of historicity" that Watsuji contends never fully and concretely appears in Heidegger's work. Moreover, if spatiality and temporality form a linked, coextensive, and unitary whole, then "in a culture, historicity and nature experienced and lived through [*fūdosei*] are two sides of the same coin; one side cannot be separated from the other. There are no historical formations that lack the character of a *fūdo*, just as there are no forms of *fūdo* without a historical character."[6]

II. Nature, History, Transcendence

Because nature and history are dimensions that form an inseparable spatiotemporal whole within a culture, a given culture and the self that belongs to and gives expression to it are neither simply a function of nature, nor do they fully transcend it. Cultural development and change are both products of geoclimatic conditions and creative responses to them, and it is in this transformative reception of environmental conditions that Watsuji locates something like human freedom or transcendence.

Transcendence first becomes possible on the ground of a certain kind of self-understanding, one that is acquired when we grasp what is demonstrated by our cultural forms of responding to nature, namely, the human capacity to freely shape this response. Liederbach maintains in this regard that for Watsuji our relation to *fūdo* is the locus for a process of self-understanding in which we are able to *discover* our freedom as a mode of transcendence. In the course of establishing this point, he draws our attention to this passage: "That is, the human being [*ningen*] discovers itself in *fūdo*. From the standpoint of the individual, this becomes awareness of the body, but in the context of the more concrete ground of human existence [*ningen sonzai*], this [self-discovery] becomes apparent through the *ways* in which we form a community, and in *forms* of consciousness, and thus in the *ways* that we construct language, and even more in things like our modes of production, the styles of our buildings, and so on. Transcendence, as the structure of human existence, must include all of these things."[7] Liederbach notes that the self-understanding of *ningen* is enlarged through this self-disclosure in *fūdo*, because *ningen* realizes that it is determined by being-in-relation (both to other selves and to nature) and grasps its capacity to shape this relationality and so contribute to its historical development. In other words, *fūdo* is a context within which *ningen* discovers both that it is determined and, at the same time, that it is capable of transcending its limitations.[8]

Thus the various artifacts and practices of a culture ranging from, for example, clothing styles and cuisines to architecture and to festivals, according to Watsuji "are in their origin what we ourselves have produced in and through our own freedom. We have not, however, devised these things without connection to the phenomena of *fūdo* such as the cold, the heat, and the humidity. We see ourselves in *fūdo*, and, in this self-understanding, we encounter our own free self-formation [*wareware jishin no jiyū naru keisei* 我々自身の自由なる形成]."[9] Sensu stricto, we collectively encounter ourselves *through* rather than *in* the *fūdo* in which we live, since we see ourselves reflected in the culture that arises in tandem with it. To grasp how culture and its structure, processes, and products can function as a mirror in which the self is able to see itself, we can draw, as Watsuji did not, on Marx's concept of objectification (*Vergegenständlichung*). For Marx the human being is *Homo laborans*. It must work to derive a life for itself from the world around it, but this is accomplished in conscious and creative ways. Hence the human being can deliberate about and gain a reflective distance from life rather than simply be in it. Where the spider or ant or beaver construct through blind instinct, we work on nature consciously, conceiving our creations in images and plans in the imagination that govern how and what we construct in working on nature. We transform what initially exists as an idea into a concrete thing with material reality. The product of our labor embodies in this way the contents of our consciousness, so that we see ourselves reflected in our work.

This means that in looking upon a world that we have made, we are able to see that in producing our life, we live it as a project. And this, in turn, entails more specifically that our freedom in relation to the *fūdo* in which we are embedded is found in our ability to shape our identity through the creation of artifacts and practices that emerge in, from, and through this *fūdo*. While what comes to ordinary awareness is our capacity to freely produce creations that both constitute and articulate a certain self-understanding, there is also another moment in the transcendence of *ningen* in relation to nature that is uncovered through philosophical reflection, namely, the way these artifacts and practices, as *constructions*, can alter—in conjunction with practical, affective, and linguistic comportments—what is disclosed as nature. This power to affect the substance of our self-understanding and the content of our disclosures is not unlimited, however, since these creations are constrained by and expressive of the specific climatic conditions to which they are a response.

Moreover, in engaging in certain activities or making use of an array of equipment in responding to the vicissitudes of nature, we do not, as a whole, devise such measures on the scene and impromptu. Instead we enter into practices and make use of constructions that are already present and that can be deployed against the elements, such as, to use Watsuji's examples, levees, drainage ditches, and charcoal braziers. Our response is a cultural one; such measures show that "we possess an inherited understanding accumulated over many years since the time of our ancestors."[10] And while we inherit this collective rejoinder to nature in an assortment of practices and artifacts—just as we inherit the language we speak, as well as a suite of possible emotional responses and practical dispositions that we can take up—insofar as such cultural forms of reacting to the determinants of the natural world are also an expression of human transcendence, they are not static and unchanging. This means, most significantly for Watsuji, that the content of our self-understanding, and the disclosure of nature to which it is tied, can and does change.

Our capacity to respond to the impositions of nature, in sum, arises from the spatiotemporal structure of human existence. We draw both on the spaces and places of the natural world and on the techniques and technology of an inherited tradition through a productive and temporally unfolding power of creation, one that reveals the link between temporality and transcendence. Hence Watsuji observes that "not only the past but also a *fūdo* are imposed on us. Of course, our existence has a free character in addition to this imposed one. . . . What suffers imposition is at the same time free; in this we are able to see the historical nature of our being."[11]

For Watsuji, this dialectic of freedom and determination within a *fūdo* frames the movement of human history:

> Human beings are not simply burdened with a "past" in general but are burdened with a particular "*fūdo*-based past" [*fūdoteki kako* 風土的過去] such that the general and formal structure of historicity is enriched by a particular substance. . . . But also, this particular substance which is *fūdo*, merely as *fūdo*, is not independent of history since it does not, as it were, enter into history as a substance afterwards. Rather, from the outset there is only "historical *fūdo*." In short, in the historical and *fūdoic* [*fūdoteki* 風土的] double-structure of human being, history is *fūdo-based history* [*fūdoteki rekishi* 風土的歴史] and *fūdo* is *historical fūdo* [*rekishiteki fūdo* 歴史的風土]. Treating history and *fūdo* each in isolation is merely an abstraction from the concrete ground shown above.[12]

There is, in sum, no history without a *fūdo* and no *fūdo* without a history.[13] In the former instance, Watsuji's interest in the nature of the historical past is less in the relation between a natural setting and the multitude of individual events that fill the past than it is in the relation between this setting and the broader cultural developments that emerge from the past. Watsuji's contention in this regard is that tradition, or the presence of the past in the present, is inherently bound up with the places and spaces of the natural world. Thus *fūdo* lies at the ground of both the material scaffolding of a culture and the meanings that have come to be sedimented in its collective way of life: "It goes without saying that—as tools—clothing, food, and shelter assume the character of a *fūdo*; but, even more fundamentally, if the human being is already subjected to the determination imposed by *fūdo* when it apprehends itself, then the form of this *fūdo* cannot but become the *form of this self-understanding*."[14] Culture, in the tangible form of equipment, tools, and artifacts, and in the intangible form of patterns of meaning such as the roles and the self-interpretations that we can take up, always comes to us out of a past whose material ground is nature. Hence the history of one region, for instance, will be inseparable from salt mines and salt traders, that of another from a long tradition of seafaring or from the rich volcanic soil of the surrounding landscape and the class of prosperous smallholders it supports.

While the past, based in *fūdo* and carried into the present in the form of tradition, is experienced as determinative for us, we are able to transcend this determination to some extent, not by leaving behind our culture or *fūdo*—since these are part of the very setting that makes possible human life and activity—but through the production of new equipment and artifacts and the creation of new ways of thinking, and so of speaking, acting, and feeling, all of which, in turn, open up nature in novel ways and thus also furnish new modes of self-understanding. So although there are certain limitations on what can come to be disclosed as a *fūdo* that are imposed by the sheer givenness of particular geospheric conditions, because disclosure has a temporal character, the contents of our experience of nature can change over time. In this sense it can be said that, like human beings, nature has a history.

Take, for example, the landscape of a particular hill chain and the forests and lakes surrounding it. In pre-Christian times this area might have been understood as the abode of the gods. Later, for both the "barbarians" who lived there and the imperial Roman garrison stationed on the other side of its watershed, it is likely to have shown up as an ideal location for defense and concealment. Its sacred character might have been recaptured in the later construction of a medieval monastery complex at its center, though one can imagine that for the young poets and writers who wandered through the ruins of this complex in the Romantic period, a different but perhaps related kind of experience was to be had of the views on offer. Here there would have been a vision of nature as inner source and of God as the current of life running through and striving in nature that emerges as an inner impulse or voice, one that we come to fully know by expressing what we discover within.[15] For later artists, painters, and writers, the aesthetic pleasure that this view provided might simply have been enough. And it is not difficult to envisage how, in the twentieth century, one section of this topography might have been set aside as a recreational area for hiking and for an uphill leg of the Tour de France, with the crests of the hills in this section designated for the use of telecommunications masts and meteorological stations. The area around the ruins of the monastery, meanwhile, might have been transformed into a protected cultural zone, while the rest of the hill chain may have come to be incorporated into a national park system that helps to protect endangered plant and animal species.

Every *fūdo* has a history of this kind, one that depends largely upon the people who inhabit it. And this means that if one people leave or are forced out of a locale and another people come to live in this place, especially if they have come from distant lands and bring with them a very different material and spiritual culture that originated in these places, the history of a *fūdo* can change in thoroughgoing ways. Consider the settler societies of North America, Australasia, and southern Africa, for instance. What comes to be disclosed as nature, as well as the corresponding self-interpretations that have come to be available, are directly linked to this transplanted cultural infrastructure (although not reducible to it, as we have seen). And while this infrastructure eventually registers changes that are brought about by this relation to a new precinct of nature, cultural features that grew out of a very different place stubbornly persist: hence we have the spectacle of nations on these continents blanketed in architectural styles originating in northern Europe or of children in countless homes across the American South awaiting a sleigh-riding, reindeer-driving, chimney-climbing Santa Claus fully equipped for arctic weather. These examples bring to light a related but distinct mode of transcendence in which essential arenas in the continuing life of a culture can take their impetus from and be sustained by something other than the current natural habitat in which a people reside.

In other instances it is not people, but a cultural product that is on the move: the connection between a place and the cultural artifacts created there is, Watsuji notes, by no means absolute. He points to the example of the way the Old Testament, which was born of life in the desert—and which cannot be properly understood without an understanding of the special character of desert life—has cast a spell over Europe for more than a thousand years, or the way the Koran, begotten of the same desert, today maintains a powerful hold over the Indian subcontinent (and, he might have added, Malaysia, Indonesia, Turkey, Africa, and the Balkans).[16]

All of these forms of transcendence appear to open up a certain type of freedom from the determination of nature, but they also share a certain kind of limitation: they are collective structures, events, or processes that operate at the level of the human being in general. That is, this examination has shown that the human being taken collectively and as a whole is able to transcend the *fūdo* in which it finds itself, but it has not shown that this same capacity belongs to the individual human being, to that particular self who must—to be a self at all—take up and give expression to a culture that is inseparable from a particular region of nature.

Watsuji's dialectic of freedom and determination within a *fūdo* seems, in short, too roughly hewn to accommodate both the forms of transcendence that are evident in, for example, the complex identities of immigrants, of those who have lived in multiple countries, of those who live in multiple milieus at the same time (say, for instance, a Turkish-Armenian immigrant in California who has a business in Russia and so spends half of every year there, or a Syrian Indian Christian professor working in Japan who passes her summers in India), of those who develop a very different character from their compatriots even as they live together in the same place, and the idea that *fūdo* in a very important sense literally makes us who we are.

To make sense of such cases while retaining Watsuji's basic insight about the unity of people with their *fūdo*, we also need a subtler account, on a much smaller scale, of the ways the self is both constituted by and is also able to transcend its *fūdo*. In what follows we will give an indication of some of the issues involved that any such account must take into consideration. We saw earlier that certain features of a particular *fūdo*, such its wide open spaces or its location near the sea, its particular scents and colors and flavors and so on, subject me to a sense that sediments over time into a sense for or taste for something, that is, into a sensibility, as well as helps to shape a particular perspective on and orientation toward the world. Thus Watsuji maintains that the land one grows up on, and continues to live on, affects one to the very bottom of one's existence. He observes that those who move away from a place for a long time lose the whole wondrous sense of and absorption in a particular *fūdo* in the same way that those who leave their land at a very young age lose their native language. This sense of place, however, is given only over time. If you take a person out of a place early enough in life (such as in the case of international adoption), who one becomes (and can become) can change radically.[17] On the other hand, if I move to another *fūdo* far removed from my own later in life, I bring with me a particular sense for things derived from my time in this earlier milieu. (This phenomenon is captured in the various versions of the old adage that you can take a person out of a place, but you can't take a place out of a person.) Nevertheless the very receptivity that made possible this process of sedimentation can be understood as that which also opens me up to the acquisition of new and different preferences and tastes acquired from living in another *fūdo*. This adds yet another layer of sedimentation to my sensibility, and may even break up or transform and enrich earlier layers.

Another form of distance and difference between self and *fūdo* becomes apparent when we consider that the interwoven natural and cultural texture of any *fūdo* is so dense and fertile that that the receptivity or openness of the self to what is encountered requires a direction or tendency such that one feature rather than another of what surrounds us exerts a stronger influence on us, so that we come to identify with one aspect of the natural and cultural topography we find ourselves amid rather than another. One person, for example, may identify more strongly with the sensibility of the Deep South of the United States (and hence come to understand herself above all as a southerner), whereas someone else might be far more powerfully shaped by a particular geographical landscape in the same region and the opportunities for certain leisure activities it affords, so that he comes to see himself first and foremost as a fly fisherman, for example. What seems to be decisive here is the way one thing rather than another strikes the imagination, prompting one to bring some circles of sense in one's environment closer to the self rather than others. Hence the strong identification with one aspect of one's milieu rather than another shows that the self is much more than the simple expression of its *fūdo*. This form of transcendence, I suggest, can be studied with profit as an instance of what Watsuji calls the individual dimension of human beings.

III. Overcoming Subjectivism: Disclosure as Mediation

In our account of the human capacity for transcendence, we have been careful not to exaggerate the distance between self and nature, which is never absolute. This has enabled us to show that the subjectivity of the self cannot be reduced to the objectivity of nature, even as they are united in a continuous whole. A parallel conception of the difference between self and nature also plays a decisive role in thwarting the reduction of the objectivity of nature to the subjectivity of the self in the phenomenon of disclosure.

The previous chapter devoted much time and philosophical energy to showing that our perceptual experience of *fūdo*, or *fūdosei*, must be understood as the *disclosure* of nature. Yet something difficult, but essential, still seems to elude our grasp in all of this—namely, how we are to make full sense of the claim that it is nature itself that is encountered in the event of disclosure. How can I know that it is nature per se—rather than a subjective construal of nature—that appears in my experience of a given *fūdo*? After all, given that a *fūdosei* presents itself phenomenologically as an encounter with a living reality laden with qualities and values, the best and most parsimonious explanation would seem to be that these appearances are the result of subjective interpretations of, or projections onto, facts that are themselves neutral or indifferent.

One of the main objections to this kind of explanation is that it assumes the "real" world is a qualitatively featureless and neutral domain of entities existing in themselves that shows up to the external and disengaged standpoint of science, a domain onto which qualities and values are then projected or out of which they are constructed. Yet, as I have tried to show, even if the standpoint of science arrives at a certain kind of objectively valid knowledge of the world, this achievement does not entail an objectivist ontology of this kind. Moreover any projectivist explanation of our experience of qualities and values is confronted with the dilemma that one will have to use such terms in one's explanation of what is being projected, which then does not so easily allow one to explain away the term in question.[18] As Margaret Little puts it, "It is very difficult to explain the entire practice of using Ø without seeing some things as, in fact, Ø."[19]

Even if these difficulties do not, finally, prove insuperable for attempts to explain (away) how our lived experience of nature appears to the first-person point of view, projectivist explanations still presuppose a dualistic framework in which a subject projects characteristics onto the objects it faces. On Watsuji's view, of course, there is no such separation of the elements of experience: the subject is united with the objects of experience through its intentional comportments. Insofar as intentional comportments are inseparable from what is disclosed through them, the role that such stances play in any perception is decisive; disclosure is nonetheless not a result of the constructive activity of the subject. Instead the richness and depth of our experience is a consequence of what is disclosed to the practical, affective, and linguistic comportments of the subject of that experience, rather than of the projection of qualities and values onto the entities we encounter.

This understanding of disclosure as the process of mediating a dimension of meaning that belongs to the things themselves is a conception that is already found in and required by the very idea of *fūdo*. Insofar as *fūdosei*—or *fūdo* as it is experienced and lived through—is the disclosure of nature, we have to understand ourselves as rooted in the particularity and specificity of a region of nature, one that transcends our perception in its otherness and its resistance, shaping and constraining what can be disclosed, since nature must already be given for it to be lived through and hence opened up and made manifest *as* something or other. And to the extent that consciousness is not simply coextensive with the whole of nature, there is always something of nature that does not show itself, something that remains hidden or withdrawn. Yet that part of nature which does appear in experience is not simply a sheer, unmediated givenness; on Watsuji's view, something can appear as "some" thing only insofar as it already possesses a certain sense or meaning that is disclosed by activity, affectivity, and language. Disclosure is thus neither merely the result of the positing activity of the subject, nor is it an annunciation of the object, a self-giving of the thing in its total and univocal meaning. Instead the appearances, as grasped in these modes of apprehension, are always already mediated.

Nonetheless there seems to be a certain tension here between, on the one hand, the claim that the things of nature have a meaning of their own—one that we must accommodate—and the idea, on the other, that we never encounter the meanings of things independently of the way our practical, affective, and linguistic comportments present them to us. This difficulty can be overcome if we accept that meanings reside in things, but view our comportment as that which brings out and completes these meanings so that things are able to be encountered as what they are. Comportments are thus disclosive insofar as in presenting or articulating the intelligible sense of a thing, they allow us to grasp its meaning, and so to understand it *as* something or other. This entails that things appear in our experience "as" what they are because of our comportments toward them, but *not* that things depend on these comportments to appear or become manifest at all; this would be patently absurd, since obviously some version of the things I encounter can appear to infants, animals, and people from other cultures who do not share my language or the relevant emotions or practices. We can compare such instances to the way something can be disclosed to perception but is still not fully intelligible, such as the manner in which we experience an object or implement belonging to an unfamiliar culture. In this case, we lack the words and practices to understand what we are seeing, so that the thing does not appear *as* what it is. Thus the idea is not that comportments disclose *simpliciter,* but that by articulating the intelligibility of things, they more fully disclose them as what they are.

Each of the forms of shared comportment we have treated recapitulates this general format. At the level of practical comportments, what is articulated and understood is the dimension of practical intelligibility that belongs to things. So, as Merleau-Ponty has shown, the potential actions of the body, by forming an intentional arc toward the world, illuminate the possible actions that can be taken in it. Our basic directedness toward the world in terms of our possible projects and activities means that every act of perception on our part is already intentionally related to a perceived world through the capacities of the body. If the body is able to do something, such as climb or swim, things in the world show up as able to be climbed up or swum in. Thus it is because I can ski that the snow shows up as ski snow and the mountain shows up as possessing slopes for skiing. Though this form of practical intelligibility belongs to the snow and to the mountain itself, it is a *nascent* dimension of sense, that is, one that only fully appears through and is brought out by the capacities, skills, and knowledge sedimented in the body.

While this kind of disclosure to perception of a meaning that belongs to things depends upon the capacities of the body, it also relies on the emotions and moods that are evoked by what is perceived. Here it is the values and qualities that belong to the things of the world—rather than the practical sense of a thing—that come to presentation more fully or are disclosed in a more complete way to perceptual experience. Unlike our practical comportments, however, our emotions and moods are directly elicited by and so function as responses to a situation they at the same time help to interpret or compose. So although something in a scene can "speak" to certain emotions, such that feelings are reactions to a phenomenon that presents itself in a certain way, this response is also a mode of cognition that grasps and more fully discloses the thing as what it is. Our feelings of wonder or awe are elicited by the view of a canyon from above, for instance, even as these emotions articulate and so make fully present the grandeur that resides in the scene. On the other hand, this coupling of feeling and perception also enables us to experience, to take Watsuji's examples, the monotony and dullness in a succession of cloudy days or in the dragging along, month after month, of the shriveling cold and cutting wind of winter.[20] "Such characteristics of climate," Watsuji says, "are intertwined with the depth of our experiences far more than we realize."[21]

This understanding of disclosure as the expressive articulation and so completion of an intelligibility that inheres in things is matched perhaps most readily to the linguistic dimension of our experience of the world. Linguistically structured comportments, like practical and affective ones, disclose by articulating or expressing the sense or meaning of a thing, so that it appears *as* something or other. Watsuji's depictions of the climate and flora he encountered in his travels are a good illustration of the way linguistically structured perceptions cohere with, present, and complete the meanings that things have. To take but one of his examples: while the climate of a certain region might be characterized by that peculiar interrelation of heat and humidity that supports the dense vegetation distinctive to the area, it is the constant overlapping of thought (in the shape of the words that pass through our minds) and perception as we make our way through the landscape that shows the surrounding foliage as luxuriant but also as wild, promiscuous, and disordered.[22]

This discussion has shown that perception is never the simple mirroring of what is present; it always includes and involves meaning, and so the understanding of something "as" something. Inasmuch as things are understood rather than simply given, there is no pure, immediate, or uninterpreted given: the given is always mediated. But to the extent that things are given at all, the way they are is not something that is up to us; things are not arrayed before us as mute sense data onto which we would then project our own meanings. They have a being and a meaning of their own that guides and constrains the way they come to presentation. Thus the claim that the given is always already understood turns out to mean that the given is always an interpretation, but that this interpretation, insofar as it is made possible by an intelligibility that belongs to the world, just *is* an appearance of the thing itself.

Watsuji himself does not, of course, bring the notions of perception and interpretation, mediation and articulation, together in this way. Yet we must interpret his notion of disclosure in this manner if we are to make sense of his claims about the ontological significance of *fūdo*. The precise nature of this significance can be elucidated more fully by clarifying the relationship between *fūdo* and *fūdosei*. I propose that each be seen as a particular dimension of an ontology of lived experience. More specifically, a *fūdo* can be understood as a domain of possibility that is actualized as *fūdosei*. As such a condition of possibility, a *fūdo* is characterized—most importantly—by intelligible properties (such as practical significance and qualities and values like beauty, gracefulness, ugliness, serenity, danger, sublimity, etc.) that depend on a subject to experience them. And although these subject-related properties, as qualitative and normative entities (including those that express practical imperatives) elicit actions and attitudes, they are not any less real than entities that are not subject-dependent. This is because such properties can be understood as objects of awareness brutely *there* to be experienced, and so as constituting a part of the world to which we are sensitive.

In this regard it can be said that each *fūdo* possesses a nascent intelligibility that is completed in the experience of those who encounter it. This appears as and in the concrete character of a region of nature as lived through, or what Watsuji calls *fūdosei*. *Fūdosei*, then, is neither objective nor subjective, but arises as a coproduction of human beings and the *fūdo* they inhabit. Each of these interactional domains represents local variants on the lifeworldy dimension of nature, a dimension whose robust ontological status is a consequence of the broader philosophical promotion of lived experience to an ultimate ontological horizon.

IV. Overcoming Subjectivism: Nondualism

In some ways the underlying worry about subjectivism remains relatively untouched by these considerations, since on this account the appearances are mediated through comportments that belong to us, such that they are the result of our interpretive and so in this sense "subjective" construals. That is, despite all that we have said about the capacity of our practical, affective, and linguistic engagements to disclose the natural world, it is still *we* who open up and disclose it. One might wonder how it is that these modes of comportment, which are part of *our* way of being in the world, can constitutively articulate the things of nature as what *they* are. Hence the question remains: How can we know that the way nature appears to us through our disclosive stances is not a "mere" appearance in the pejorative sense, that is, a misrepresentation of things from our standpoint rather than the advent of nature itself?

The difficulty here is that to know whether we can take our experience of nature at face value, we would need to be able to step outside of our modes of disclosure, namely, our language, our affectivity, our body, and our actions and practices, in order to compare the intelligibility that belongs to nature with the way we have disclosively articulated that intelligibility. Since this is not possible, it also seems impossible to ever know whether we have successfully crossed the gap between nature and the way it appears to us.

Watsuji himself seems not to have thought that this kind of subjectivism posed a serious philosophical difficulty for the concept of *fūdo*. His descriptive accounts of the various *fūdo* of the world take our lived experience of nature at face value without explanation or justification. One reason for this may have been that this sort of subjectivism relies on the kind of dualist presuppositions Watsuji rejects in his critique of objectivism. Moreover two of the most important sources of Watsuji's thinking, namely, the Buddhist metaphysics of nondualism and Heidegger's phenomenology, cast serious doubt, in different ways, on the viability of various forms of dualism. Watsuji nonetheless seems to lean on these sources without a substantive account of how the recovery of the lifewordly dimension of nature must be linked to the reunion of the subjective and objective poles of experience that is achieved in these respective philosophical positions. To compensate for this shortcoming, we will attempt to construct the outlines of just such an account here, explicitly setting out what appears to have been mostly implicit in Watsuji's thinking about these questions.

To move past the serious obstacles posed by the problem of subjectivism, we will need to take a wider view of the issues here and bring into view the ground that makes possible the unveiling of nature in our linguistic, affective, and practical modes of disclosure. For Watsuji, this ground is ontological and is found in the belonging together of self and nature. We have already seen how self and *fūdo* constitute and depend on one another through self-understanding and disclosure. But Watsuji indicates that there is also another and quite different sense in which self and nature form a relational whole, namely, as moments within a more basic and encompassing reality. It is extremely difficult for us to recognize and grasp this profound unity of the self with the space of nature that environs it, since what is in reality a single, undivided scene has come to be divided into two separate and distinct entities through a process of abstraction: "It is only by adding predetermined abstractions to what is in fact a concrete scene or landscape [*keikan* 景観] that we are able to extract a 'nature' which stands opposed to 'human beings.' "[23] In short, for Watsuji not only is it the case that human beings and nature interlace and are continuous with one another in the acts of perception and self-apprehension; they also belong together as aspects of a single, unitary ontological phenomenon.

Watsuji approaches this idea from two distinct directions. On one side, he depicts this unity in terms of the Buddhist metaphysics of nondualism; from the other side, he draws on the philosophical language and concepts of Heideggerean phenomenology in order to reveal the continuity of subject and object at the ground of our experience of nature. In the former instance, the bulk of Watsuji's attention and energy is taken up, in his work as an intellectual historian of Buddhism, with the problem of subject-object dualism and, in his philosophical work proper, with the relation between self and other. Notwithstanding this, he does come to specifically address the nondual structure of the relation between self

and nature, albeit in a limited way. There are two examples of this in particular that I want to examine because, taken together, they show the way
Watsuji links the nondualism of self and nature to an ontology of lived
experience. In the first example, which is taken from *Ethics*, he maintains
that in the perception of a beautiful flower, the beauty of the flower cannot be explained by reducing it to one of the physical constituents of
experience that show up to the scientific standpoint. He suggests that
this is because this beauty is the truth of the flower, and this truth has a
nondual ground:

> A natural form's being beautiful has no relation or connection to the
> nature of natural science. No matter how much research in botanical
> science advances, no matter how minutely developed research in the
> physics of light and color becomes, the *beauty* of a flower cannot be
> explained. This is because the *way* that a flower is beautiful is based on
> human existence; it is not a property of a thing called a "flower" which
> is separate from human existence. Rather, in the feeling of a flower's
> beauty, human beings receive their own existence as coming forth
> from the origin of this flower. If a poet or artist captures this beauty
> and artistically crystallizes it, then although the flower here is not a
> natural object, but rather something whose *color and form alone* he or
> she is concerned to depict, this on the contrary opens up the true life
> of the flower.[24]

Watsuji's enigmatic reference in this passage to the link between
the mode of existence of a beautiful flower and human existence points
to the nondual ground that unites human beings and nature. While he
does not expand on this idea here, in *The Practical Philosophy of Early Buddhism* he uses the same example to show that the unity and continuity in
experience between purportedly subjective and objective elements are
founded on this ground. In his commentary on the Buddhist concept
of sensation (*vedanā*) in this text, he analyzes the nature of perceptual
experience and contends that perception has a holistic character. When
we perceive, we perceive whole things rather than isolated sensations, and
this is an encounter that always has an affective or emotional tone. He
illustrates this point with a phenomenological description of the perception of a flower, pointing out that this experience never simply consists
in the bare sensation of elements such as color or shape; we always perceive a particular flower, and we always perceive it as a whole. Moreover,
because perception always already includes affective feeling, feelings are
not, as an objectivist ontology would have it, psychological entities possessed by subjects that subsequently add emotional color to objects that

are "really" neutral. Feelings do not simply issue from the subject—they are also determined by the object:

> With regard to feelings that exist as psychological entities, for example in the experience of the feeling of the beauty of an objectively existing flower, it is not the case that this flower is actually neither beautiful nor ugly; in this example this flower is already beautiful. It is not possible to experience a flower that is *not* beautiful as beautiful. Concretely, the *way* in which a beautiful flower *exists*, and the *experience* of feeling the beauty of that flower are one and the same. We first are able to consider "feeling" as a psychological entity when we pull these elements apart into the subjective and the objective in an abstract fashion.[25]

Watsuji shows that from the standpoint of metaphysical nondualism, our perceptual encounter with a beautiful flower cannot be reduced to either the subjective or the objective pole of experience. Rather our perception of a flower's beauty and the mode of existence of a beautiful flower must be grasped as two aspects of the same phenomenon.

These examples underscore the way metaphysical nondualism challenges the commonly accepted dichotomy between fact and value. This distinction is usually made in terms of facts that are viewed as "out there" in the world and objective, and values that are seen as "inside" the mind and subjective. For the metaphysics of nondualism, however, facts and values cannot be pulled apart in this way, since this construal of values as internal and subjective, and facts as external and objective, maps onto the distinction between inner and outer that is entailed by a subject-object ontology.

V. Overcoming Subjectivism: Phenomenology

Given the philosophical and conceptual richness of metaphysical non-dualism and the alternatives it opens up to an approach that objectifies nature, it comes as a surprise to find that Watsuji did not explicitly draw much further on this theory in developing the concept of *fūdo*. One explanation for this might be that—as multiple commentators have suggested—Watsuji was not, fundamentally, a religious thinker. In this instance, at least, he does not engage in a sustained way with Buddhist philosophy, preferring instead to use the philosophical language of phenomenology to argue for the ontological unity of self and nature. This can be seen in what is perhaps the most well-known passage in *Fūdo*, in which he illustrates the sense in which self and nature are continuous with and belong to one another with an analysis of the ordinary experience of feeling chilly on a cold day: "That we feel cold is a clear and indisputable fact for anyone. But what is this coldness? Is it that air at a certain temperature, i.e., cold air as a physical object, stimulates the sensory organs in our bodies, and we as psychological subjects experience it as a certain mental state? . . . But is this really the case? How can we know the independent existence of coldness *before we feel cold?* This is impossible. It is *through* the experience of feeling cold that we discover coldness."[26] Watsuji contends that the phenomenon of coldness and the subject who experiences it do not exist as separate and independent entities. Rather we discover coldness in feeling it, and we feel cold through an intentional relationship to coldness. Yet viewing the cold as an intentional object would seem to suggest that coldness is solely a moment of subjective experience. Coldness, however, is not a merely subjective feeling; it is an objective entity that transcends the subject. This impasse raises the question of how the subjective sensation of feeling cold can establish a relation with the transcendent entity that is the coldness of the outside air. From Watsuji's viewpoint, this question involves a misunderstanding of the nature of the intentional object:

The intentional object is not some kind of psychological content. Therefore, objective coldness, and coldness as an independent experience, are not intentional objects. When we *feel* the cold, we do not feel the "sensation" of coldness, rather we directly *feel* the "chilliness of the air" or "the cold." In other words, the cold "felt" within intentional bodily experience is not "something subjective" [*shukanteki na mono* 主観的なもの] but "something objective" [*kyakkanteki na mono* 客観的なもの]. It may be said, therefore, that the intentional "relation" itself of *feeling* the cold is already a relation to the chilliness of the air. The cold air as a transcendent entity is first constituted only in this intentionality. Therefore, the problem of how the feeling of coldness relates to the external coldness of the air does not arise in the first place. Considered in this manner, the distinction between subject and object and hence the distinction related to this between a "we" and "cold air" existing independently of each other involves a certain misunderstanding. When we *feel* cold, we ourselves already dwell in the coldness of the outside air. Our coming into relation with the cold means nothing other than that we ourselves are *out* in the cold. In this sense, as Heidegger emphasizes, our way of being is characterized by "standing out" (*ex-sistere*) and, therefore, intentionality. . . . When the *cold* is discovered from the *outset*, we ourselves are already out in the cold. So that which is most primordially "being outside" is not a "thing" or "object" like the cold air, but we ourselves. "Standing out" is a fundamental determination [*konponteki kitei* 根本的規定] of our own structure, and intentionality is also founded on this.[27]

These passages are intended to show that our experience of nature is neither a purely subjective nor a purely objective phenomenon, because Dasein's existence as "standing out" collapses the distinction between inner and outer. Watsuji recognizes that Heidegger's breakthrough here was in showing that insofar as Dasein exists "out there," beyond itself and in the world, such that it extends into a world that extends into it, experience is never purely internal or external, subjective or objective, but rather is always a single scene in which these dimensions are unified. On this view, the coldness of the air and my being cold are not to be understood as an interaction between two completely separate and distinct entities, namely, a subject who has an inner experience (coldness) of an external, objective phenomenon (the cold); they are two aspects of the same, single, unitary phenomenon.

Like other thinkers in the phenomenological tradition, Watsuji discovers in the close description of lived experience something difficult, elusive, and strange. Yet he does not, as he had in his account of the dual structure of the human being as individual and social, enter headlong into the dialectical intricacies of articulating what he finds. Nonetheless the philosophical restraint—or caution—he exercises here did not come without a cost: something very significant remains unsaid, and perhaps unthought, which bears directly on the relation between human beings and nature.

This can be brought out without entering in a comprehensive way into the intricacies of Heidegger's philosophy on this particular point; we will follow Watsuji's example by instead building on what seems essential in Heidegger. At the same time, we will need to venture far beyond anything Watsuji himself offers by way of explanation with respect to these questions. We can begin by returning to Watsuji's example and posing a question about it: If being cold is an experience that cannot be explained in dualistic terms, how are we to explain it? How, indeed, can we account for any experience (and hence consciousness or subjectivity) within the framework of the ontological unity and continuity between subject and object? To answer this, I suggest we briefly turn at this point to the philosophy of Merleau-Ponty and bring concepts from his work together with what we have gained from Heidegger, because Merleau-Ponty's account highlights something crucial about the structure of experience that is less obvious in Heidegger, namely, that the belonging together of subject and object constitutes a unity, but that—as in the logic of nondualism—this unity (to borrow Nishida's phrase) is a continuity of discontinuity.

Merleau-Ponty's work is in many ways a development of Heidegger's thought; he too, gives an account of experience in terms of the intertwining and so indivisibility of self and world, bringing new insights, arguments, and evidence to elucidate what he calls, following Heidegger, *être au monde*. Most of these are directed toward the development of his great insight that the body has a central role in the interweaving of subject and object by constituting the primordial world of perception. But the philosophical attention he gives to the body has more than merely epistemological significance; he also discovers in the body, and so in the very way we exist, a form of ontological continuity between the self and the world.

This continuity is a relation of difference within unity and is paradigmatically disclosed in the experience of perception. Merleau-Ponty observes in this regard that in the phenomenon of doubling and reversibility in tactile and visual sensation we have the bodily experience of being both a subject for ourselves and a thing in the world. When my hands are clasped together, my body both feels and is the felt object; it is in an ambiguous situation in which it can alternate the roles of touching and being touched. There is an essential reversibility in this ability of what Merleau-Ponty calls the *body-subject* to move between being subject and being object.[28] This is also true of the body-subject seeing itself, since in visual experience it can be both seer and seen. Nevertheless, touching and touched, seer and seen do not coincide. There is in perception and necessary to it a dehiscence or fission of the self from the world. For perception to take place, there must be an *écart*, a gap, between what perceives and what is perceived, since perceiving something is distinct from being it.[29]

At the same time, touching and touched and seer and seen are also united in having their source in one and the same body-subject. The self in this regard just *is* the world. Furthermore, the self can also be identified with the world in another sense, namely, insofar as the world, as Merleau-Ponty puts it, "is made of the very stuff of the body."[30] It is this continuity between my own flesh and that of the world, moreover, that makes possible the very activities of touching and seeing, since touching and seeing require hands and eyes that are themselves part of the visible and tangible world.[31] Our organs and powers of perception belong to the things perceived.

In his late writings, Merleau-Ponty maintains that these continuities take the form of an originating event of sense, one that is ontologically more primordial than either a sense-giving subject or a sense-bearing object, both of which are abstractions from an original unitary dimension of what he calls the "flesh" (*la chair*). This is a unity composed of difference, such that while perception is an opening onto a world that it simultaneously belongs to and emerges from, this continuity will not mean that the self perfectly coincides with things, since then there would be no experience at all. Rather the subject is interwoven with the world while nonetheless also being a divergence or gap (*écart*) in the being of the whole that makes possible its experiential presence to things. We are an opening onto the world that must itself be understood as part of and continuous with that very same world. As Merleau-Ponty puts it in quoting Valéry, perception is the "flaw" in the great diamond of the world.[32]

In order to uncover the significance of this claim for our narrower concerns about the relation between self and nature, we have to grasp the radical, even uncanny conception of experience that is being advanced here: in conceiving experience as an opening within the unity and continuity of subject and object, Merleau-Ponty understands the embodied subject of sensible perception as the spacing or distance in which the world gives itself to itself in and through us. Here we can draw a parallel to Heidegger's radical rethinking of the human as that which holds opens the site for the appearance of being. Because Dasein *is* its disclosure in this way, we can understand experience as the appearance of the world within the openness that I am.

Watsuji for his part does not appear to have been aware of Merleau-Ponty's work, and that part of Heidegger's thought that most closely resembles Merleau-Ponty's late ontology of the flesh is found in ideas that only come clear in writings after *Being and Time*. Had he been in contact with either of these sources, Watsuji would have been able to set out the relation between self and nature in the wake of what is opened up by the later Heidegger and Merleau-Ponty, while circumscribing its focus. Since "nature" for Watsuji includes human nature, the self is not a transcendent or Promethean figure standing above or outside of nature; it is an immanent agent that participates in nature, one part of nature acting on another. Unlike Heidegger and Merleau-Ponty, however, Watsuji does not enter into what this relational structure entails for the way we understand experience, and in this case, the experience of nature. Yet if, as I have argued, experience is an event of disclosure understood as a gap or break that belongs to and remains within a wider whole, then in our encounter with nature as *fūdo*, it can be said that this experience is the disclosure of a nature that presents *itself* to us.

VI. The Fullness of Nature

The implications of this account of the disclosure of nature are immense. Insofar as our capacity to perceive belongs to the things perceived, the comportments and dispositions that realize these capacities can also be said to belong to what they would disclose. And if, as I have tried to show, this process of disclosure articulates and so completes a nascent intelligibility that belongs to things, then what is encountered and perceived through the sentiments, language, and practices that belong to a culture is never only or merely a culturally constructed image of nature. Furthermore, because nature as it appears in the lifeworld, namely, as a richly concrete and living reality, is disclosed through these shared comportments, it can be said that our lived experience of nature is the very face of nature itself. If nature can be identified in this manner with the way it appears to us in the first-person standpoint, namely, as alive and expressive, as meaningful and replete with particular qualities and values, then what is promised in the concept of *fūdo* is nothing less than the partial reenchantment of nature.

Notwithstanding the conceptual ambition of this sweeping vision and its aspiration to grasp human perception from the standpoint of the whole, there is a final objection to this attempt to identify nature with the way it appears—one that can be developed in another direction. And this is that what we experience as nature cannot be part of what nature "really" is, because the entities that compose this aspect of nature, the colors, properties, characteristics, qualities, and values we attribute to and perceive in it, depend on a subject to apprehend them in order to be what they are. While this point presupposes the equation of objectivity, or that which can be understood independently of human sensibility, with reality, we have already been given reason enough to mistrust such a straightforward equivalence. The rejection of ontological objectivism, however, is not limited to thinkers in the phenomenological tradition. John McDowell, to take an important example, has criticized the equation of that which exists independently of human perception, or mind independently, with reality, on the grounds that there are certain phenomena, such as so-called secondary qualities, that are not intelligible except from within the standpoint of a particular point of view, so that the attempt to account for or make intelligible all of reality from an objective, third-person point of view must fail.

McDowell claims, for instance, that what the color red *is* is not conceivable independently of the way the color red *looks*, and the way a color looks is not something that can be fully explained from a third-person standpoint by giving an exact account of the reflectancy of the object, that is, its disposition to absorb certain wavelengths of light and reflect others. We can see this if we consider that what the color red *is* cannot be made intelligible to a blind person in this way. Knowing the way the color red looks requires one to occupy a certain point of view. This undermines a projectivist explanation of color as well, since one would need to isolate what a color is from how it looks in order to identify it as that element which is seen from a third-person point of view as being projected.[33]

The problem, then, is that color cannot be accounted for by a more encompassing explanation from an objective standpoint, yet our experience presents it as something that is part of the world to which we are sensitive. McDowell thinks that we can take this experience at face value if we understand colors (as well as other secondary qualities) as a special kind of dispositional property of objects. On this construal, colors and other secondary qualities would be properties that have the power to produce certain perceptual states in observers with the appropriate sensory apparatus under suitable conditions, and they would not be intelligible apart from sentient responses to them; that is, they are subject-dependent: "Thus an object's being red is understood as something that obtains in virtue of the object's being such as (in certain circumstances) to look, precisely, red." Moreover "an object's being such as to look red is independent of its actually looking red to anyone on any particular occasion; so notwithstanding the conceptual connection between being red and being experienced as red, an experience of something as red can count as a case of being presented with a property that is there anyway—there independently of the experience itself,"[34] though not independent of our sensibility. A red object continues to be red even if the lights are turned off or the person in the presence of the object is color-blind.[35] Such properties qualify as real because they are, as one commentator on McDowell puts it, "fully describable without reference to any effect had on a particular occasion to a particular sentient being."[36]

In the same way that our perceptual experience gives us color and other secondary qualities as if they were features of things, our experience of nature presents us with aesthetic and other kinds of qualities and values as if these were part of the very "fabric of the world."[37] And just as in the case of color, we have good reason to take these experiences at face value, that is, to treat the phenomenal appearances of these qualities and values as subject-dependent yet real properties. This is because the failure of projectivist and narrow, naturalistically reductivist accounts of such experiences is a failure to conceive of these concrete phenomena independently of the way they appear, namely, as either purely naturalistic determinants of human responses or as all-too-human projections onto neutral objects.[38] This is very good evidence that, like color, these entities are not something "really" different from the way they look to an involved observer.

While McDowell's argument allows us to see how it is possible for subject-dependent entities to count as real, and this provides a philosophical justification for taking our experience of nature at face value, I want to both draw on and go beyond this to develop a related but different idea. The example of color allows us to enter into the issues involved here with special clarity. McDowell demonstrated that what a color is, is not fully captured by the language of electromagnetic radiation, the language of an external, scientific standpoint; to know what a color is, one must know the way it looks. What a color *is* cannot be distinguished from the way it *appears*. Yet everything that can be perceived would seem to be governed by a similar logic, though in the case of entities that are not dispositional properties of objects, the connection between the appearance of a thing and its "whatness," or what it is, is less rigorous.[39] A sequoia tree, a cubic foot of hydrogen sulfide gas, and a river agate exist as what they are independently of human perception. But a complete description of what each of these things is must include reference to the shape and size of the tree, the smell of the gas, and the smoothness of the stone, and this suggests that each of these entities exists most fully or completely only *as* what it is in being perceived.

Watsuji appears to have been on the cusp of establishing the same point when he showed that our experience of coldness and the coldness of the air cannot be separated from one another in dualistic fashion into subjective and objective components. The temperature of the air does not depend upon its being perceived to exist, but to fully be what it is in this instance, namely, cold air, it must enter into someone's experience. The distinction here is between *temperature*, which no one feels, and *coldness*, which, as Watsuji put it, "as a transcendent entity is first constituted only in the intentional relation."[40]

So on the view I wish to argue for, experience is central to reality insofar as that part of reality that can be perceived is most fully what it is only in appearing to consciousness. This is not to say that this aspect of reality requires experience, but only that it is somehow incomplete and not fully what it is without the perception of it such that it can make an appearance. This means that the first-person standpoint, or the viewpoint of consciousness, is the dimension in which certain aspects of reality come most fully into being through the event of perception. And this, in turn, entails the thought that consciousness is an essential part of reality itself rather than a contingent bonanza, a superfluous addition to the world.

There is a final set of considerations that lend additional support to the idea that the reality of our world is emergent rather than sheerly and objectively *there*, already complete in itself, that it comes most fully into being in unfolding with and through the active participation of human and animal perception. And this is the irreducible plurality and almost gratuitous variety of the dimensions in the sensible givenness of things, from visual, tactile, olfactory, auditory, and gustatory, to the thermal, magnetic, electrical, and gravitational planes of sensible experience. It is as if the things of the world were made to be seen, touched, tasted, smelled, heard, and felt. And if the notion of purposiveness here is taken in a metaphorical sense, this impression is one that is consonant with the relational ontology of nondualism: like everything else, that which can be perceived is—and can be what it is—only in relation to other things, including a relation to beings that can experience them. It is not that for such things being is equivalent to being perceived; it is that to fully or completely be, for them, is to be perceived. They depend on us in that they rely on our perception of them to appear, and so to be fully what they are. If we return with this revision of our ordinary understanding of experience to the question of the relation between self and *fūdo*, the fuller ontological significance of the claim that a *fūdo* depends upon the self to be disclosed now becomes clearer. And this is that nature as it is experienced and lived through—nature reenchanted—is what nature most fully is.

Conclusion

In seeking out the unities that emerge in our experience of the human and natural worlds, Watsuji has shown how the natural and the cultural are interwoven in a setting that is partly constitutive of and partly constituted and opened up by a group of people inhabiting a particular place. Such ontological commitments mean that we need to somehow think nature together with culture, and the self as what belongs to, emerges from, and shapes this matrix.

The manner in which culture comes together with and opens up nature in the concept of *fūdo* endows the lifeworldly dimension of nature with a kind of ontological dignity, returning us to a richer, premodern conception of experience, one that restores a certain fullness to being. This rehabilitation of the appearances is a restitution, a philosophical rejoinder to the kind of scientism and objectivism that can be traced back to the achievement of a specific form of objectively valid knowledge by the scientific rationalism of the early modern period. In this new dispensation, no loss has been felt more keenly than the loss of our orientation in the lifeworld. Thus the idea that we must take the appearances seriously goes against the grain of centuries of philosophic and scientific thought; it is a remarkable claim with profound implications for our view of reality when we consider the sorts of things we find in the appearances, such as moral and aesthetic qualities and values. This return to the *Lebenswelt* thus also makes possible a return to a partially reenchanted nature, and so holds out the promise of a reconciliation with the world—one that answers our striving to be at home in it.

In other, very significant ways, however, we already belong to the world. Watsuji's conception of nature as the matrix of the self shows that the self is inconceivable apart from the natural world that surrounds it and in which it inheres. This constitutive unity of the self with its *fūdo*, moreover, has novel and important implications for contemporary concerns about the troubled relationship between human beings and nature. One of the major themes to emerge in response to this crisis is a rethinking of our place in the world such that we come to see ourselves as part of the wider community of nature. Yet the argument can be made that the concept of "nature" is too general for a lived and experiential sense of our continuity with the dynamic and concrete natural environment in which we are embedded. Here I suggest we can look to Watsuji's notion of the self as constituted by its immersion in a specific locale, which places nature in relation to the self at a level that allows us to see *how* the self is continuous with nature: my tastes and preferences for certain foods, certain kinds of weather, certain colors, certain leisure activities, certain experiences, and so on, that help make me who I am, all arise from the *fūdo* in which I live. In this way my self is engulfed by and emerges as an expression of my *fūdo*; if I can come to see this clearly, I can perhaps more fully identify with and feel the imperative to care for the local natural environment in which I have my very being. To speak instead of a relation to nature as a whole can be a subtle way of distancing ourselves from it; it certainly can be difficult to see how I can care for or experience an ethical obligation toward something so vast and abstract.

The phenomenon of climate change illustrates especially well the concrete and practical implications for ethical life of the idea that who I am is tied directly to *where* I am and where I have been. This issue has been examined by Bruce Janz explicitly in connection with Watsuji's concept of *fūdo* to introduce a useful and relatively novel element into the climate change discussion. Janz contends that the notion of *fūdo* shifts the ground beneath the discussion of how an ethics of climate should be formulated. The prevailing tendency is to see climate ethics as a form of environmental ethics, although this subfield then faces the same difficulties and impasses in environmental ethics concerning the grounds on and extent to which nonhuman entities can be objects of ethical concern. Janz sees that the concept of *fūdo* demonstrates that "it is also possible to think of climate ethics not as a form of environmental ethics, but rather, to conceive of climate as a different object of reflection. Or, put more carefully, perhaps not an object of ethical reflection, but a context of ethical reflection, a place that frames ethics itself."[1] This is so because the notion of *fūdo* enables us to see that natural environments—and their climates and geographies above all—afford ways of being. These shape the structure of cities and schedules, buildings and interactions, as well as the structure of ideas, habits, and values.

Given that climate change alters such a milieu, Janz points out that what is damaged or lost when climate is damaged or lost are not only biological and physical characteristics of the planet, such as the reduction or loss of species or habitats, but also that "ecology of concepts and experiences" that underwrites and animates a collective way of life. Hence the disappearance of certain climates reduces the diversity of *fūdos* and thus the range of possible spaces in which new and different kinds of human experiences, values, concepts, and forms of life can emerge.

Because there is no way to adequately compensate for this kind of destruction—the kind of damage and loss here is not only environmental but also existential—the imperative must be to avert such an outcome altogether. Among the host of measures that have been formulated in response to the threat of global warming, the path marked out by Watsuji's work is philosophical, though not for all that any less decisive or significant. His thought introduces an integrative mode of analysis that approaches phenomena in terms of the encompassing conditions, structures, and wholes within which they are emplaced. This untiring focus on formations and totalities is grounded in his understanding of the underlying relatedness of all things. Moreover it is not difficult to see the relevance of this kind of approach to other concerns that fall within the realm of moral experience, such as the relations between different races or religions, between genders, and between the human and the animal.

To the extent that Watsuji's philosophy continually builds toward an inclusive perspective on things, it can be seen as a form of what I call *topological* thinking. Thinking can be characterized as topological insofar as it reverses the usual and taken-for-granted ontological primacy of discrete objects or entities over the places, contexts, structures, fields, and relations in which these are located and by which these are engulfed. Topos and entity, moreover, belong to one another in such a way that one could not exist without the other.

Understanding Watsuji's topological approach can help one place ethical concerns within a wider explanatory perspective; it is also a useful and productive way to orient oneself to Watsuji's philosophy as a whole, since two of the most important philosophical concepts he employs, *aidagara* and *fūdo*, are topological notions. Taken together, these concepts provide the framework for a topological account of the self, which moves beyond the problematic modern understanding of human beings as individual subjectivities fully detached from the other people among whom they live and from the natural environment that surrounds them. Instead Watsuji's work shows that the relational network of *aidagara* is itself situated in a specific spatiotemporal locale characterized by a particular geography, culture, and history.

This means that the self, in effect, is emplaced in and encompassed by a place and a space that is both geocultural *and* social. But this is not a merely passive relation; the self acts upon and so partly constitutes both other selves and a specific *fūdo*, while both of these, in turn, act upon and help make the self what it is. The self, then, comes to be what it is through relational contact with others and with a particular geocultural climate, while both of these *also* depend on the self to be what they are.

Self, others, and *fūdo* belong to one another in and through this relational exchange, with each functioning as a component of the larger experiential whole.

Aidagara and *fūdo* are hence the place and space of the self, but not of a self that would be "in" or "on" these topoi as a cat on a mat or a shoe in a box, as if each one were an absolutely distinct entity that would then come into relation with the other. Rather *aidagara* and *fūdo* are dimensions of the basic space and place in and through which the self is able to be continuous with the world. Yet this continuity does not mean that the self is simply reducible to that which surrounds it; instead this is a form of unity constituted by the very difference and distance between self, other, and *fūdo*.

This topological understanding of the self converges with the turn to place in philosophy initiated by philosophers such as Edward Casey and Jeff Malpas. Continuities and synthetic connections can be established, for example, between Casey's concept of "wild" nature and Watsuji's concept of *fūdo*, so that each enriches the other. This link can be seen in Casey's construal of wild nature as composed of wild places whose singularity arises from the complex network of experiential dimensions that belong to each locale, so that an understanding of such places can only be local and nontransferrable. But the significance of Casey's work for carrying further some of what has been set down in Watsuji's thought extends well beyond the question of nature to the category of place as a whole.

For Casey too place is constitutive of our being. We have to retrieve the significance of our lived experience of being "implaced," which has been subordinated in the history of philosophy to the concepts of time, being, and space. This retrieval has special value in our current dispensation, a postmodern form of life in which we find ourselves alienated from nature and from the capacity to really be at home in a place, drifting instead through the homogeneous global space of superhighways and shopping malls. Against this placeless anomie, a recovery of our sense of place has the capacity to "direct and stabilize us, to memorialize and identify us, to tell us who and what we are in terms of *where we are* (as well as where we are *not*)."[2]

Like Casey, Malpas sees us as bound to place; place is not merely a contingent site for and ontologically separate from human life and activity. But the philosophical significance of place for Malpas lies less in our experience of it than in the ways human thought, identity, and experience are established in and through it. Malpas and Casey both distinguish place from space and understand place to be a more fundamental and overarching concept, a unitary structure that encompasses both space and time, subjectivity and objectivity. Malpas examines in addition the way self and other also fit into the unified framework of place. Points of contact, overlap, and continuity with Watsuji's thought abound, and even the most important contrast harbors a productive tension. Whereas Watsuji criticizes the Heidegger of *Being and Time* for overlooking the constitutive role of space and place in the being of Dasein, Malpas has done much to show that Heidegger must be counted as one of the founders of place-oriented thinking. He maintains that almost from the beginning, place runs through Heidegger's thought, directly and indirectly, in his use of topological concepts and images and in the themes and motifs of his work.[3]

In addition to the relevance of Watsuji's work for this resurgence in contemporary discussions about the philosophical significance of place, his topological approach also opens onto other, older intellectual vistas. Because his understanding of *aidagara* and *fūdo* as topological dimensions of the structure of the self breaks convincingly with dualistic accounts of a disengaged self that faces the world and its places and people as though they were really fully separate objects, this understanding of the self also allows us to place Watsuji in relation to his most important philosophical contemporaries, namely, those thinkers in the first generation of the Kyoto School with whom, to some degree or other, he is usually associated. There is something of a family resemblance, for example, between *aidagara* and *fūdo* and other topological concepts such as the absolute nothingness of Nishida, the absolute dialectic of Tanabe, and the field of *śūnyatā* of Nishitani. Yet there are also some important methodological and thematic differences here as well. Much of the philosophical reflection on nondualism in the Kyoto School, for instance, is either oriented by what can be called, with certain caveats, an explicitly "religious" standpoint, as in the work of Tanabe and Nishitani, or else it takes the form of abstract conceptualization in the service of speculative metaphysics, as for example in Nishida's attempt to gain a comprehensive grasp of the nondual whole by systematically mapping its logical structure.[4] While both of these approaches have their place and importance in philosophical inquiry, one of Watsuji's most valuable contributions to this question is the exploration of concrete structures of experience, which, while neither originating nor culminating in an obviously religious standpoint, nevertheless exemplify the profoundly nondual nature of the self.[5]

Watsuji's close and concrete description of ordinary yet essential features of our nondual way of being in the world also allows his views to be related quite readily to the work of thinkers in the classical phenomenological tradition; moreover there is little doubt that he has something singular and significant to contribute to the project of overcoming dualism in this tradition. Here we find another ontology in which consciousness and thing, self and world, intertwine and mutually determine one another. Heidegger, for instance, is concerned to show the way our practices, language, affectivity, and historicity determine both the mode of being of Dasein as well as what appears or becomes manifest to it; Merleau-Ponty the ways—in addition to these—the structure and capacities of our body help to constitute the perceived world while, at the same time, belonging to and emerging from that same world.

In looking beyond Japanese philosophy to the wider philosophical world in these ways, Watsuji's work expands and opens up our sense of what being-in-the-world, which has been a phenomenon of the greatest significance for contemporary phenomenology, and nondualism, which has been a concept of the first importance in East Asian philosophy, are and can be. Watsuji's theory of *fūdo* thus offers a novel, wide-ranging, and complex view of how the self comes to be what it is—a view that moves beyond the problematic modern understanding of human beings as individual subjectivities ontologically decoupled from the natural and social environment that surrounds them. In this vision, we find instead that the self and its consciousness are rooted in a source far greater and more profound than the awareness of a single individual: not only are we immersed in, and emerge from, the depths of the historical and social world, but our lives both shape, and flow from, the vast life of nature.

Notes

Introduction

1. Note that Japanese names are written in the Japanese fashion of surname followed by given name, unless these are names of Japanese living and working in the West who have adopted Western-style name order in their publications.

2. Watsuji ostensibly went to Germany to gain fuller exposure to contemporary trends in German and European philosophy, though he never made use of the letter of introduction to Heidegger that Tanabe Hajime supplied him with. See Inaga, "Japanese Philosophers Go West," 118.

3. Martin Heidegger, "A Dialogue on Language between a Japanese and a Inquirer," in *On the Way to Language*, 1–54; Heidegger, *Unterwegs zur Sprache*, 79–146. Two good sources for the connections between Heidegger and the Kyoto School, as well as Asian thought, are Parkes, *Heidegger and Asian Thought* and Parkes, "Rising Sun over Black Forest."

4. Parkes, *Heidegger and Asian Thought*, 7.

5. Ibid., 5.

6. Malpas, *Place and Experience*, 40.

7. Malpas, *Heidegger's Topology*, 35.

8. James Heisig, foreword to Goto-Jones, *Re-Politicising the Kyoto School as Philosophy*, xiv.

9. As Ikimatsu Keizō observes, Watsuji had real difficulty in fluidly uniting *aidagara* and *fūdo*. He suggests that nature as *fūdo* never really enters into Watsuji's various discussions of *aidagara* in a significant way. See Ikimatsu, "Watsuji fūdoron no shomondai." This would seem to claim too much, but the point is well taken.

10. Sakabe, "Surrealistic Distortion of the Landscape," 348.

11. Maurice Merleau-Ponty, "On the Phenomenology of Language" in *Signs*, 84.

Chapter 1

1. See Lurie, "Fudoki Gazetteers," 45–49.

2. See Frédéric, *Japan Encyclopedia*, 194; Lurie, "Fudoki Gazetteers"; *Records of Wind and Earth*; *Harima Fudoki*. The latter is an entire *fudoki*, including extensive explanation and historical context provided in the introduction.

3. I am by and large, though not entirely, following Wittkamp's summary here, "Between Topos and Topography," 15–29.

4. The division here is not, to repeat, an absolute one. The adventurer, diarist, and painter Sugae Masumi (1754–1829), for example, wrote travel diaries containing *waka* as well as detailed descriptions of the land and people of northern Japan (see Wittkamp, "Between Topos and Topography," 20, 27). Sugae, moreover, was not an exception in this regard. The writings of his contemporaries Furukawa Koshōken and Tachibana Nankei are also characterized by a similar blending of genres. See, for instance, Bolitho, "Traveler's Tales."

5. The approximate date of authorship of the *Jinkokuki* comes from Asano Kenji, editor of the *Jinkokuki/Shin jinkokuki*, who estimates it to have been written between 1532 and 1569 (see 290).

6. Yonemoto, *Mapping Early Modern Japan*, 56, 72.

7. In his *Eisei shinpen* (*New Book of Hygiene*) of 1898, for example, Mori examines the relationship between hygiene and natural environment. See Yoshino, "The Development of Bioclimatological Thought in Japan."

8. Ikkai, *Ichigo no jiten—Kaze*, 88.

9. Ibid., 89.

10. This stands in opposition to and undermines what can be called a designative theory of linguistic meaning according to which the meaning of a word is equivalent to what it designates, so that the meaning of a word such as *fūdo* is merely enhanced rather than supplied by these contexts.

11. Saussure, *Course in General Linguistics*, 114.

12. Wittgenstein, *Philosophical Grammar*, 21.

13. Though this is not to deny the performative function of language.

14. Humboldt, *On Language*, 106.

15. See Maraldo, "Between Individual and Communal," 77.

16. This information can be found in Inaga, "Japanese Philosophers Go West"; Berque, "The Question of Space"; and in Watsuji's letters to his wife during this trip in *Watsuji Tetsurō zenshū*, vol. 25 (hereafter *WTZ* followed by volume and page numbers).

17. *WTZ* 8, 2.

18. See Befu, "Watsuji Tetsurō's Ecological Approach," 106–120. These thinkers are mentioned in the last chapter of *Fūdo* (*WTZ* 8, 205–241).

19. *WTZ* 8, 206–207. All translations from Watsuji's Japanese in this and other volumes are my own.

20. *WTZ* 8, 208.

21. Goto-Jones, "Politicizing Travel and Climatizing Philosophy," 50.

22. See Herder, "Ideas for a Philosophy," 290.

23. *WTZ* 11, 137; *WTZ* 8, 210–213.

24. *WTZ* 11, 137; *WTZ* 8, 210, 216–218.

25. See Herder, "Ideas for a Philosophy," 285.

26. *WTZ* 8, 210–213.

27. See Liederbach, "Zur Entstehungsgeschichte von Watsuji Tetsurō's Fūdo," 160–161.

28. See Takashima, *Gendai Nihon no Kōsatsu*.

29. See Ikimatsu, "Watsuji fūdoron no shomondai," 140, and Iizuka, *Iizuka Kōji chosakushū*, 313–342.

30. *WTZ* 8, 13.

31. See, for example, Carter and McCarthy, "Watsuji Tetsurō." And in his introduction to the English translation of *Rinrigaku*, Carter claims that by *fūdo* "Watsuji means to include not only weather patterns of a region but the natural geographic setting of a people plus the social environment of family, community, society, lifestyle, and even the technological apparatus that supports community survival and interaction" (5).

32. In endorsing Berque's translation of *fūdo* as "milieu," for example, Arisaka argues for a broad definition of *fūdo*: "The term 'milieu' is more appropriate than 'climate,' since for Watsuji the notion of a *fūdo* includes not only the natural environment but also the social and historical environment at the same time" ("Space and History," 190).

33. Couteau, "Watsuji Tetsurō's Ethics of Milieu," 277.

34. *WTZ* 8, 7.

35. *WTZ* 11, 167–191.

36. Watsuji does maintain, however, that even the smallest garden and the smallest piece of village land have the character of the region's land imprinted on them. See *WTZ* 11, 157. As Gary Snyder puts it: "A place on earth is a mosaic within larger mosaics—the land is all small places, all precise tiny realms replicating larger and smaller patterns" (*The Practice of the Wild*, 27).

37. Ibid., 27–28. At the end of this passage Snyder refers the reader to Dodge, "Living by Life."

38. Mill, *Three Essays on Religion*, 66.

39. Watsuji notes that it is because primeval forests are now so rare that we make such an effort to protect them. See *WTZ* 11, 101.

40. Kort, "'Landscape' as a Kind of Place-Relation," 38.

41. Katz, "Preserving the Distinction," 81.

42. This historical and philosophical analysis of the term *shizen* draws on Tellenbach and Kimura, "The Japanese Concept of Nature," 153–162; Kimura, "Self and Nature"; Berque, *Japan*, 135–143; Odin, "The Japanese Concept of Nature."

43. Tellenbach and Kimura, "The Japanese Concept of Nature," 155.

44. Animals do not constitute part of a *fūdo* but, along with the plants that do, are a mediating entity between human existence and *fūdo*, since human beings produce particular kinds of food, clothing, and shelter in interaction with a particular plant and animal kingdom. See *WTZ* 11, 162.

45. *WTZ* 11, 166.

46. *WTZ* 8, 75–77.

47. This information can be found in Liederbach, "Zur Entstehungsgeschichte."

48. For accounts of Kuki's life and activities while in Europe, see Pincus, *Authenticating Culture*; Benfy, *The Great Wave*; Light, *Shūzō Kuki and Jean-Paul Sartre*.

49. For this assessment of Watsuji's intellectual development, see Inaga, "Japanese Philosophers Go West."

50. A handful of scholars, such as Berque, Mochizuki, Sato, Couteau, and Bernier, however, have grasped the radical philosophical potential and significance of the concept of *fūdo*. See, e.g., Taro, "Climate and Ethics"; Sato and Turzynski, "The Criticism of Science"; Bernier and Couteau, "Logique du lieu et mésologie"; and much of Berque's oeuvre.

51. Tosaka, *Tosaka Jun zenshū*, 97–102.

52. Nakashima, "Nationalizing Nature."

53. *WTZ* 11, 112.

54. Nakashima, "Nationalizing Nature," 122.

55. See Sevilla, *Watsuji Tetsurō's Global Ethics of Emptiness*, especially chapter 3.

56. See *WTZ* 11, 428.

57. See *WTZ* 11, 60, 154.

58. The development of this point in the next four paragraphs comes from *WTZ* 11, 94–95, 103–104, 118, 146, 158–161, 172, 191–192.

59. Watsuji observes that a complete description that could cover the whole of what is shared in a common past between even old friends, or parents and children, is beyond the power of human beings to construct, because such an enormous quantity of scenes and events constitutes the past of just a single relationship of this kind. See *WTZ* 11, 7.

60. Sevilla, *Watsuji Tetsurō's Global Ethics of Emptiness*, 99.

61. Ibid., 97, 113.

62. See *WTZ* 11, 419–420, 429–431, 434.

63. Sevilla, *Watsuji Tetsurō's Global Ethics of Emptiness*, 105. I have been aided in constructing this overview of these issues by Sevilla's account of the changes in the second volume of *Ethics*, as well as by his analysis of the way the third volume fits into this story.

64. Watsuji is aware, for instance, of what he sees as the dangers of overemphasizing geography in understanding society. He raises examples of the problems that can arise in expanding the subject of geography to cover too broad an area, and notes that there are instances of geographical thinking that go too far and become a form of geographical determinism. See *WTZ* 11, 149–150.

65. Kamata, "Watsuji Tetsurō," 36.

66. *WTZ* 8, 7.

67. Berque, "The Japanese Thought of Milieu (*Fūdo*)," 61–63.

68. My translation. See Bernier and Couteau, "Logique du lieu et mésologie," 51.

69. *WTZ* 8, 1.

70. See *WTZ* 11, 108.

71. *WTZ* 11, 156.

Chapter 2

1. *WTZ* 8, 1.

2. *WTZ* 8, 11.

3. *WTZ* 8, 136, 29, 198, 137. Unfortunately Watsuji employs some of these

depictions of the *fūdo* of Japan to make some highly specific and outlandish claims about the link between the national personality of the Japanese and their climate. As we noted in the first chapter, however, this approach does not cohere with Watsuji's basic philosophical positions and orientation.

4. *WTZ* 11, 99.

5. *WTZ* 11, 99.

6. Watsuji notes, contrary to this, that such representations of the weather, climate, and landscape emerge only through a process of abstraction that erases the essential character and identity of such phenomena as a "moment of human existence" (*ningen sonzai no keiki* 人間存在の契機) (*WTZ* 11, 99).

7. For a more extensive commentary regarding this point, see MacArthur, "Naturalizing the Human."

8. *WTZ* 11, 109.

9. For a brief but clear account of this historical background, see Taylor, "Engaged Agency and Background in Heidegger," 317–336.

10. See Husserl, *The Crisis of European Sciences*, 23, 32, 36–38, 44, 51.

11. I am indebted to David Carr's admirably clear article "Husserl's Problematic Concept of the Life World" for key elements of this summary of the significance of the emergence and development of the natural sciences for Husserl.

12. See Husserl, *The Crisis of European Sciences*, 51–52. Also see 3, 23, 32.

13. Ricoeur, *Oneself as Another*, 135.

14. See Ihde, *Expanding Hermeneutics*, 111.

15. For a brief but informative description of the geographical naturalism underlying modern ontological individualism, see Berque, "Milieu et identité humaine," 386–387.

16. See the following by Berque: "A Basis for Environmental Ethics"; "Overcoming Modernity"; "Offspring of Watsuji's Theory of Milieu (Fûdo)"; "From Watsuji's Concept of 'Human,'" 138–144.

17. *WTZ* 11, 107–108.

18. *WTZ* 11, 109.

19. *WTZ* 11, 109.

20. Husserl, *The Crisis of European Sciences*, 48–49.

21. Carr, "Husserl's Problematic Concept of the Life-World," 334.

22. *WTZ* 11, 108.

23. Watsuji makes this point using the language and vocabulary of phenomenology in *Ningen no gaku to shite no rinrigaku*. See *WTZ* 9, 137.

Chapter 3

1. See *WTZ* 10, 11.

2. Gadamer, "The Hermeneutics of Suspicion," 318.

3. *WTZ* 9, 137.

4. See *WTZ* 9, 176.

5. *WTZ* 9, 176.

6. Quoted in Kisiel, "The Paradigm Shifts of Hermeneutic Phenomenology."

7. *WTZ* 8, 9–10; compare *WTZ* 9, 160. Here Watsuji says that standing out (*ex-sistere*) is the source of intentionality for Heidegger, and that the phenomenon of standing out is linked both to Heidegger's notion of temporality and to what makes an object an object of intentionality.

8. See Heidegger, *The Metaphysical Foundations of Logic*, 135–136; *Gesamtausgabe* 26, 169–170.

9. Heidegger, *Being and Time*, Stambaugh translation, 129 (hereafter *BT*); Heidegger, *Sein und Zeit*, 133 (hereafter *SZ*). The last sentence quoted follows the previous sentence in a footnote.

10. Hence Heidegger famously claims that animals are poor in world (*Weltarm*). Human beings, on the other hand, are open to and opened by things.

11. Moran, "Intentionality," 338.

12. Heidegger, *BT*, 40; *SZ*, 42.

13. Lafont, "Hermeneutics," 271.

14. Heidegger, *BT*, 109; *SZ*, 116.

15. Heidegger, *BT*, 55, 57; *SZ*, 59, 61.

16. Heidegger, *BT*, 58; *SZ*, 62.

17. Heidegger, *BT*, 25; *SZ*, 29.

18. See *WTZ* 8, 2.

19. Berque thinks it is this feature of Heidegger's fundamental ontology above all that validates Watsuji's criticism. See, for example, "A Basis for Environmental Ethics," "*Sabaku* de Watsuji Tetsurô," and "The Question of Space."

20. Nagami, "The Ontological Foundation," n. 24.

21. See Liederbach, "Faktizität, Existenz, Klima," 86; Liederbach, *Martin Heidegger im Denken Watsuji Tetsurôs*, 109.

22. See Mine, *Haideggā to Nihon no tetsugaku*, 108.

23. Arisaka, "The Ontological Co-Emergence of 'Self and Other.'"

24. Olafson, *Heidegger and the Ground of Ethics*, 20.

25. Heidegger, *BT*, 120; *SZ*, 113.

26. Heidegger, *BT*, 107; *SZ*, 114.

27. Heidegger, *BT*, 118; *SZ*, 111.

28. Heidegger, *BT*, 58; *SZ*, 62.

29. McMullin, *Time and the Shared World*, 6.

30. Heidegger, *Basic Problems of Phenomenology*, , 164; *Gesamtausgabe* 24, 234.

31. Dreyfus, "Being-with-Others," 146.

32. Ibid.

33. *WTZ* 10, 185.

34. See *WTZ* 10, 185.

35. *WTZ* 11, 98.

36. *WTZ* 9, 162.

37. *WTZ* 8, 10.

38. *WTZ* 8, 18.

39. Olafson, *Heidegger and the Ground of Ethics*, 29.

40. Watsuji, *Watsuji Tetsurō zenshū bekkan 2*, 206.

41. *WTZ* 8, 18. Thus Watsuji declares that the temporality of individual consciousness is an abstraction from a history of being-in-relation-to-others.

42. In order to give an accurate rendition of Watsuji's interpretation of Heidegger, we use the term Watsuji uses, agreeing, however, with Sheehan that, strictly speaking, Dasein does not "transcend." See Sheehan, "A Paradigm Shift in Heidegger Research," 194–196.

43. See *WTZ* 8, 10.

Chapter 4

1. Carman, "The Principle of Phenomenology," 105, n. 17.
2. See *WTZ* 9, 154–155.
3. *WTZ* 10, 65.
4. *WTZ* 10, 71.
5. *WTZ* 10, 54.
6. *WTZ* 10, 36–37.
7. See *WTZ* 10, 73.
8. See *WTZ* 9, 141.
9. *WTZ* 10, 73.
10. *WTZ* 9, 141.
11. And this experience is quite distinct, in turn, from the mutual interpenetration of consciousnesses that is found among people with whom we are intimate or well acquainted. See *WTZ* 10, 73–74.
‹ 12. *WTZ* 10, 73.
13. *WTZ* 10, 54.
14. *WTZ* 10, 74.
15. On the nature of the game and for a comparison between the game and dialogue, see Hans-Georg Gadamer, "On the Problem of Self-Understanding" and "Man and Language," in *Philosophical Hermeneutics*, 53–57, 66; *Gesammelte Werke* (1990), 128–131, 151–152.
16. See *WTZ* 10, 73: "Such an act, in which self and other are connected, must be understood from the standpoint of the practical interconnection of acts itself, rather than from that of an individual consciousness."
17. See *WTZ* 10, 37.
18. See *WTZ* 10, 37.
19. See *WTZ* 11, 37.
20. See Krueger, 'Watsuji's Phenomenology of Embodiment," and "The Space between Us."
21. Yuasa, *The Body*, 48.
22. Watsuji, *WTZ* 10, 69.
23. See, for example, *WTZ* 10, 71.
24. See *WTZ* 10, 63–71.
25. Krueger, "The Space between Us," 60.
26. *WTZ* 9, 177.
27. Scheler, *The Nature of Sympathy*, 260.
28. Watsuji maintains in this regard that a human being is also the sum of all of the roles she takes up. See *Watsuji Tetsurō zenshū bekkan 2*, 207.

222

NOTES TO PAGES 98-113

29. Heidegger, *BT*, 129; *SZ*, 133.
30. See Heidegger, *BT*, 134; *SZ*, 143.
31. *WTZ* 10, 86–87.

Chapter 5

1. See Mine, "Das Menschliche Dasein als Zwischensein."
2. Geertz, "'From the Native's Point of View,'" 31.
3. Watsuji's remarks concerning this notion are at *WTZ* 10, 24.
4. *WTZ* 10, 25.
5. See *WTZ* 10, 24.
6. *WTZ* 10, 246.
7. See *WTZ* 10, 16–17.
8. See *WTZ* 9, 20.
9. Maraldo, "Between Individual and Communal," 85.
10. Naoki Sakai has criticized this process of individuation as a rebellion or the guise of a rebellion "that is always launched in anticipation of a pre-arranged resolution: it is a moment of deviation, but it always assumes a return to normalcy" (*Translation and Subjectivity*, 88). As Sevilla has pointed out, however, the possibility of social change can be found in Watsuji's suggestion that the individual might leave one social body for another or even found an entirely new group himself. See Sevilla, "Watsuji's Balancing Act."
11. See *WTZ* 11, 154–155.
12. See *WTZ* 10, 142–143.
13. See Sevilla, "Watsuji's Balancing Act," for an account of the evolution of Watsuji's thinking here.
14. Couteau, "Watsuji Tetsurō's Ethics of Milieu," 283.
15. See LaFleur, "Buddhist Emptiness in the Ethics and Aesthetics of Watsuji Tetsurō," 242, and Shields, "The Art of Aidagara," 279.
16. Kalmanson, "Levinas in Japan," 201.
17. See, respectively, *WTZ* 10, 195; *WTZ* 10, 127; *WTZ* 10, 22.
18. LaFleur, "Buddhist Emptiness," 250. David Dilworth maintains that Watsuji "seems to have refused, at least philosophically and methodologically, to embrace the solution of religion" ("Watsuji Tetsurō," 17).
19. For examples of this identification, see, e.g., *WTZ* 9, 152; *WTZ* 10, 36; *WTZ* 10, 197–198.
20. See *WTZ* 10, 195, 197–199.
21. See *WTZ* 10, 195–196.
22. Watsuji says that our ultimate origin is also the ultimate destination to which we return. This is what "origin as futurity" (*honraisei soku miraisei* 本来性即未来性) means. See *WTZ* 10, 195–6.
23. *WTZ* 10, 142.
24. See *WTZ* 10, 127.
25. Sevilla, "Watsuji's Balancing Act," 122.
26. Ibid., 123.

27. See *WTZ* 10, 38–40.
28. See Sevilla, "The Buddhist Roots."
29. See Nāgārjuna, *The Fundamental Wisdom of the Middle Way*, 28–30; Westerhoff, *Nāgārjuna's Madhyamaka*, 27–28.
30. See *WTZ* 10, 71, 195.
31. *WTZ* 9, 473.
32. The practical subject is always already directed to and extends out toward others in this way because this orientation and condition have their ground in the very division between one subject and another that makes possible their union. See *WTZ* 10, 173.
33. See *WTZ* 10, 166.
34. *WTZ* 10, 163–164.
35. See *WTZ* 10, 187.

Chapter 6

1. *WTZ* 11, 93.
2. Malpas, *Heidegger and the Thinking of Place*, 115.
3. Heidegger, *BT*, 96; *SZ*, 103.
4. See *WTZ* 10, 183–186.
5. *WTZ* 10, 186–188.
6. McCarthy, "The Spatiality of the Self," 186.
7. See *WTZ* 10, 186–187.
8. See *WTZ* 10, 186.
9. *WTZ* 11, 93.
10. Heidegger, *BT*, 94, 97, 98; *SZ*, 101, 104, 106.
11. See Cerbone, "Heidegger on Space and Spatiality," 129–144; Malpas, *Heidegger and the Thinking of Place*, especially chapter 6, "Place, Space, and World."
12. Dreyfus—among others who have complained about this account—says of it that "the discussion of spatiality is one of the most difficult in *Being and Time*, not because it is deeper than any other discussion but because it is fundamentally confused" (*Being-in-the-World*, 129).
13. *WTZ* 10, 19.
14. *WTZ* 10, 22.
15. Gadamer, "Die Vielfalt der Sprachen," 339–349. My translation.
16. *WTZ* 10, 20.
17. Maraldo, "Between Individual and Communal," 83.
18. See *WTZ* 10, 22.
19. *WTZ* 9, 143.
20. *WTZ* 9, 156.
21. *WTZ* 9, 143.
22. See *WTZ* 10, 173.
23. *WTZ* 9, 162.
24. See *WTZ* 9, 161.
25. See *WTZ* 9, 163–164.

26. For an analysis of other such examples, see Lebra, "*Migawari*," 107–124.

27. See *WTZ* 8, 145, 164.

28. See Taylor, "Merleau-Ponty and the Epistemological Picture," 34; Taylor, "Foundationalism," 111.

29. See Dreyfus, "Overcoming the Myth of the Mental." See Gibson, *The Ecological Approach to Visual Perception.*

30. Dreyfus, "Intelligence without Representation."

31. Gibson, *The Ecological Approach to Visual Perception*, 3.

32. *WTZ* 8, 197.

33. I say "almost" because, as William Britt has reminded me, it is not evident whether it can be said that some version of weather still conditions the experience of astronauts, or, again, if weather conditions even our internal experiences (e.g., introspection, dreams, bodily pain, and so on).

34. *WTZ* 8, 11.

35. Malpas, *The Intelligence of Place*, 3.

36. Ingold, "Earth, Sky, Wind, and Weather." The quote which Ingold cites comes from Nelson, *Make Prayers to the Raven*, 33.

37. *WTZ* 11, 100–103.

Chapter 7

1. Tsuda Masao points out that Watsuji can be said to have expanded Heidegger's notion of *Befindlichkeit* to include an attunement to *fūdo*, so that this passive and receptive relation to the world as determinative for Dasein would be another fundamental *existentiale* of Dasein. See Tsuda, "Fūdo to moraru."

2. Watsuji uses several terms to refer to this phenomenon, the most frequent two being *jiko o miidasu* 自己を見いだす and *jiko ryōkai* 自己了解. The former term is frequently translated as "self-discovery," but this term suggests that something one has been unaware of newly comes to consciousness. But self-understanding is always already there; even if only implicitly, I always understand myself and my possibilities and projects. These two expressions are also used interchangeably by Watsuji with "seeing oneself" (*onore o miru* 己れを見る), "self-disclosure" (*jiko kaiji* 自己開示), and "grasping oneself" (*jiko hasoku* 自己把捉). I have generally used the term *apprehend* to cover these meanings.

3. See *WTZ* 11, 8.

4. Heidegger, *BT*, 64–65, 70–72, 78; *SZ*, 68–70, 74–77, 84.

5. Foltz, *Inhabiting the Earth*, 51.

6. Heidegger, *BT*, 60; *SZ*, 63.

7. Heidegger, *BT*, 75; *SZ*, 80–81.

8. Heidegger, *BT*, 66; *SZ*, 70.

9. Heidegger, *BT*, 66; *SZ*, 71.

10. Heidegger, *BT*, 66; *SZ*, 71.

11. Heidegger, *BT*, 66; *SZ*, 70.

12. The first set of quotations are from Stambaugh's translation, *BT*, 66; *SZ*, 70. The final sentence is from the Macquarrie and Robinson translation, 100; *SZ*, 70.

13. Heidegger, *BT*, 355; *SZ*, 388–389.

14. Heidegger, *SZ*, 381. Stambaugh translates the key portion of the relevant passage as "*nature* in the surrounding world as the 'historical ground.' " This almost makes it seem as if Heidegger posits a domain of nature that is coextensive with and incorporated through historicity into his notion of world, but the original German reads: "die *Umweltnatur* als 'geschichtlicher Boden.' " *Umweltnatur* is elsewhere translated by Stambaugh as "the surrounding world of nature," a rendering that I have also followed here.

15. *WTZ* 8, 23.

16. See *WTZ* 11, 137.

17. The following summary of Liederbach's interpretation of Watsuji comes from *Martin Heidegger im Denken Watsuji Tetsurôs* and "Faktizität, Existenz, Klima."

18. This appears in *WTZ* 9, 1–192.

19. *WTZ* 9, 182.

20. Heidegger, *BT*, 26; *SZ*, 30.

21. Heidegger, *BT*, 31; *SZ*, 35.

22. *WTZ* 9, 181.

23. Kojima, "Japan," 369.

24. *WTZ* 9, 183.

25. *WTZ* 9, 183.

26. See *WTZ* 9, 144; *WTZ* 10, 38.

27. See *WTZ* 9, 179.

28. Liederbach draws our attention to Watsuji's claim at *WTZ* 9, 162 that Heidegger completely overlooks what is even more basic than the understanding of being, namely, the practical interconnection of acts, that is, the *Existenz* of Dasein.

29. *WTZ* 9, 182.

30. Liederbach, "Faktizität, Existenz, Klima," 88.

31. Kojima, "Japan," 369.

32. Mine, "Das Menschliche Dasein als Zwischensein," 66.

33. See *WTZ* 9, 162, 165.

34. *WTZ* 9, 148.

35. *WTZ* 9, 30.

36. The account in the next three paragraphs is a summary of *WTZ* 9, 30–33.

37. Mengzi, *Mengzi*, 107.

38. Mengzi, *Mencius*, 111.

39. *WTZ* 9, 33.

40. Heidegger, *Metaphysical Foundations of Logic*, 129; *Gesamtausgabe* 26, 162.

41. Liederbach, *Heidegger im Denken Watsuji Tetsurôs*, 113.

42. *WTZ* 9, 176–177.

43. *WTZ* 9, 148.

44. The summary that follows is drawn from *WTZ* 9, 28–34; *WTZ* 4, 506–551.

45. *WTZ* 10, 25.

46. *WTZ* 4, 549.

47. *WTZ* 9, 148.

48. *WTZ* 4, 549.

49. Dahlstrom, "Heidegger's Method," 781.

50. Ibid.

51. Merleau-Ponty, *Phenomenology of Perception*, 40.

52. Ibid., 7.

53. See *WTZ* 10, 77–78.

54. *WTZ* 10, 47.

55. *WTZ* 10, 48.

56. *WTZ* 10, 78. But he does not further elaborate on this here; instead his aim in addressing this issue was to show an example of the way the contents of consciousness can be communal and shared.

57. *WTZ* 9, 140.

58. *WTZ* 10, 78.

59. Schatzki, "Landscapes as Temporalspatial Phenomena," 81.

60. *WTZ* 10, 39.

61. *WTZ* 10, 78.

62. See Gadamer, "Man and Language," 63; *Gesammelte Werke* (1990), 149.

63. *WTZ* 10, 529–531. Watsuji's point is mostly about understanding each other in psychological and social terms, though his abiding concern is with the thing being discussed, or *koto* こと. He is interested in what this shows about the nature of the relation between the speakers. The relationship between the speakers is mediated and expressed by the matter or issue we speak of (the *koto*), such that one can see from this exchange the degree of intimacy the speakers have with one another, what their attitudes toward one another are, and so forth—but speaking to one another also involves another kind of mutual understanding, namely, the understanding of a world.

64. Gadamer, *Truth and Method*, 454; *Warheit und Methode*, 462.

65. See Watsuji's essay "On Mono no Aware" in *WTZ* 4, 144–155.

66. *WTZ* 11, 107.

67. *WTZ* 11, 104, 172.

68. *WTZ* 11, 107.

69. Tuan, *Space and Place*, 55–56.

70. Berque, *Japan*, 135.

Chapter 8

1. See Blattner, "Temporality," 311–324, for a convincing argument showing that originary temporality is modally indifferent with respect to authenticity and inauthenticity.

2. Malpas, *Heidegger's Topology*, 107.

3. Arisaka, "Spatiality, Temporality," 39. As Arisaka points out, Heidegger later acknowledges that the attempt to found the spatiality of being-in-the-world on temporality is untenable.

4. *WTZ* 8, 1–2.

5. *WTZ* 8, 16.

6. *WTZ* 8, 119.

7. *WTZ* 8, 18.

8. Liederbach, "Watsuji Tetsurô on Spatiality," 135.

9. *WTZ* 8, 12.

10. *WTZ* 8, 12.

11. *WTZ* 8, 21. Here I have only slightly emended Geoffery Bownas's translation. See Watsuji, *Climate and Culture*, 15.

12. *WTZ* 8, 16–17.

13. Jeff Malpas reminds us that the same kind of integrated spatiotemporal analysis is especially prominent within twentieth-century historiography, which has explicitly thematized the interplay of climatic, geological, and topographical factors and human action, society, and culture. He observes that Paul Vidal de la Blache and Lucien Febvre played a foundational role in the rise of this kind of geographically oriented history. See *Heidegger and the Thinking of Place*, 138–140. Watsuji read both de la Blache and Febvre, but their influence on him was limited since, as he notes in the postface added to *Fūdo* in 1948, he read both of them after writing this text. Moreover, while he approves of de la Blache's and Febvre's criticism of Friedrich Ratzel's approach as a form of environmental determinism, he decided against making any major revisions to the manuscript of *Fūdo* because his study of *fūdo* (*fūdogaku* 風土学) is not to be directly identified with the notion of "human geography" advanced by these two scholars.

14. *WTZ* 8, 21–22.

15. I take this summary of some of the central philosophical tenets of Romanticism from Taylor, *Sources of the Self*, 368–390.

16. *WTZ* 8, 201.

17. See *WTZ* 11, 103.

18. This point is made by John McDowell in "Aesthetic Value, Objectivity, and the Fabric of the World," in *Mind Value, and Reality*, 122–124.

19. Little, "Moral Realism II," 228.

20. See WTZ 8, 197.

21. *WTZ* 8, 198.

22. See *WTZ* 8, 197.

23. *WTZ* 11, 155.

24. *WTZ* 11, 106.

25. *WTZ* 5, 123–124.

26. *WTZ* 8, 8.

27. *WTZ* 8, 9–10.

28. See Merleau-Ponty, *The Visible and the Invisible*, 93.

29. See Dillon, *Merleau-Ponty's Ontology*, 159.

30. Merleau-Ponty, "Eye and Mind," 125.

31. Ibid., 161.

32. Merleau-Ponty, *Phenomenology of Perception*, 241.

33. McDowell, "Aesthetic Value," 122–124.

34. John McDowell, "Values and Secondary Qualities," in *Mind, Value, and Reality*, 133, 134.

35. de Gaynesford, *John McDowell*, 175.

36. Ibid., 167.

37. This phrase comes from Mackie, "The Subjectivity of Values," 289–309.

38. See, for example, the account broadly sketched out by Taylor in "McDowell on Value and Knowledge."

39. In speaking of the "appearances" here I am referring to that which appears in the perceptual experience of a sentient being—not only visual appearances such as things, events, qualities, and values, but also smells, sounds, tastes, and so on.

40. This way of putting the distinction between *temperature* and *coldness* was first suggested to me by William Britt.

Conclusion

1. Janz, "Watsuji Tetsuro, *Fudo*, and Climate Change."

2. Casey, *Getting Back into Place*, xv.

3. Malpas, *Heidegger and the Thinking of Place*, 1.

4. Tanabe and Nishitani's work may be considered "religious" from a Western standpoint. The issue is complicated, since the word for religion (*shūkyō* 宗教) was coined in Japan in the mid-nineteenth century to translate this Western concept. This is also not to ignore the deep Buddhist influences to be found in Watsuji's work. See, for example, LaFleur, "Buddhist Emptiness"; Nagami, "The Ontological Foundation."

5. Excavating the shared topological structure that underlies *aidagara* and *fūdo* allows us to understand each domain as a concrete and quotidian facet of the nondual whole. We should note that in this regard, Watsuji's rendition of nondualism extends beyond the frequently noted framework of a form of the metaphysics of dependent origination in which the self negates the social whole and the social whole negates the self.

Bibliography

Abe, Yoshishige, et al., eds. *Watsuji Tetsurō zenshū*. Vol. 4. Tokyo: Iwanami shoten, 1977.
————. *Watsuji Tetsurō zenshū*. Vol. 5. Tokyo: Iwanami shoten, 1977.
————. *Watsuji Tetsurō zenshū*. Vol. 8. Tokyo: Iwanami shoten, 1977.
————. *Watsuji Tetsurō zenshū*. Vol. 9. Tokyo: Iwanami shoten, 1977.
————. *Watsuji Tetsurō zenshū*. Vol. 10. Tokyo: Iwanami shoten, 1977.
————. *Watsuji Tetsurō zenshū*. Vol. 11. Tokyo: Iwanami shoten, 1962.
————. *Watsuji Tetsurō zenshū*. Vol. 25. Tokyo: Iwanami shoten, 1992.
————. *Watsuji Tetsurō zenshū bekkan*. Vol. 2. Tokyo: Iwanami shoten, 1992.
Arisaka, Yoko. "The Ontological Co-Emergence of 'Self and Other' in Japanese Philosophy." *Journal of Consciousness Studies* 8 (2001): 197–208.
————. "Space and History: Philosophy and Imperialism in Nishida and Watsuji." PhD diss., University of California, Riverside, 1996. Proquest (304285706).
————. "Spatiality, Temporality, and the Problem of Foundation in *Being and Time*." *Philosophy Today* 40 (1996): 36–46.
Boteva-Richter, Bianca. *Der Methodentransfer nach Watsuji Tetsuro: Ein abendländisch-asiatischer Vorschlag für das Arbeiten im interkulturellen Bereich.* Nordhausen: Traugott Bautz, 2009.
Befu, Harumi. "Watsuji Tetsurō's Ecological Approach: Its Philosophical Foundation." In *Japanese Images of Nature: Cultural Perspectives,* edited by Pamela Asquith and Arne Kalland. Surrey: Curzon Press, 1997.
Benfy, Christopher. *The Great Wave: Gilded Age Misfits, Japanese Eccentrics, and the Opening of Old Japan.* New York: Random House, 2004.
Bernier, Bernard, and Pauline Couteau. "Logique du lieu et mésologie: Nouveaux paradigmes pour la position transcendantale." *Ebisu* 40–41 (2008): 45–53.
Berque, Augustin. "A Basis for Environmental Ethics." *Diogenes* 52 (2005): 3–12.
————. *Ecoumène-Introduction à l'étude des milieux humains.* Paris: Belin, 2016.
————. "From Watsuji's Concept of 'Human' to beyond the Limits of Modern Ontological Topos." In *Cultural Diversity and Transversal Values,* edited by. S. Wauchope. Paris: UNESCO, 2006.
————. "The Japanese Thought of Milieu (*Fūdo*): From Peculiarism to the Quest of the Paradigm." In *Japanese Culture and Society: Models of Interpretation,* edited by Josef Kreiner and Hans Dieter Ölschleger. Munich: Iudicium Verlag, 1996.

BIBLIOGRAPHY

———. *Japan: Nature, Artifice and Japanese Culture.* Translated by Ros Schwartz. London: Pilkington Press, 1997.

———. "Milieu et identité humaine." *Annales de Géographie* 113 (2004): 385–99.

———. "Offspring of Watsuji's Theory of Milieu (Fûdo)." *GeoJournal* 60 (2004): 389–396.

———. "Overcoming Modernity, Yesterday and Today." *European Journal of East Asian Studies* 1 (2001): 89–102.

———. "The Question of Space: From Heidegger to Watsuji." *Ecumene* 3 (1996): 373–383.

———. "*Sabaku* de Watsuji Tetsurô, Présentation et traduction." *Ebisu* 29 (2002): 7–26.

Blattner, William. "Temporality." In *A Companion to Heidegger,* edited by Hubert L. Dreyfus and Mark A. Wrathall. Malden, Mass.: Wiley-Blackwell, 2005.

Bolitho, Harold. "Traveler's Tales: Three Eighteenth-Century Travel Journals." *Harvard Journal of Asiatic Studies* 50 (1990): 485–504.

Carman, Taylor. "The Principle of Phenomenology." In *The Cambridge Companion to Heidegger,* edited by Charles Guignon. Cambridge: Cambridge University Press, 2006.

Carr, David. "Husserl's Problematic Concept of the Life World." *American Philosophical Quarterly* 7 (1970): 331–339.

Carter, Robert. Introduction to *Watsuji Tetsurō's Rinrigaku: Ethics in Japan,* by Tetsurō Watsuji. Translated by Yamamoto Seisaku and Robert E. Carter. Albany: SUNY Press, 1996.

Carter, Robert, and Erin McCarthy. "Watsuji Tetsurō." In *The Stanford Encyclopedia of Philosophy* (Spring 2017 Edition), edited by Edward N. Zalta. https://plato.stanford.edu/archives/spr2017/entries/watsuji-tetsuro.

Casey, Edward S. *Getting Back into Place: Toward a Renewed Understanding of the Place-World.* Bloomington: Indiana University Press, 1993.

Cerbone, David R. "Heidegger on Space and Spatiality." In the *Cambridge Companion to Heidegger's* Being and Time, edited by Mark A. Wrathall. Cambridge: Cambridge University Press, 2013.

Couteau, Pauline. "Watsuji Tetsurō's Ethics of Milieu." In *Frontiers of Japanese Philosophy,* edited by James W. Heisig. Nagoya, Japan: Nanzan Institute for Religion and Culture, 2006.

Dahlstrom, Daniel O. "Heidegger's Method: Philosophical Concepts as Formal Indications." *Review of Metaphysics* 47 (1994): 775–795.

de Gaynesford, Maximilian. *John McDowell.* Cambridge: Polity Press, 2004.

Dillon, M. C. *Merleau-Ponty's Ontology.* Bloomington: Indiana University Press, 1988.

Dilworth, David. "Watsuji Tetsurō (1889–1960): Cultural Phenomenologist and Ethician." *Philosophy East and West* 24 (1974): 3–22.

Dreyfus, Hubert. *Being-in-the-World: A Commentary on Heidegger's* Being and Time, *Division I.* Cambridge, Mass.: MIT Press, 1990.

———. "Being-with-Others." In *The Cambridge Companion to Heidegger's* Being and Time, edited by Mark Wrathall. Cambridge, Mass.: Cambridge University Press, 2013.

———. "Intelligence without Representation—Merleau-Ponty's Critique of Mental Representation." *Phenomenology and the Cognitive Sciences* 1 (2002): 367–383.

———. "Overcoming the Myth of the Mental: How Philosophers Can Profit from the Phenomenology of Everyday Expertise." *Proceedings and Addresses of the American Philosophical Association* 79 (2005): 47–65.

Dodge, Jim. "Living by Life: Some Bioregional Theory and Practice." *CoEvolution Quarterly* 32 (1981): 6–12.

Foltz, Bruce. *Inhabiting the Earth: Heidegger, Environmental Ethics, and the Metaphysics of Nature.* Atlantic Highlands, N.J.: Humanities Press, 1995.

Frédéric, Louis. *Japan Encyclopedia.* Translated by Käthe Roth. Cambridge, Mass.: Belknap Press of Harvard University Press, 2002.

Gadamer, Hans-Georg. "Die Vielfalt der Sprachen und das Verstehen der Welt." In *Gesammelte Werke*, vol. 8. Tübingen: J. C. B. Mohr (Paul Siebeck), 1993.

———. *Gesammelte Werke.* Vol. 2. Tübingen: J. C. B. Mohr (Paul Siebeck), 1990.

———. "The Hermeneutics of Suspicion." *Man and World* 17 (1984): 313–323.

———. *Philosophical Hermeneutics.* Translated and edited by David E. Linge. Berkeley: University of California Press, 1977.

———. *Truth and Method.* 2nd revised edition. Translated by Joel Weinsheimer and Donald G. Marshall. New York: Continuum, 2004.

———. *Warheit und Methode: Grundzüge einer philosophischen Hermeneutik.* In *Gesammelte Werke*, vol. 1. Tübingen: J. C. B. Mohr (Paul Siebeck), 1990.

Geertz, Clifford. "'From the Native's Point of View': On the Nature of Anthropological Understanding." *Bulletin of the American Academy of Arts and Sciences* 28 (1974): 26–45.

Gibson, James J. *The Ecological Approach to Visual Perception.* London: Lawrence Erlbaum, 1986.

Goto-Jones, Christopher. "Politicizing Travel and Climatizing Philosophy: Watsuji, Montesquieu and the European Tour." *Japan Forum* 14 (2002): 41–62.

———, ed. *Re-Politicising the Kyoto School as Philosophy.* New York: Routledge, 2008.

Harima Fudoki: A Record of Ancient Japan Reinterpreted. Edited and translated by Edwina Palmer. Leiden: Brill, 2016.

Heidegger, Martin. *Basic Problems of Phenomenology.* Translated by Albert Hofstadter. Bloomington: Indiana University Press, 1988.

———. *Being and Time.* Translated by John Macquarrie and Edward Robinson. New York: Harper, 1962.

———. *Being and Time.* Translated by Joan Stambaugh. Albany: SUNY Press, 2010.

———. *Die Grundprobleme der Phänomenologie.* In *Gesamtausgabe*, vol. 24. Frankfurt am Main: Vittorio Klostermann, 1975.

———. *The Metaphysical Foundations of Logic.* Translated by Michael R. Heim. Bloomington: Indiana University Press, 1984.

———. *Metaphysische Anfangsgründe der Logik im Ausgang von Leibniz.* In *Gesamtausgabe*, vol. 26. Frankfurt am Main: Vittorio Klostermann, 1978.

———. *On the Way to Language.* Translated by Peter D. Hertz. New York: Harper and Row, 1971.

———. *Sein und Zeit.* 19th edition. Tübingen: Max Niemeyer Verlag, 2006.

————. *Unterwegs zur Sprache.* In *Gesamtausgabe*, vol. 12. Frankfurt am Main: Vittorio Klostermann, 1985.

Herder, Johann Gottfried. "Ideas for a Philosophy of the History of Mankind." In *Herder on Social and Political Culture*, edited and translated by F. M. Barnard. Cambridge: Cambridge University Press, 1969.

Humboldt, Wilhelm von. *On Language: On the Diversity of Human Language Construction and Its Influence on the Mental Development of the Human Species.* Edited by Michael Losonsky. Translated by Peter Heath. Cambridge: Cambridge University Press, 1999.

Husserl, Edmund. *The Crisis of European Sciences and Transcendental Phenomenology.* Translated by David Carr. Evanston, Ill.: Northwestern University Press, 1970.

Ihde, Don. *Expanding Hermeneutics: Visualism in Science.* Chicago: Northwestern University Press, 1999.

Iizuka, Kōji. *Iizuka Kōji chosakushū.* Vol. 6. Tokyo: Heibonsha, 1975.

Ikkai, Tomoyoshi. *Ichigo no jiten—Kaze.* Tokyo: Sanseidō, 1996.

Ikimatsu, Keizō. "Watsuji fūdoron no shomondai." In *Hito to shisō: Watsuji Tetsurō*, edited by Yuasa Yasuo. Tokyo: San-ichi, 1973.

Inaga, Shigemi. "Japanese Philosophers Go West: The Effect of Maritime Trips on Philosophy in Japan with Special Reference to the Case of Watsuji Tetsurō (1889–1960)." *Japan Review* 25 (2013): 113–144.

Ingold, Tim. "Earth, Sky, Wind, and Weather." *Journal of the Royal Anthropological Institute* 13 (2007): S19–S38.

Janz, Bruce B. "Watsuji Tetsuro, *Fudo*, and Climate Change." *Journal of Global Ethics* 7 (2011): 173–184.

Jinkokuki/Shin jinkokuki. Edited by Asano Kenji. Tokyo: Iwanami shoten, 1995.

Kalmanson, Leah. "Levinas in Japan: The Ethics of Alterity and the Philosophy of No-Self." *Continental Philosophy Review* 43 (2010): 193–206.

Kamata, Manabu. "Watsuji Tetsurō to fūdosei no mondai." *Bulletin of the Faculty of Literature of Hirosaki Gakuin University* 39 (2003): 33–41.

Katz, Eric. "Preserving the Distinction between Nature and Artifact." In *The Ideal of Nature: Debates about Biotechnolgy and the Environment*, edited by Gregory E. Kaebnick. Baltimore: Johns Hopkins University Press, 2011.

Kimura, Bin. "Self and Nature—An Interpretation of Schizophrenia." *Zen Buddhism Today* 6 (1988): 1–10.

Kisiel, Theodore. "The Paradigm Shifts of Hermeneutic Phenomenology: From Breakthrough to the Meaning-Giving Source." *Gatherings: The Heidegger Circle Annual* 4 (2014): 1–13.

Kojima, Hiroshi. "Japan." In *Encyclopedia of Phenomenology*, edited by Lester Embree. Dordrecht: Kluwer, 1997.

Kort, Wesley A. "'Landscape' as a Kind of Place-Relation." In *The Place of Landscape: Concepts, Contexts, Studies*, edited by Jeff Malpas. Cambridge, Mass.: MIT Press, 2011.

Krueger, Joel. "The Space between Us." In *Levinas and Asian Thought*, edited by Leah Kalmanson, Frank Garrett, and Sarah Mattice. Pittsburgh: Duquesne University Press, 2013.

————. 'Watsuji's Phenomenology of Embodiment and Social Space." *Philosophy East and West* 63 (2013): 127–152.

LaFleur, William. "Buddhist Emptiness in the Ethics and Aesthetics of Watsuji Tetsurō." *Religious Studies* 14 (1978): 237–250.

Lafont, Cristina. "Hermeneutics." In *A Companion to Heidegger*, edited by Hubert L. Dreyfus and Mark A. Wrathall. Malden, Mass.: Blackwell, 2004.

Lebra, Takie Sugiyama. "*Migawari*: The Cultural Idiom of Self-Other Exchange in Japan." In *Self as Person in Asian Theory and Practice*, edited by Roger T. Ames. Albany: SUNY Press, 1994.

Liederbach, Hans Peter. "Faktizität, Existenz, Klima: Das Problem des In-der-Welt-seins zwischen Martin Heidegger und Watsuji Tetsurô." *Synthesis philosophica* 19 (2004): 83–100.

————. *Martin Heidegger im Denken Watsuji Tetsurôs: Ein japanischer Beitrag zur Philosophie der Lebenswelt*. Munich: Iudicium, 2001.

————. "Watsuji Tetsurô on Spatiality: Existence within the Context of Climate and History." *Kwansei University Department of Sociology Bulletin* 114 (2012): 123–138.

————. "Zur Entstehungsgeschichte von Watsuji Tetsurô's Fūdo: Die Veränderungen des Klimabegriffs von der Erstveröffentlichung 1929 bis zur Buchfassung 1935." *Nachrichten der Gesellschaft für Natur- und Völkerkunde Ostasiens* 167/170 (2001): 159–179.

Light, Stephen. *Shūzō Kuki and Jean-Paul Sartre: Influence and Counter-Influence in the Early History of Existential Phenomenology*. Carbondale: Southern Illinois University Press, 1987.

Little, Margaret. "Moral Realism II: Non-Naturalism." *Philosophical Books* 35 (1994): 225–233.

Lurie, David. "Fudoki Gazetteers." In *The Cambridge History of Japanese Literature*, edited by Haruo Shirane and Tomi Suzuki with David Lurie. Cambridge: Cambridge University Press, 2016.

MacArthur, David. "Naturalizing the Human or Humanizing Nature: Science, Nature, and the Supernatural." *Erkentniss* 61 (2004): 29–51.

Mackie, J. L. "The Subjectivity of Values." In *Morality and the Good Life*, edited by Thomas L. Carson and Paul K. Moser. New York: Oxford University Press, 1990.

Malpas, Jeff. *Heidegger and the Thinking of Place: Explorations in the Topology of Being*. Cambridge, Mass.: MIT Press, 2012.

————. *Heidegger's Topology: Being, Place, World*. Cambridge, Mass.: MIT Press, 2006.

————. *The Intelligence of Place: Topographies and Poetics*. Edited by Jeff Malpas. London: Bloomsbury, 2015.

————. *Place and Experience: A Philosophical Topography*. Cambridge: Cambridge University Press, 1999.

Maraldo, John. "Between Individual and Communal, Subject and Object, Self and Other: Mediating Watsuji Tetsurô's Hermeneutics." In *Japanese Hermeneutics: Current Debates on Aesthetics and Interpretation*, edited by Michael F. Marra. Honolulu: University of Hawai'i Press, 2002.

Mayeda, Graham. *Time, Space, and Ethics in the Philosophy of Watsuji Tetsurō, Kuki Shūzō, and Martin Heidegger*. New York: Routledge, 2006.

McCarthy, Erin. *Ethics Embodied: Rethinking Selfhood through Continental, Japanese, and Feminist Philosophies*. Lanham, Md.: Lexington Books, 2010.

———. "The Spatiality of the Self." Ph.D. diss., University of Ottawa, 2000. Proquest (304662078).

McDowell, John. *Mind Value, and Reality*. Cambridge, Mass.: Harvard University Press, 1998.

McMullin, Irene. *Time and the Shared World: Heidegger on Social Relations*. Evanston, Ill.: Northwestern University Press, 2013.

Mengzi. *Mencius: An Online Teaching Translation*. Translated by Robert Eno. May 2016. http://www.indiana.edu/~p374/Mengzi.pdf.

———. *Mengzi: With Selections from Traditional Commentaries*. Translated by Bryan W. Van Norden. Indianapolis: Hackett, 2008.

Merleau-Ponty, Maurice. "Eye and Mind." In *The Merleau-Ponty Aesthetics Reader: Philosophy and Painting*, edited by Galen A. Johnson. Evanston, Ill.: Northwestern University Press, 1993.

———. *Phenomenology of Perception*. Translated by Colin Smith. London: Routledge, 1962.

———. *Signs*. Translated by Richard C. McCleary. Evanston, Ill.: Northwestern University Press, 1964.

———. *The Visible and the Invisible*. Translated by Alphonso Lingis. Evanston, Ill.: Northwestern University Press, 1968.

Mill, John Stuart. *Three Essays on Religion*. Edited by Louis J. Matz. Peterborough, Ontario: Broadview Press, 2009.

Mine, Hideki. "Das Menschliche Dasein als Zwischensein: Grundriss der Philosophie Tetsuro Watsujis." *Synthesis philosophica* 37 (2004): 65–81.

———. *Haideggā to Nihon no tetsugaku: Watsuji Tetsurō, Kuki Shūzō, Tanabe Hajime*. Kyoto: Minerva Shobō, 2002.

Mochizuki, Taro. "Climate and Ethics: Ethical Implications of Watsuji Tetsuro's Concepts: 'Climate' and 'Climaticity.'" *Philosophia Osaka* 1 (2006): 43–55.

Moran, Dermot. "Intentionality: Some Lessons from the History of the Problem from Brentano to the Present." *International Journal of Philosophical Studies* 21 (2013): 317–358.

Nagami, Isamu. "The Ontological Foundation in Tetsurō Watsuji's Philosophy: Kū and Human Existence." *Philosophy East and West* 31 (1981): 279–296.

Nāgārjuna. *The Fundamental Wisdom of the Middle Way: Nāgārjuna's Mūlamadhyamakakārikā*. Translated by Jay L. Garfield. Oxford: Oxford University Press, 1995.

Nakashima, Koji. "Nationalizing Nature: Discourses of 'Fudo' and National Environmentalism in Modern Japan." *Geographical Reports of Kanazawa University* 10 (2002): 115–125.

Nelson, Richard. *Make Prayers to the Raven: A Koyukon View of the Northern Forest*. Chicago: University of Chicago Press, 1986.

Odin, Steven. "The Japanese Concept of Nature in Relation to the Environmental Ethics and Conservation Aesthetics of Aldo Leopold." *Environmental Ethics* 13 (1991): 345–360.

Olafson, Frederick. *Heidegger and the Ground of Ethics.* Cambridge: Cambridge University Press, 1998.

Parkes, Graham, ed. *Heidegger and Asian Thought.* Honolulu: University of Hawaii Press, 1987.

———. "Rising Sun over Black Forest: Heidegger's Japanese Connections." In *Heidegger's Hidden Sources: East Asian Influences on His Work,* by Reinhard May. Translated by Graham Parkes. London: Routledge, 1996.

Pincus, Leslie. *Authenticating Culture in Imperial Japan: Kuki Shūzō and the Rise of National Aesthetics.* Berkeley: University of California Press, 1996.

Records of Wind and Earth: A Translation of Fudoki with Introduction and Commentaries. Translated by Michiko Y. Aoki. Ann Arbor, Mich.: Association for Asian Studies, 1997.

Ricoeur, Paul. *Oneself as Another.* Translated by Kathleen Blamey. Chicago: University of Chicago Press, 1995.

Sakabe, Megumi. "Surrealistic Distortion of the Landscape and the Reason of the Milieu." In *Culture and Modernity: East-West Philosophic Perspectives,* edited by Eliot Deutsch. Honolulu: University of Hawaii Press, 1991.

Sakai, Naoki. *Translation and Subjectivity: On "Japan" and Cultural Nationalism.* Minneapolis: University of Minnesota Press, 1997.

Sato, Yasukuni, and Angela Turzynski. "The Criticism of Science and Its Assimilation in Modern Japanese Thought: Phenomenology and Science in the Work of Watsuji Tetsuro." *Review of Japanese Culture and Society* 7 (1995): 40–47.

Saussure, Ferdinand de. *Course in General Linguistics.* Edited and translated by Roy Harris. Peru, Ill.: Open Court, 2006.

Schatzki, Theodore. "Landscapes as Temporalspatial Phenomena." In *The Place of Landscape: Concepts, Contexts, Studies,* edited by Jeff Malpas. Cambridge, Mass.: MIT Press, 2011.

Scheler, Max. *The Nature of Sympathy.* Translated by Peter Heath. New Brunswick, N.J.: Transaction Publishers, 2008.

Sevilla, Anton Luis. "The Buddhist Roots of Watsuji Tetsurô's Ethics of Emptiness." *Journal of Religious Ethics* 44 (2016): 606–635.

———. "Watsuji's Balancing Act: Changes in the Understanding of Individuality and Totality from 1937 to 1949." *Journal of Japanese Philosophy* 2 (2014): 105–134.

———. *Watsuji Tetsurô's Global Ethics of Emptiness: A Contemporary Look at a Modern Japanese Philosopher.* Cham, Switzerland: Palgrave Macmillan, 2017.

Sheehan, Thomas. "A Paradigm Shift in Heidegger Research." *Continental Philosophy Review* 34 (2001): 183–202.

Shields, James. "The Art of *Aidagara*: Ethics, Aesthetics, and the Quest for an Ontology of Social Existence in Watsuji Tetsurô's *Rinrigaku*." *Asian Philosophy* 19 (2009), 265–283.

Snyder, Gary. *The Practice of the Wild.* San Francisco: North Point Press, 1990.

Takashima, Zenya. *Gendai Nihon no kōsatsu.* Tokyo: Kobushi shobō, 1998.

Taylor, Charles. "Engaged Agency and Background in Heidegger." In *The Cambridge Companion to Heidegger,* edited by Charles B. Guignon. New York: Cambridge University Press, 1993.

———. "Foundationalism and the Inner-Outer Distinction." In *Reading McDowell on Mind and World,* edited by Nicholas Smith. New York: Routledge, 2002.

———. "McDowell on Value and Knowledge." *Philosophical Quarterly* 50 (2000): 242–249.

———. "Merleau-Ponty and the Epistemological Picture." In *The Cambridge Companion to Merleau-Ponty,* edited by Taylor Carmen and Mark B. N. Hansen. New York: Cambridge University Press, 2005.

———. *Sources of the Self: The Making of Modern Identity.* Cambridge, Mass.: Harvard University Press, 1989.

Tellenbach, Hubertus, and Bin Kimura. "The Japanese Concept of Nature." In *Nature in Asian Traditions of Thought,* edited by. J. Baird Callicot and Roger T. Ames. Albany: SUNY Press, 1989.

Tosaka, Jun. *Tosaka Jun zenshū.* Vol. 5. Tokyo: Keisō shobō, 1966.

Tsuda, Masao. "Fūdo to moraru (4) Watsuji rinrigaku nōto." *Gifu University Regional Studies Research Report* 5 (1999): 87–98.

Tuan, Yi-Fu. *Space and Place: The Perspective of Experience.* Minneapolis: University of Minnesota Press, 2001.

Watsuji, Tetsurō. *Climate and Culture: A Philosophical Study.* Translated by Geoffery Bownas. New York: Greenwood Press, 1988.

———. *Watsuji Tetsurō's* Rinrigaku: *Ethics in Japan.* Translated by Yamamoto Seisaku and Robert E. Carter. Albany: SUNY Press, 1996.

Westerhoff, Jan. *Nāgārjuna's Madhyamaka: A Philosophical Introduction.* Oxford: Oxford University Press, 2009.

Wittgenstein, Ludwig. *Philosophical Grammar.* Translated by A. Kenny. Oxford: Blackwell, 1974.

Wittkamp, Robert F. "Between Topos and Topography: Japanese Early Modern Travel Literature." In *Asian Crossings: Travel Writing on Japan, China, and Southeast Asia,* edited by Steve Clark and Paul Smethurst. Hong Kong: Hong Kong University Press, 2008.

Yonemoto, Marcia. *Mapping Early Modern Japan: Space, Place, and Culture in the Tokugawa Period, 1603–1868.* Berkeley: University of California Press, 2003.

Yoshino, Masatoshi. "The Development of Bioclimatological Thought in Japan from Ancient Times to the Present." *Global Environmental Research* 13 (2009): 5–12.

Yuasa, Yasuo. *Toward an Eastern Mind-Body Theory.* Translated by Nagatomo Shigenori and T.P. Kasulis. Albany: SUNY Press, 1987.

Index

affectivity, 86, 148; as *Befindlichkeit*, 70; disclosure and, 177, 194, 197
aida, 103, 185
aidagara, 9, 11, 14, 74, 78–81, 87–88, 101, 105, 122, 123, 215n9, 228n5; Dasein as, 8; definition of, 13, 84–85; expression and, 136–38; mutual interpenetration of consciousnesses and, 90, 169; shared intentionality and, 168; space and, 126, 128; as topological concept, 211–13. *See also* being-in-relation-to-others
animals, 32, 35, 39, 160, 165; disclosure and, 67, 194, 208; ethics and, 211; history of the concept of *fūdo* and, 20; as mediating *fūdo*, 217n44; world and, 146, 220n10
appearances, 55, 115, 206, 209; definition of, 228n39; disclosure and, 162, 166, 178; as expressions, 157, 167; mediation and, 194, 197; of nature, 5, 15–16, 146, 181, 193; phenomenology and, 65, 68, 73, 156–57
architecture, 32, 187
Arisaka, Yoko, 31, 74, 184, 217n32, 220n23, 226n3
artifacts, 39, 47, 130, 164–65, 187–90; atmospheres and, 139–40, 143; definition of, 134; distinction between nature and artifact, 37; as expressions, 134–36, 138, 157; interpretive understanding and, 134–35; space and, 143–44
atmosphere, 20, 36, 129; artifacts and, 134, 138–41; of nature, 140–44; social tenor and, 88–89, 130–31, 134, 170
attunement, 70, 71, 224n1. *See also Befindlichkeit*

authenticity, 226n1, 108, 183
autonomous, 76, 91–92, 117, 138, 150

Befindlichkeit, 70, 224n1
being-in-relation-to-others, 8, 13–14, 82, 84–85, 159; expressions of, 137–38, 157–58; *fūdo* and, 181; Heidegger and, 74, 78–79; mutual interpenetration of consciousnesses and, 88, 90; as ontological category, 74, 79, 81, 99, 104, 136; practical interconnection of acts and, 102; self-understanding and, 150; shared intentionality and, 168–69; space and, 81, 123, 127; subjective extendedness and, 119–20, 136; temporality and, 220n41; tools and, 136
being-in-the-world, 6, 13–14, 214; being-in-relation-to-others and, 73, 75, 77–79, 81; explanation of, 69–73, 76; *ex-sistence* and, 67; history and, 153–54; intentionality and, 12, 63, 66, 68; space and, 123–25, 127–28, 183, 185, 234n3; Watsuji's appropriation of, 64, 100, 156, 158, 161
being-toward-death, 74, 183, 185
being-toward-life, 185
being-with, 74–75, 77. *See also* coexistence
Bernier, Bernard, 47, 218n50, 218n68
Berque, Augustin, viii, 8, 47, 216n16, 217n42, 218n50, 218n67, 220n19, 226n70; on modern ontological *topos*, 58, 219n15, 219n16; on relation between nature and culture, 178–79; on translating *fūdo*, 24, 217n32;
body-subject, 94, 203
Buddhism, 3, 7–8, 228n4; cosmology of, 20, 32; emptiness and, 6, 106, 110,